ALSO BY M. SCOTT PECK, M.D.

THE ROAD LESS TRAVELED:
A New Psychology of Love,
Traditional Values and Spiritual Growth

# PEOPLE
## OF THE
# LIE
## THE HOPE
## FOR
## HEALING
## HUMAN
## EVIL

# M. SCOTT PECK, M.D.

A TOUCHSTONE BOOK
Published by *SIMON & SCHUSTER, Inc.*
NEW YORK

Designed by Karolina Harris

Manufactured in the United States of America

5 7 9 10 8 6 4
18   17                                    Pbk.

Library of Congress Cataloging in Publication Data
Peck, M. Scott (Morgan Scott), date
People of the lie.

1. Good and evil—Psychological aspects.
2. Psychology, Pathological. 3. Psychiatry and
religion. I. Title.
RC455.4.R4P4   1983      616.89      83-13631

ISBN 0-671-45492-7
ISBN 0-671-52816-5 Pbk.

The author is grateful for permission to use excerpts from the
following works:
"A Devout Meditation in Memory of Adolph Eichmann" from
*Raids on the Unspeakable* by Thomas Merton. Copyright ©
1966 by The Abbey of Gethsemani, Inc. Reprinted by
permission of New Directions Publishing Corporation.
*The Heart of Man* by Erich Fromm. Copyright © 1964 by Erich
Fromm. Reprinted by permission of Harper & Row,
Publishers, Inc.

*(continued on page 271)*

FOR LILY—
*who serves so many ways,
only one of which has been
to wrestle with demons.*

# CONTENTS

# HANDLE WITH CARE

☰ THIS IS A DANGEROUS BOOK.

I have written it because I believe it is needed. I believe its over-all effect will be healing.

But I have also written it with trepidation. It has potential for harm. It will cause some readers pain. Worse, some may misuse its information to harm others.

I have inquired of several preliminary readers whose judgment and integrity I particularly respect: "Do you think this book about human evil is itself evil?" Their answer was no. One, however, added, "Some of us in the Church have a saying that even the Virgin Mary can be used for sexual fantasy."

While this crude but pithy response is realistic, I do not find it greatly reassuring. I apologize to my readers and to the public for the harm this book may cause, and I plead with you to handle it with care.

One meaning of care is love. Be gentle and loving with yourself if you find what is written causing you pain. And please be gentle and loving with those neighbors you may come to understand as evil. Be careful—full of care.

Evil people are easy to hate. But remember Saint Augustine's advice to hate the sin but love the sinner.* Remember when you

---

* Saint Augustine, *The City of God*, ed. Bourke (Image Books, 1958 ed.), p. 304.

recognize an evil person that truly, "There but for the grace of God go I."

In labeling certain human beings as evil, I am making an obviously severely critical value judgment. My Lord said, "Judge not, that ye be not judged." By this statement—so often quoted out of context—Jesus did not mean we should never judge our neighbor. For he went on to say, "Thou hypocrite, first cast out the beam out of thine own eye; and then shalt thou see clearly to cast out the mote out of thy brother's eye."* What he meant was that we should judge others only with great care, and that such carefulness begins with self-judgment.

We cannot begin to hope to heal human evil until we are able to look at it directly. It is not a pleasant sight. Many observed that my previous book, *The Road Less Traveled*,† was a nice book. This is not a nice book. It is about our dark side, and in large part about the very darkest members of our human community—those I frankly judge to be evil. They are not nice people. But the judgment needs to be made. It is the principal thesis of this work that these specific people—as well as human evil in general—need to be studied scientifically. Not in the abstract. Not just philosophically. But scientifically. And to do that we must be willing to make judgments. The dangers of such judgments will be elaborated at the beginning of the concluding section of the book. But I ask you for the present to bear in mind that such judgments cannot be made safely unless we begin by judging and healing ourselves. The battle to heal human evil always begins at home. And self-purification will always be our greatest weapon.

This book has been most difficult to write for many reasons. Preeminent among them is that it has always been a book in process. I have not learned about human evil; I am learning. In fact, I am just beginning to learn. One chapter is entitled "Toward a Psychology of Evil" precisely because we do not yet have a body of scientific knowledge about evil sufficient to be dignified by calling it a psychology. So let me add another note of caution: Do not regard anything written here as the last word. Indeed, the purpose of the book is to lead us to dissatisfaction with our current state of ignorance of the subject.

* Matthew 7:1–5.
† Simon and Schuster, 1978.

I referred earlier to Jesus as my Lord. After many years of vague identification with Buddhist and Islamic mysticism, I ultimately made a firm Christian commitment—signified by my non-denominational baptism on the ninth of March 1980, at the age of forty-three—long after I had begun working on this book. In a manuscript he sent me an author once apologized for his "Christian bias." I make no such apology. I would hardly have committed myself to something I regarded as a bias. Nor do I desire to disguise my Christian outlook. In fact, I couldn't. My commitment to Christianity is the most important thing in my life and is, I hope, pervasive and total.

But I am concerned that this outlook will, when most apparent, unnecessarily bias some readers. So I ask you to be careful in this respect also. Great evil has been committed throughout the centuries—and is still being committed—by nominal Christians, often in the name of Christ. The visible Christian Church is necessary, even saving, but obviously faulty, and I *do* apologize for its sins as well as my own.

Crusades and inquisitions have nothing to do with Christ. War, torture, and persecution have nothing to do with Christ. Arrogance and revenge have nothing to do with Christ. When he gave his one recorded sermon, the first words out of Jesus' mouth were, "Blessed are the poor in spirit." Not the arrogant. And as he was dying he asked that his murderers be forgiven.

In a letter to her sister, Saint Theresa of Lysieux wrote, "If you are willing to serenely bear the trial of being displeasing to yourself, then you will be for Jesus a pleasant place of shelter."* To define a "true Christian" is a risky business. But if I had to, my definition would be that a true Christian is anyone who is "for Jesus a pleasant place of shelter." There are hundreds of thousands who go to Christian churches every Sunday who are not the least bit willing to be displeasing to themselves, serenely or otherwise, and who are not, therefore, for Jesus a pleasant place of shelter. Conversely, there are millions of Hindus, Buddhists, Muslims, Jews, atheists, and agnostics who are willing to bear that trial. There is nothing in this work that should offend the latter. Much may offend the former.

I feel compelled to make another "nonapology." Many readers

* *Collected Letters of St. Thérèse of Lisieux,* trans. F. J. Sheed (Sheed and Ward, 1949), p. 303.

are likely to be concerned about my use of masculine pronouns in relation to God. I think I both understand and appreciate their concern. It is a matter to which I have given much thought. I have generally been a strong supporter of the women's movement and action that is reasonable to combat sexist language. But first of all, God is not neuter. He is exploding with life and love—even sexuality of a sort. So "It" is not appropriate. Certainly I consider God androgynous. He is as gentle and tender and nurturing and maternal as any woman could ever be. Nonetheless, culturally determined though it may be, I subjectively experience His reality as more masculine than feminine. While He nurtures us, He also desires to penetrate us, and while we more often than not flee from His love like a reluctant virgin, He chases after us with a vigor in the hunt that we most typically associate with males. As C. S. Lewis put it, in relation to God we are all female.*
Moreover, whatever our gender or conscious theology, it is our duty—our obligation—in response to His love to attempt to give birth, like Mary, to Christ in ourselves and in others.

I shall, however, break with tradition and use the neuter for Satan. While I know Satan to be lustful to penetrate us, I have not in the least experienced this desire as sexual or creative—only hateful and destructive. It is hard to determine the sex of a snake.

I have made multiple alterations of detail in every one of the many case histories given in this book. The cornerstones of both psychotherapy and science are honesty and accuracy. Nonetheless, values often compete, and the preservation of confidentiality takes precedence in this book over the full or accurate disclosure of irrelevant detail. The purist, therefore, may distrust my "data." On the other hand, if you think you recognize one of my specific patients in this book, you will be wrong. You will, however, probably recognize many people who conform to the personality patterns I will describe. That will be because the many alterations of case-history details have not, in my judgment, significantly distorted the reality of the human dynamics involved. And this book has been written because of the commonality of such dynamics, as well as their need to be more clearly perceived and understood by us human beings.

* *That Hideous Strength,* Macmillan (Paperback Edition, New York, 1965), p. 316.

The length of the list of people to be thanked for their support of this work makes such listing impractical, but the following deserve special mention: my faithful secretary, Anne Pratt, who without benefit of word processor, cooperatively typed the seemingly endless manuscript versions and revisions over the course of five years; my children, Belinda, Julia, and Christopher, who have suffered from their father's workaholism; those of my colleagues who have affirmed me through their courage to also face the terrible reality of human evil, particularly my wife, Lily, to whom this work is dedicated, and my dear "atheist" friend, Richard Slone; my editor, Erwin Glikes, who encouraged me so greatly by his belief in the need for the book; all the brave patients who have submitted to my fumbling ministrations and have thereby been my teachers; and, finally, two great modern students of human evil and mentors for me, Erich Fromm and Malachi Martin.


                                        M. SCOTT PECK, M.D.
                             *New Preston, Connecticut 06777*

# 1

# THE MAN
# WHO MADE A PACT
# WITH THE DEVIL

GEORGE HAD ALWAYS BEEN a carefree person—or so he thought—until that afternoon in early October. It is true that he had the usual concerns of a salesman, a husband and father of three, and the owner of a house with a roof that occasionally leaked and a lawn that always needed mowing. It is also true that he was an unusually neat and orderly person who tended to worry more than most if the lawn got a little high or the house paint a little chipped. And it is true that in the evenings, just as the sun was setting, he always experienced a strange mixture of sadness and dread. George did not like sunset time. But that lasted only a few minutes. Sometimes when he was busy selling or when the sky was gray, he did not notice the sunset time at all.

George was a topnotch salesman, a natural. Handsome, articulate, with an easy manner and a gift for storytelling, he had taken over the southeastern states territory like a meteor. He sold plastic container lids, the kind that snap easily over coffee cans. It was a competitive market. George's company was one of five national manufacturers of such products. Within two years of taking over the territory from a man who was no slouch himself, George, with his genius for orderliness, had tripled the sales At thirty-four he was making close to sixty thousand dollars a year in salary and commissions without even having to work very hard. He had made it.

The trouble started in Montreal. The company suggested that he go there for a plastics manufacturers' convention. Since it was autumn, and neither he nor his wife, Gloria, had seen the fall foliage of the north, he decided to take her with him. They enjoyed it. The convention was just another convention, but the foliage was exquisite, the restaurants were excellent, and Gloria was in a reasonably good mood. On their last afternoon in Montreal they went to see the cathedral. Not because they were religious; Gloria was a lukewarm Protestant at best, and he, having endured a fanatically religious mother, had a distinct antipathy to churches. Still it was one of the sights and they were sightseeing. He found it gloomy and uninteresting and was happy when Gloria had had enough of it. As they were walking out toward the sunlight he spied a small contribution box near the massive door. He stopped in indecision. On the one hand he had no genuine desire to give a penny to this or any church. On the other, he felt a small unreasonable fear that he might be jeopardizing the stability of his life if he didn't. The fear embarrassed him; he was a rational man. But then it occurred to him that it would be quite rational to make a small contribution, just as it is rational to pay an admission price to a museum or an amusement park. He decided to give the change in his pocket if it was not a large amount. It wasn't. He counted fifty-five cents in small coins and dumped them in the box.

That was the moment when that first thought hit him. It struck him like a blow, an actual punch, totally unexpected, dazing him, confusing him. It was more than a thought. It was as if the words were suddenly written out in his mind: "YOU ARE GOING TO DIE AT 55."

George reached into his pocket for his wallet. Most of his cash was in traveler's checks. But he had a five and two one-dollar bills. He tore them from his wallet and stuffed them into the box. Then he took Gloria by the arm and almost shoved her through the doorway. She asked him what was wrong. He told him he was suddenly feeling ill and wanted to return to their hotel. He did not remember walking down the cathedral steps or hailing a taxi. It was only when he was back in their hotel room, lying in bed vaguely pretending to be sick, that his panic began to subside.

By the next day, as they were flying back to their home in

North Carolina, George was feeling peaceful and confident. The incident was forgotten.

Two weeks later, driving on a sales trip in Kentucky, George came to a sign announcing a curve in the road and a forty-five-mile-an-hour speed limit. As he passed the sign another thought came to him, etched in his mind as before in large sharply hewn letters: "YOU WILL DIE AT 45."

George felt uneasy the remainder of the day. This time, however, he was able to consider his experience a little more objectively. Both thoughts had to do with numbers. Numbers were just numbers, nothing else, little abstracts without meaning. If they had meaning, why would they change? First 55, now 45. If they were consistent, then he might have something to worry about. But they were just numbers without significance. By the next day he was his old self again.

A week passed. As George drove into the outskirts of a small village a sign announced that he was entering Upton, North Carolina. The third thought came: "YOU WILL BE MUR-DERED BY A MAN NAMED UPTON." George began to be seriously worried. Two days later, driving past an old abandoned railroad station, the words flashed again: "THE ROOF OF THAT BUILDING WILL COLLAPSE WITH YOU INSIDE, KILLING YOU."

Thereafter the thoughts came almost every day, always when he was driving, working his territory. George started dreading the mornings on which he faced business trips. He was preoccupied when he was working, and he lost his sense of humor. Food ceased to taste good. It was difficult to get to sleep at night. But it was all still bearable until the morning he drove across the Roanoke River. Immediately afterward he had the thought: THAT'S THE LAST TIME YOU'LL EVER CROSS THAT BRIDGE.

George considered telling Gloria about his thoughts. Would she think he was crazy? He couldn't bring himself to do it. But lying in bed that night with Gloria snoring softly beside him, he hated her for having peace of mind while he wrestled with his dilemma. The bridge across the Roanoke was one of his most traveled routes. To avoid it he would have to go several hundred miles out of his way each month or else drop several clients. Goddamn it, it was absurd. He couldn't let his life be dictated by mere thoughts, mere figments of a perverse imagination. There was not the slightest shred of evidence that these thoughts represented any kind of reality. On the other hand, how could he know they weren't real? That's it—he could prove they weren't real. If he were to go over the Roanoke Bridge again and not die, it would prove the thought to be false. But if the thought were true . . .

At one o'clock in the morning George reached the decision to risk his life. Better to die than live tormented in this way. He dressed silently in the darkness and slipped out of the house. Seventy-three miles back to the Roanoke Bridge. He drove very carefully. When the bridge finally loomed up before him in the night, there was such a tightness in his chest he could hardly breathe. But he went ahead. Over the bridge. Two miles down the road. Then he turned around and drove back across the bridge toward home. He'd made it. He'd proved the thought was wrong! Silly, ridiculous thought. He began to whistle. By the time he let himself back into the house at dawn he was ecstatic. He felt well for the first time in two months. There was no more fear.

Until three nights later. Returning home in the afternoon from another day's trip, he passed a deep excavation at the side of the road near Fayetteville. BEFORE IT IS FILLED, YOUR CAR WILL DRIVE STRAIGHT INTO THAT EXCAVATION AND YOU WILL BE KILLED. At first George almost laughed about this latest thought. The thoughts were just thoughts; hadn't he proved it? Yet that night he could not get to sleep once again. It was true he had proven the thought about the Roanoke Bridge to be false. But that did not necessarily mean this new thought about the excavation was false. This one just might be the real one. Couldn't it be that the Roanoke Bridge thought was designed to lull him into a false sense of security? That he really was destined to drive into the excavation? The more he considered it, the more anxious he became. Sleep was impossible.

Perhaps if he went back to the site of the excavation, it would make him feel better, just as it had when he went back to the bridge. Admittedly, the idea didn't make much sense; even if he did return to the excavation and make the trip back successfully, he still might slip up and drive into it at a later date, as forecast.

Yet he was so anxious it was perhaps worth the try. Once more George dressed in the middle of the night and slipped out of the house. He felt like a fool. Almost to his surprise, however, after he had reached Fayetteville and stopped at the edge of the excavation and started the return trip home, he did feel better—markedly better. His confidence came back. He had the feeling that he was again master of his destiny. He fell asleep as soon as he was home. For a few hours he had some peace.

The pattern of George's illness now became more fixed and devastating. Every day or two on the road he would have a new thought about his death. Following the thought his anxiety would rise to a point at which it was no longer bearable. At that point he would feel compelled to drive back to the spot where he had experienced the thought. Once he had done this, he felt fine again until the next day and the next thought. Then the cycle would start over.

George stood it for six more weeks. Every other night he was driving around the Carolina countryside. He slept less and less. He lost fifteen pounds. He dreaded going on the road, facing his job. His work performance slipped. A few customers were beginning to complain. He was irritable with his children. Finally, one evening in February, he broke down. Weeping in exasperation, he told Gloria of his torment. Gloria knew of me from a friend. She called me the next morning, and that afternoon I saw George for the first time.

I explained to George that he was suffering from a classical obsessive-compulsive neurosis; that the "thoughts" that bothered him were what we psychiatrists called obsessions, and that the need to return to the scene of the "thought" was a compulsion. "You're right!" he exclaimed. "It is a compulsion. I don't want to go back to where I have these thoughts. I know it's silly. I want to just forget about it and go to sleep. But I can't. It's like something is forcing me to think about it and forcing me to get up at night and go back. I can't help myself. I'm compelled to go back. You know, that's the worst part of it. If it were just these thoughts, I think I could stand it, but it's this compulsion to go back that's killing me, that's robbing me of my sleep, that's driving me nuts as I spend hours debating in my mind: 'Should I or shouldn't I go back?' My compulsions are even worse than—what do you call them?—my obsessions. They're what's driving me crazy." Here George paused, looking at me anxiously. "Do you think I'm going crazy?"

"No," I replied. "You're still very much a stranger to me, but on the surface of things I don't see any sign that you are going crazy or that you have anything worse than a severe neurosis."

"You mean other people have these same kinds of 'thoughts' and compulsions?" George asked eagerly. "Other people who aren't crazy?"

"That's correct," I answered. "Their obsessions may not be about dying and their compulsions may be something else. But the pattern of unwanted thoughts and the taking of undesired actions is just the same." I went on to recount to George a few of the more common obsessions from which people might suffer. I told him, for instance, of people who have great difficulty in leaving their homes for vacations because they keep worrying whether they really did remember to lock the front door and keep having to return to check it. "I've done that!" George exclaimed. "I've even had to check three or four times to see whether I'd left the stove on. That's great. You mean, I'm just like everybody else?"

"No, George, you're not like everybody else," I said. "While many people—often very successful people—suffer mildly from their need to be safe and certain, they're not up all night being driven around by their compulsions. You have a major neurosis that is crippling your life. It's a curable neurosis, but the cure—psychoanalytic psychotherapy—is going to be quite difficult and will take a long time. You're not going crazy, but I do think you have a major problem, and I think if you don't get extensive treatment, you're likely to continue to be crippled."

Three days later when George returned to see me for the second time, he was a different man. During our first session he had been weepy as he told me of his agony and almost pathetically eager for reassurance. Now he radiated confidence and aplomb. Indeed, he had a manner of casual *savoir-faire*, which we were later to identify as his "Joe Cool" appearance. I attempted to learn more about the circumstances of his life, but there was little to grab hold of.

"I don't really have anything that's bothering me, Dr. Peck, except these little obsessions and compulsions, and I haven't had any of those since I saw you last. Oh, I admit I have concerns, but that's different from real worries. I mean I'm concerned about whether we ought to paint the house this summer or wait until next. But that's a concern, not a worry. We have plenty of money in the bank. And I'm concerned about how the children are doing in school. Deborah, our oldest, who's thirteen, is probably going to need braces. George junior—he's eleven—doesn't get very good grades. He's not retarded or anything, just more interested in sports. And Christopher, who's six, he's just starting school. He's got the neatest disposition. I guess you could say he's the apple of my eye. I must admit that in my heart I favor him a bit more than the older two, but I make an effort not to show it, and I think I succeed—so that's not a problem. We're a stable family. Good marriage. Oh, Gloria has her moods. Occasionally I even think she's downright bitchy, but I guess all women are like that. Their periods, you know, and that sort of thing.

"Our sex life? Oh, that's fine. No problem there. Except, of course, when Gloria's in a bitchy mood, and then neither of us feels like it—but that's par for the course, isn't it?

"My childhood? Well, I can't say it was really always happy. When I was nine my father had a nervous breakdown. He had to be hospitalized at the state hospital. Schizophrenia, I guess they called it. I suppose that's the reason I was worried last time you might think I was going crazy. I must admit it was a load off my mind when you told me I wasn't. You see, my father never came out of it. Oh, he came home a few times on passes from the hospital, but they never worked out. Yes, I guess he was pretty crazy at times, but I really don't remember very much about it. I can remember having to visit him in the hospital. That I hated. It used to embarrass me to death. And it was such a creepy place. By the middle of high school I refused to visit him anymore, and he died when I was in college. Yes, he died young. A blessing, I would say.

"But I don't think any of that really disturbed me. My sister, who was two years younger, and I got plenty of attention. Mom was with us all the time. She was a good mother. She's a bit religious, overly so for my taste. She was always dragging us to churches, which I also hated. But that's the only thing I can fault her for, and besides that stopped as soon as I went to college. We weren't well off financially, but there was always enough to get by. My grandparents had some money, you see, and they helped us out a lot—my mother's parents. I never knew my father's parents. Anyway, we were really close to my grandparents. For a while, when my father was first in the hospital, we even lived with them. I especially loved my grandmother.

"That reminds me, I remembered something after our last meeting. Talking about compulsions brought it back to my mind that I also had a compulsion when I was around thirteen. I don't know how it started, but I got this feeling that my grandmother would die unless I touched a certain rock each day. It wasn't a big deal. The rock was on my way home from school, so all I had to do was just remember to touch it. It was a problem only on the weekends. Then I had to find time each day to do it. Anyway, I grew out of it after a year or so. I don't know how. I just naturally grew out of it, like it was a phase or something.

"It makes me think I'm also going to grow out of these obsessions and compulsions I've been having recently. I told you, I haven't had a single one since I saw you. I think maybe it's over. Possibly all I needed was the little talk we had earlier in the week. I'm most grateful to you for it. You can't imagine what a reassurance it was for me to know that I wasn't going crazy and that other people have the same kind of funny thoughts. I think that reassurance has probably done the trick. I doubt that I need this—what do you call it?—psychoanalysis. I agree, it may be too early to tell, but it seems to me a very long and expensive procedure for something I'm likely to grow out of by myself. So I'd rather not make another appointment. Let's just see what happens. If my obsessions or compulsions come back, then I'll go ahead with it, but for the moment, I'd like to let it ride."

I mildly attempted to remonstrate with George. I told him it seemed to me that nothing substantial had changed in his existence. I suspected that his symptoms would shortly recur in some form or other. I said I could understand his desire to wait and see what happened, however, and that I would be happy to see him again whenever he wanted. He had made up his mind and clearly was not going to enter therapy as long as he was feeling comfortable. There was no point in fighting about it. The only reasonable course for me was to sit back and wait.

I did not have to wait long.

Two days later George called me, frantic. "You were right,

Dr. Peck, the thoughts have come back. Yesterday as I was driving back from a sales meeting, a few miles after I'd rounded a sharp curve, I suddenly had the thought: YOU HIT AND KILLED A HITCHHIKER STANDING AT THE SIDE OF THE ROAD AS YOU DROVE AROUND THAT CURVE. I knew it was just one of my crazy thoughts. If I had really hit someone, I would have felt a bump or heard a thump. But I couldn't get the thought out of my mind. I kept envisioning the body lying in the gutter at the side of the road. I kept thinking he might not be dead and might need help. I kept worrying I would be accused of being a hit-and-run driver. Finally, just before I got home, I couldn't stand it any longer. So I turned around and drove fifty miles all the way back to that curve. Of course there was no body there, no sign of an accident, no blood in the grass. So I felt better. But I can't go on like this. I guess you're right. I guess I do need this psychoanalysis."

So George resumed therapy, and continued in it because his obsessions and compulsions continued. Over the next three months while he was seeing me twice a week he had many more of his thoughts. Most were about his own death, but some were about being the cause of someone's else's death or being accused of some crime. And each time, after a longer or shorter period of obsessing about it, George would finally give in and return to the scene where the thought had first occurred to obtain relief. His agony continued.

During these first three months in therapy I gradually learned that George had a great deal more to worry about than just his symptoms. His sex life, which he had told me was fine, proved abysmal. Gloria and he had intercourse once every six weeks, and then as an almost violent, quick animalistic act when both of them were drunk. Gloria's "bitchy moods" turned out to last for weeks. I met with her and found her to be significantly depressed, filled with hatred toward George, whom she described as a "weak, sniveling slob." George in turn slowly began to express an enormous amount of resentment toward Gloria, whom he saw as a self-centered, totally unsupportive and unloving woman. He was completely alienated from his two older children, Deborah and George junior. He felt that Gloria had been responsible for turning them against him. In the whole family, Christopher was the only one with whom he had a relationship, and he recognized that he was probably spoiling the boy "to keep him out of Gloria's clutches."

Although he had acknowledged from the beginning that his childhood had been less than ideal, as I pushed him to recollect it, George slowly started to realize that it had been more damaging and frightening than he liked to believe. He was able to remember, for instance, his eighth birthday, when his father killed his sister's kitten. He was sitting on his bed before breakfast, daydreaming of the presents he might receive, when the kitten came tumbling into the room. His father came in right after it, crazy with rage, carrying a broom. The kitten had apparently made a mess on the living room rug. As George crouched on his bed, screaming for him to stop, his father proceeded to beat the kitten to death with the broom in the corner of the bedroom. That was a year before his father finally had to go to the state hospital.

George was also able to recognize that his mother was almost as deranged as his father. One night, when he was eleven, she had kept him awake until dawn, forcing him to pray on his knees for the survival of their minister, who had had a heart attack. George had hated the minister, and hated the Pentecostal church to which his mother took him every Wednesday evening, every Friday evening, and all day Sunday, year in and year out. He remembered experiencing unrelieved embarrassment and shame as his mother would speak in tongues and writhe in ecstasy during those services, shouting "O Jesus." Nor was his life with his grandparents as idyllic as he had wanted to remember it. It was true that he had had a warm and tender and probably saving relationship with his grandmother, but that relationship frequently seemed in jeopardy. During the two years they lived with his grandparents—after his father was hospitalized—his grandfather beat his grandmother almost weekly. Each time George was afraid that his grandmother would be killed. Often he was fearful of leaving the house, feeling that somehow, even by his helpless presence, he might be able to prevent her murder.

These pieces of information, and others, had to be pried out of George. He repeatedly complained that he did not see the point of dwelling on the seemingly unsolvable problems of his present life and remembering the painful facts of his past. "All I want," he said, "is to get rid of these ideas and my compulsions. I don't see how talking about unpleasant things that are over and done with is going to help me get rid of these symptoms." At the same time George talked almost incessantly about his obsessions and compulsions. On each occasion of a new "thought" he described it with extraordinary detail and seemed to relish recounting the agonies of deciding whether or not to give in to his compulsion to return. It shortly became clear to me that George was actually using his symptoms to avoid dealing with many of the realities of his life. "One of the reasons you have these symptoms," I explained, "is that they act as a smoke screen. You are so busy thinking and talking about your obsessions and compulsions that you don't have the time to think about the more basic problems that are causing them. Until you are willing to stop using this smoke screen, and until you have dealt in much greater depth with your miserable marriage and your ghastly childhood, you're going to continue to be tortured by your symptoms."

It also became clear that George was equally reluctant to face the issue of death. "I know I'm going to die someday, but why think about it? It's morbid. Besides, nothing can be done about it. Thinking about it isn't going to change it." I attempted, without much success, to point out to George that his attitude was almost ludicrous. "Actually, you're thinking about death all the time," I said. "What do you think your obsessions and compulsions are all about, if not death? And what about your anxiety at the time of sunset? Isn't it clear to you that you hate sunsets because the sunset represents the death of the day and that reminds you of your own death? You're terrified of death. That's okay. So am I. But you're trying to avoid that terror rather than face it. Your problem is not that you think about death but the way you think about it. Until you are able to think about death—despite its terror—voluntarily, you will continue to think about it involuntarily in the form of your obsessions." But no matter how well I phrased the issue, George seemed to be in no hurry to deal with it.

He was, however, in a vast hurry to be relieved of his symptoms. Despite the fact that he preferred talking about them to talking about death or his alienation from his wife and children, there was no doubt that George was suffering greatly from his obsessions and compulsions. He took to calling me from the road when he was experiencing them. "Dr. Peck," he would say, "I'm in Raleigh and I just had another one of my thoughts a couple of hours ago. I promised Gloria I'd be home for dinner. But I can't be if I go back where I had the thought. I don't know what to do. I want to go home, but I feel I have to go back. Please, Dr. Peck, help me. Tell me what to do. Tell me I can't go back. Tell me I shouldn't give in to the compulsion."

Each time I would patiently explain to George that I was not going to tell him what to do, that I did not have the power to tell him what to do, that only he had the power to make his own decisions and it was not healthy for him to want me to make his decisions for him. But my response made no sense to him. Each session he would remonstrate with me. "Dr. Peck, I know if you were to tell me I can't go back anymore, I wouldn't. I'd feel so much better. I don't understand why you won't help me. All you keep saying is it's not your place to tell me what to do. But that's why I'm coming to see you—for you to help me—and you won't. I don't know why you're being so cruel. It's as if you don't even want to help me. You keep saying I've got to make up my own mind. But that's just what I can't do, don't you see? Don't you see the pain I'm in? Don't you want to help?" he would whine.

It went on, week after week. And George was visibly deteriorating. He developed diarrhea. He lost more weight and began looking more and more haggard. He became weepy much of the time. He wondered whether he shouldn't be seeing a different psychiatrist. And I myself began to doubt that I was handling the case correctly. It looked as if George might soon need to be hospitalized.

But then something suddenly seemed to change. One morning, a little less than four months after he began therapy, George came to his session whistling and obviously cheerful. I immediately commented on the change. "Yes, I certainly am feeling well today," George acknowledged. "I don't really know why. I haven't had one of my thoughts or the need to go back for four whole days now. Maybe that's why. Maybe I'm beginning to see the light at the end of the tunnel." Yet despite the fact that he was not preoccupied with his symptoms, George seemed no more eager to deal with the painful realities of his home life or his childhood. Having resumed his Joe Cool manner, he rather facilely talked about these realities at my urging, but without any real feeling. Then just before the end of the session, out of the blue, he asked me, "Dr. Peck, do you believe in the devil?"

"That's an odd question," I replied. "And a very complicated one. Why do you ask?"

"Oh, no particular reason, just curious."

"You're evading." I confronted him. "There must be a reason."

"Well, I guess the only reason is that you read a lot about these weird cults that worship Satan. You know, like some of these far-out groups in San Francisco. There's a lot in the papers about them these days."

"That's true," I agreed. "But what brought it to your mind? Why did you suddenly think about it this morning, right now in this particular session?"

"How should I know?" George asked. He appeared annoyed. "It just came into my mind. You've instructed me to tell you everything that comes into my mind, so I did. All I was doing was what I'm supposed to do. It came into my mind and I told you. I don't know why it came into my mind."

There seemed no way to proceed further. We had come to the end of the session, and the matter was dropped. The following session George was still feeling well. He had gained a couple of pounds and no longer looked haggard. "I had another one of my thoughts two days ago," he reported, "but it didn't bother me. I told myself I'm not going to let these silly thoughts bother me anymore. They obviously don't mean anything. So I'm going to die one of these days—so what? I didn't even have the desire to go back. It hardly crossed my mind. Why should I go back about something that's so silly? I think maybe I've finally got this problem licked."

Once more, since he was again no longer obsessed with his symptoms, I attempted to help him focus more deeply on his marital problems. But his "Joe Cool" manner was impenetrable; all his responses seemed superficial. I had an uneasy feeling. George did seem to be getting better. Ordinarily I would have been delighted, but I did not have the slightest understanding of why. Nothing in his life, or in the way he was dealing with life, had changed. Why, then, was he getting better? I pushed my uneasiness into the back of my mind.

Our next session was an evening one. George entered looking well and more "Joe Cool" than ever. As customary, I let him begin the session. After a brief silence, rather casually and without the slightest sign of anxiety, he announced, "I guess I have a confession to make."

"Oh?"

"Well, you know, I've been feeling better lately, and I haven't told you why."

"Oh?"

"You remember a couple of sessions ago I asked you if you believed in the devil? And you wanted to know why I was thinking about it? Well, I guess I wasn't quite honest with you. I do know why. But I felt silly telling you."

"Go on."

"I still feel a bit silly. But, you see, you haven't been helping me. You wouldn't do anything to prevent me from going back to those spots where my thoughts came to me. I had to do something to keep myself from giving in to my compulsions. So I did it."

"Did what?" I asked.

"I made a pact with the devil. I mean, I really don't believe in the devil, but I had to do something, didn't I? So I made this agreement that if I did give in to my compulsion and go back, then the devil would see to it that my thought came true. Do you understand?"

"I'm not sure," I responded.

"Well, for instance, the other day I had this thought near Chapel Hill: THE NEXT TIME YOU COME THIS WAY YOU WILL DRIVE OVER THAT EMBANKMENT AND BE KILLED. Ordinarily, of course, I would have stewed about it for a couple of hours, and finally I would have gone back to the embankment just to prove that the thought wasn't true. Right? But having made this pact, you see, I couldn't go back. Because as part of the agreement, if I went back, the devil would see to it that I did drive over that embankment and would be killed. Knowing I would be killed, there was no reason for me to go back. In fact, there was an incentive not to go back. Now do you understand?"

"I understand the mechanics of it," I replied noncommittally.

"Well, they seem to work," George said happily. "Twice now I've had the thoughts, and neither time have I had to go back. I must admit I have a little bit of the guilties about it though."

"The 'guilties'?"

"You know, a feeling of guilt. I mean, people aren't supposed to make a pact with the devil and all that, are they? Besides, I don't even really believe in the devil. But if it seems to work, so what?"

I was silent. I had no idea what to say to George. I felt over-whelmed by the complexity of the case and the complexity of my own feelings. Staring at the soft light on the table that sepa-rated the two of us sitting together in my quiet, seemingly safe office, I was aware that hundreds of thoughts were rushing through my mind, all disconnected. I felt unable to find my way in this labyrinth of obsessional thinking, to come to grips with this working pact with the devil that did not exist in order to nullify the compulsion to nullify thoughts that themselves were unreal. Knowing I was unable to see the woods for the trees, I simply sat there staring at the lamp as the minutes ticked by audibly on my office clock.

"Well, what is your reaction?" George finally asked me.

"I don't know, George," I replied, "I don't know what my re-action is. I have to have more time to think about it. I don't know what to say to you yet."

I resumed staring at the light, and the clock continued to click. Another five minutes went by. George seemed quite discomfited by the silence. Finally he broke it. "Well, I guess there is a little bit more I haven't told you," he said. "And I guess there's an-other reason I have the guilties a little bit. You see, there was an-other part to my agreement with the devil. Because I don't really believe in the devil, I couldn't really believe for certain that he would see to it that I was killed if I went back. For it to work I had to have some insurance, something that would really keep me from going back. What could that be, I wondered. Then it occurred to me that the one thing I love most in the world is my son Christopher. So I made it part of the agreement that if I did give in to the compulsion and go back, the devil would see to it that Christopher died an early death. Not only would I die but Christopher would too. Now you know why I can't go back anymore. Even if the devil's not real, I'm still not willing to risk Christopher's life on the issue—I love him so much."

"So you threw Christopher's life into the bargain as well?" I repeated numbly.

"Yes—it doesn't sound good, does it? That's the part that really gives me the guilties."

I fell silent again, slowly beginning to sort things out. It was almost the end of the hour. George started making motions to get ready to go. "Not yet, George," I commanded. "Ours is the last appointment I have today. I would like to respond to you, and I feel I'm almost ready. Unless you have an urgent need to leave, I'd like you to stay and wait until I'm able to say some things."

George waited, fidgeting. It was not my intention to make him fidget. As a psychiatrist I had been trained—and had trained myself—not to be judgmental. Therapy can work only when the patient feels himself to be accepted by the therapist. Only in an atmosphere of acceptance can the patient be expected to confide his secrets so as to develop a sense of his own value. I had been practicing long enough to learn that frequently it is necessary, indeed essential, at some point in the course of the case for the therapist to oppose the patient on a particular issue and pass critical judgment on him. But I also knew that ideally this point should occur late in the course, after the therapeutic relationship had been firmly established. George had been in treatment with me a mere four months and we still had little in the way of a relationship. I was unwilling to take the risk of passing judgment on him this early, and on such a basic level as well. It seemed a very dangerous thing to do. It also seemed a dangerous thing not to do.

George could not tolerate the silent waiting any longer. In the midst of the final throes of my decision-making he blurted, "Well, what do you think?"

I looked at him. "I think, George, that I am very glad you are having the guilties, as you call them."

"What do you mean?"

"I mean that you *should* feel guilty. You have done something to feel guilty about. I would be very worried about you if you didn't feel guilty over what you have done."

George immediately became wary. "I thought psychotherapy was supposed to relieve me of my guilt feelings."

"Only those guilt feelings that are inappropriate," I replied. "To feel guilty about something that is not bad is unnecessary and sick. Not to feel guilty about something that *is* bad is also sick."

"Do you think that I'm bad?"

"I think that in making this pact with the devil you have done something that is bad. Something evil."

"But I haven't really done anything," George exclaimed. "Don't you see? It's all been in my mind. You yourself have told me that there's no such thing as a bad thought, a bad wish or feeling. 'Only what one actually does is bad,' you've said. 'The first law of psychiatry,' you called it. Well, I haven't done anything. I haven't lifted a finger against a single soul."

"But you have done something, George," I responded.

"What?"

"You made a pact with the devil."

"But that's not doing anything."

"No?"

"No. Can't you understand? It's all in my mind, a figment of my imagination. I don't even believe in the devil. I don't believe in God, for that matter, so how could I believe in the devil? If I had made a real pact with a real person, that would be another matter. But I haven't. The devil's not real. So how can my pact be real? How can you make a real pact with something that doesn't exist? It hasn't been a real action."

"You mean you didn't make a pact with the devil?"

"Damn it, I did. I told you I did. But it's not a real pact. You're trying to trip me up by playing word games."

"No, George," I replied. "You're the one who's playing the word games. I don't know any more about the devil than you do. I don't know whether it's a he, she, or an it. I don't know whether the devil's corporeal, or whether it's a force, or whether it's just a concept. But it doesn't matter. The fact remains that whatever it is, you made a contract with it."

George tried a different tack. "Even if I did, the contract's not valid. It's null and void. Any lawyer knows that a contract under duress isn't a legal contract. You can't be held liable for signing a contract when a gun is pointed at your back. And God knows I've been under duress. You've seen how I've been suffering. For months I've been pleading with you to help me, and you haven't lifted a finger. You seem to be interested in me all right, but for some reason you won't do anything to relieve my suffering. What else am I supposed to do when you won't help me? It's been torture for me these past months. Pure torture. If that isn't duress, I don't know what is."

I got up from my chair and went over to the window. I stood there for a minute looking out into the empty darkness. The moment had arrived. I turned around to face him. "Okay, George,

I'm going to say a few things to you. I want you to listen to them well. Because they're very important. Nothing is more important."

I resumed my seat and continued, still looking at him. "You have a defect—a weakness—in your character, George," I said. "It is a very basic weakness, and it is the cause of all the difficulties we've been talking about. It's the major cause of your bad marriage. It's the cause of your symptoms, your obsessions and compulsions. And now it's the cause of your pact with the devil. And even of your attempt to explain away the pact.

"Basically, George, you're a kind of a coward," I continued. "Whenever the going gets a little bit rough, you sell out. When you're faced with the realization that you're going to die one of these days, you run away from it. You don't think about it, because it's 'morbid.' When you're faced with the painful realization that your marriage is lousy, you run away from that too. Instead of facing it and doing something about it, you don't think about that either. And then because you've run away from these things that are really inescapable, they come to haunt you in the form of your symptoms, your obsessions and compulsions. These symptoms could be your salvation. You could say, 'These symptoms mean that I'm haunted. I better find out what these ghosts are, and clean them out of my house.' But you don't say that, because that would mean really facing some things that are painful. So you try to run away from your symptoms too. Instead of facing them and what they mean, you try to get rid of them. And when they're not so easy to get rid of, you go running to anything that will give you relief, no matter how wicked or evil or destructive.

"You plead that you shouldn't be held accountable for your pact with the devil because it was made under duress. Of course it was made under duress. Why else would one contract with the devil, except to rid oneself of some kind of suffering? If the devil is lurking around, as some suggest, looking for souls who'll sell out to him, I'm damn sure he's focusing all his attention on those people who are suffering some kind of duress. The question is not duress. The question is how people deal with duress. Some withstand it and overcome it, ennobled. Some break and sell out. You sell out, and, I must say, you do it rather easily.

"Easily. Easy. That's a key word for you, George. You like to think of yourself as easygoing. Joe Cool. And I suppose you are easygoing, but I don't know where you're going easy except into hell. You're always looking for the easy way out, George. Not the right way. The easy way. When you're faced with a choice between the right way and the easy way, you'll take the easy way every time. The painless way. In fact, you'll do anything to find the easy way out, even if it means selling your soul and sacrificing your son.

"As I said, I'm glad you're feeling guilty. If you didn't feel bad about taking the easy way out, no matter what, then I wouldn't be able to help you. You've been learning that psychotherapy is not the easy way out. It's a way of facing things, even if it's painful, even if it's very painful. It's the way of not running away. It's the right way, not the easy way. If you're willing to face the painful realities of your life—your terrorful childhood, your miserable marriage, your mortality, your own cowardice—I can be of some assistance. And I am sure that we will succeed. But if all you want is the easiest possible relief from pain, then I expect that you are the devil's man, and I don't see any way that psychotherapy can help you."

It was George's turn to be silent. The minutes ticked by again. We had now been meeting for two hours. Finally he spoke: "In the comic books, once someone makes a pact with the devil, he can no longer get out of it. Once he's sold his soul, the devil won't give it back. Maybe it's too late for me to change."

"I don't know, George," I responded. "As I told you, I don't know much about these things. You're the first person I've ever known who specifically made such a pact. Like you, I don't even know whether the devil really exists. But on the basis of my experience with you, I think I can hazard a very educated guess about the way things really are. I think you really did make a pact with the devil, and because you did, I think, for you, the devil became real. In your desire to avoid pain, I think you called the devil into existence. Because you had the power to call him into existence, I think you also have the power to end his existence. Intuitively, in the deepest part of me, I feel the process is reversible. I think you can go back to where you were. I think that if you change your mind and become willing to bear the duress, then the pact will be voided and the devil will have to look elsewhere for someone to make him real."

George looked very sad. "For the past ten days," he said, "I've felt better than I have in many months. I've had a few thoughts, but they really haven't bothered me at all. If I were to reverse the process, it would mean going back to where I was two weeks ago. In agony."

"I expect that's right," I agreed.

"What you're asking me to do is to voluntarily return to a state of torment."

"It's what I'm suggesting you need to do, George. Not for me, but for yourself. If it would help you if I asked you to do it, then I will."

"To actually choose a state of pain." George mused. "I don't know. I'm not sure I can do it. I'm not sure I want to do it."

I stood up. "Are you going to see me Monday, George?" I asked.

"Yes. I'll be here."

George stood up. I went over to him and shook his hand. "Until Monday, then. Good night."

That evening was the turning point in George's therapy. By Monday his symptoms had returned in full force. But there was a change. He no longer pleaded with me to tell him not to go back. He also was very slightly more willing to examine in depth his fear of death and the enormous gulf of understanding and communication that existed between him and his wife. As time went by, this willingness gradually increased. Eventually he was able to ask his wife, with my assistance, to enter therapy herself. I was able to refer her to another therapist, with whom she made great progress. The marriage began to improve.

Once Gloria was also in therapy, the major focus of our work together became George's "negative" feelings—feelings of anger, of frustration, of anxiety, of depression, and, above all, feelings of sadness and grief. He was able to see that he was quite a sensitive person, one who felt deeply the passing of the seasons, the growing up of his children, and the transience of existence. He was able to realize that in these negative feelings, in his sensitivity and tenderness and vulnerability to pain, lay his humanity. He became less Joe Cool, and at the same time his capacity to bear pain increased. Sunsets continued to hurt him, but they no longer made him anxious. His symptoms—his obsessions and compulsions—began, with ups and downs, to diminish in intensity several months after that night on which we discussed his pact with the devil. At the end of another year they had petered out entirely. Two years after it had begun, George terminated therapy, still not the strongest of men, but stronger than before.

# 2

# TOWARD
# A PSYCHOLOGY
# OF EVIL

## ≛ OF MODELS AND MYSTERY

There are different ways to look at things.

The way psychiatrists are most accustomed to understand human beings is in terms of health and disease. This viewpoint is known as the medical model. It is a very useful and effective way of looking at people.

According to this viewpoint, George was suffering from a very specific disease—namely, an obsessive-compulsive neurosis. We know a good deal about this disease. In many ways George's case was typical. For instance, obsessive-compulsive neuroses have their origins in early childhood, beginning almost always in a less than ideal toilet-training situation. George was not able to remember how he had been toilet-trained. But from the fact that his father beat a kitten to death for making a mess one can guess it was made clear to George that he had better learn to control his bowels or else. It is no accident that George grew up to become a particularly neat and methodical adult, as obsessive-compulsives so often are.

Another typical characteristic of people who are victims of this neurosis is their propensity for what psychiatrists call "magical thinking." Magical thinking can take a variety of forms, but basically it is a belief that thoughts in and of themselves may cause events to occur. Young children normally think magically. For instance, a five-year-old boy may have the thought: I wish my baby sister would die. Then he may become anxious, fearing that she actually will die *because* he wished it. Or if his sister becomes ill, he may be consumed with guilt, feeling that his thought *caused* her to become ill. Ordinarily we grow out of this tendency to think magically and by adolescence are quite certain that we do not have the power to control external events by our thoughts alone. Frequently, however, children who have been unduly traumatized one way or another do not grow out of their magical-thinking stage. This is particularly true of people with an obsessive-compulsive neurosis. Certainly George had not grown out of it. His belief that his thoughts would come true was an essential part of his neurosis. It was because he believed his thoughts would come to pass that he was compelled, time and time again, to travel mile after mile back to the scene of his thoughts so as to nullify or undo their power.

Looked at in this light, George's pact with the devil was simply another manifestation of his magical thinking. The pact seemed to George a feasible maneuver to obtain relief from his suffering precisely because he believed it would come true. Although the pact was "all in his mind," George believed he and his son would both actually die in accordance with its conditions. Restricting ourselves to the medical model, we might say of George's pact with the devil that it was merely one of the many forms his magical thinking took, and that his magical thinking was a typical feature of the common mental illness from which he suffered. And since the phenomenon can be understood in these terms, there is no need for further analysis. Case closed.

The problem is that, viewed in this light, the relationship between George and the devil seems prosaic and not very significant. How would it seem if we viewed it instead in terms of a traditional Christian religious model?

According to this model, humanity (and perhaps the entire universe) is locked in a titanic struggle between the forces of good and evil, between God and the devil. The battleground of this struggle is the individual human soul. The entire meaning of human life revolves around the battle. The only question of ultimate significance is whether the individual soul will be won to God or won to the devil. By establishing through his pact a relationship with the devil, George had placed his soul in the greatest jeopardy known to man. It was clearly the critical point of his life. And possibly even the fate of all humanity turned upon his decision. Choirs of angels and armies of demons were watching him, hanging on his every thought, praying continually for one outcome or the other. In the end, by renouncing the pact and the relationship, George rescued himself from hell to the glory of God and for the hope for mankind.

Which is the meaning of George's pact: just another neurotic symptom or the crucial turning point of his existence, with cosmic significance?

It is not my intention in this book to decry the medical model. Of all the possible models—and there are many—it remains the most generally useful one for understanding mental illness. In specific instances at specific times, however, another model may be more appropriate.

At such moments we are required to choose a vantage point. When George told me of his pact with the devil, I was faced with the choice of whether to regard it as just another typical neurotic symptom or as a moment of moral crisis. If I chose the first possibility, no immediate action was mandated on my part; if the latter, I owed it to George and the world to throw myself with all the vigor I could muster into the moral fray. Which way to decide? In choosing to see George's pact—even if it was all in his mind—as immoral, and confronting him with his immorality, I certainly picked the more dramatic alternative. Herein lies, I believe, a rule of thumb. If, at a particular moment, we are in a position in which we must choose a particular model, we should probably choose the most dramatic one—that is, the one that imparts to the event being studied the greatest possible significance.

It is usually neither necessary nor advisable, however, to adopt a single model. We North Americans see a man in the moon; some Central Americans, I am told, perceive a rabbit. Who is right? Both, of course, since each has a different vantage point, cultural as well as geographical. What we call models are simply alternative points of view. And if we want to know the moon—or any phenomenon—as best we can, we need to inspect it from as many diverse vantage points as possible.

Thus the approach of this book will be a multifaceted one. Readers who prefer their fare simple (or simplistic) will likely be uncomfortable. But the subject deserves more than incomplete clarity. Human evil is too important for a one-sided understanding. And it is too large a reality to be grasped within a single frame of reference. Indeed, it is so basic as to be inherently and inevitably mysterious. The understanding of basic reality is never something we achieve; it is only something that can be approached. And, in fact, the closer we approach it the more we realize we do not understand—the more we stand in awe of its mystery.

Then why try to understand? The very question speaks the language of nihilism, since time immemorial a diabolic voice.* Why do or learn anything? The answer is simply that it is far better—both more fulfilling and constructive—to have some glimmer of understanding of what we are about than to flounder around in total darkness. We can neither comprehend nor control it all, but as J. R. R. Tolkien said: "It is not our part to master all the tides of the world, but to do what is in us for the succour of those years wherein we are set, uprooting the evil in the fields that we know, so that those who live after may have clean earth to till. What weather they shall have is not ours to rule."†

So science seeks, as far as it might, to penetrate the mystery of the world. And ever so gradually scientists are beginning to become comfortable embracing multiple models. Physicists are no longer disheartened to look at light as both a particle and a wave. As for psychology, models abound: the biological, the psychological, the psychobiological, the sociological, the sociobiological, the Freudian, the rational-emotive, the behavioral, the existential, and so on. And while science needs those innovators who will champion a single new model as the most advanced understanding, the patient who seeks to be understood as wholly as possible would be well advised to seek a therapist capable of approaching the mystery of the human soul from all angles.

Science has not yet, however, become exactly broad-minded. This chapter is entitled "Toward a Psychology of Evil" precisely because we do not yet have a body of scientific knowledge about human evil deserving of being called a psychology. Why not? The concept of evil has been central to religious thought for mil-

---

* In account after account of exorcisms the demonic voices will propound nihilism of one variety or another.
† J. R. R. Tolkien, *The Return of the King* (Ballantine Books), 1965, p. 190.

lennia. Yet it is virtually absent from our science of psychology—which one might think would be vitally concerned with the matter. The major reason for this strange state of affairs is that the scientific and the religious models have hitherto been considered totally immiscible—like oil and water, mutually incompatible and rejecting.

In the late seventeenth century, after the Galileo affair proved hurtful to both, science and religion worked out an unwritten social contract of nonrelationship. The world was quite arbitrarily divided into the "natural" and the "supernatural." Religion agreed that the "natural world" was the sole province of the scientists. And science agreed, in turn, to keep its nose out of the spiritual—or for that matter, anything to do with values. Indeed, science defined itself as "value-free."

So for the past three hundred years there has been a state of profound separation between religion and science. This divorce—sometimes acrimonious, more often remarkably amicable—has decreed that the problem of evil should remain in the custody of religious thinkers. With few exceptions, scientists have not even sought visitation rights, if for no other reason than the fact that science is supposed to be value-free. The very word "evil" requires an a priori value judgment. Hence it is not even permissible for a strictly value-free science to deal with the subject.

All this is changing, however. The end result of a science without religious values and verities would appear to be the Strangelovian lunacy of the arms race; the end result of a religion without scientific self-doubt and scrutiny, the Rasputinian lunacy of Jonestown. For a whole variety of factors, the separation of religion and science no longer works. There are many compelling reasons today for their reintegration—one of them being the problem of evil itself—even to the point of the creation of a science that is no longer value-free. In the past decade this reintegration has already begun. It is, in fact, the most exciting event in the intellectual history of the late twentieth century.

Science has also steered clear of the problem of evil because of the immensity of the mystery involved. It is not that scientists have no taste for mystery so much as that their attitude and methodology in approaching it is generally reductionistic. Theirs is a "left brain," analytical style. Their standard procedure is to bite off tiny little pieces at a time and then to examine such pieces in relative isolation. They prefer little mysteries to big ones.

Theologians suffer under no such compunction. Their appetite is as large as God. The fact that God is invariably larger than their digestion does not deter them in the least. To the contrary, while some seek in religion an escape from mystery, for others religion is a way to approach mystery. The latter are not loath to employ the reductionistic methods of science, but they are also not reluctant to use more integrative "right brain" means of exploration: meditation, intuition, feeling, faith, and revelation. For them the bigger the mystery, the better.

The problem of evil is a very big mystery indeed. It does not submit itself easily to reductionism. We shall, however, find that some questions about human evil can be reduced to a size manageable for proper scientific investigation. Nonetheless, the pieces of the puzzle are so interlocking, it is both difficult and distorting to pry them apart. Moreover, the size of the puzzle is so grand, we cannot truly hope to obtain more than glimmerings of the big picture. In common with any early attempt at scientific exploration, we shall end up with more questions than answers.

The problem of evil, for instance, can hardly be separated from the problem of goodness. Were there no goodness in the world, we would not even be considering the problem of evil.

It is a strange thing. Dozens of times I have been asked by patients or acquaintances: "Dr. Peck, why is there evil in the world?" Yet no one has ever asked me in all these years: "Why is there good in the world?" It is as if we automatically assume this is a naturally good world that has somehow been contaminated by evil. In terms of what we know of science, however, it is actually easier to explain evil. That things decay is quite explainable in accord with the natural law of physics. That life should evolve into more and more complex forms is not so easily understandable. That children generally lie and steal and cheat is routinely observable. The fact that sometimes they grow up to become truly honest adults is what seems the more remarkable. Laziness is more the rule than diligence. If we seriously think about it, it probably makes more sense to assume this is a naturally evil world that has somehow been mysteriously "contaminated" by goodness, rather than the other way around. The mystery of goodness is even greater than the mystery of evil.*

And these mysteries are inextricable. The title of this chapter

---

* See the discussion of entropy, laziness, and original sin in M. Scott Peck, *The Road Less Traveled* (Simon & Schuster, 1978).

is itself a distortion. It should more properly read "Toward a Psychology of Good and Evil." We cannot legitimately investigate the problem of human evil without simultaneously investigating the problem of human goodness. Indeed, as I shall make clear in the final chapter, an exclusive focus on the problem of evil is actually extremely dangerous to the soul of the investigator.

Bear in mind also that just as the issue of evil inevitably raises the question of the devil, so the inextricable issue of goodness raises the question of God and creation. While we can—and, I believe, should—bite off little pieces of mystery upon which to gnash our scientific teeth, we are approaching matters vast and magnificent beyond our comprehension. Whether we know it or not, we are literally treading upon holy ground. A sense of awe is quite befitting. In the face of such holy mystery it is best we remember to walk with the kind of care that is born both of fear and love.

## A LIFE-AND-DEATH ISSUE

To proceed we need at least a working definition. It is a reflection of the enormous mystery of the subject that we do not have a generally accepted definition of evil. Yet in our hearts I think we all have some understanding of its nature. For the moment I can do no better than to heed my son, who, with the characteristic vision of eight-year-olds, explained simply, "Why, Daddy, evil is 'live' spelled backward." Evil is in opposition to life. It is that which opposes the life force. It has, in short, to do with killing. Specifically, it has to do with murder—namely, unnecessary killing, killing that is not required for biological survival.

Let us not forget this. There are some who have written about evil so intellectually that it comes out sounding abstract to the point of irrelevancy. Murder is not abstract. Let us not forget that George was actually willing to sacrifice the very life of his own child.

When I say that evil has to do with killing, I do not mean to restrict myself to corporeal murder. Evil is also that which kills spirit. There are various essential attributes of life—particularly human life—such as sentience, mobility, awareness, growth, autonomy, will. It is possible to kill or attempt to kill one of these attributes without actually destroying the body. Thus we may "break" a horse or even a child without harming a hair on its head. Erich Fromm was acutely sensitive to this fact when he broadened the definition of necrophilia to include the desire of certain people to control others—to make them controllable, to foster their dependency, to discourage their capacity to think for themselves, to diminish their unpredictability and originality, to keep them in line. Distinguishing it from a "biophilic" person, one who appreciates and fosters the variety of life forms and the uniqueness of the individual, he demonstrated a "necrophilic character type," whose aim it is to avoid the inconvenience of life by transforming others into obedient automatons, robbing them of their humanity.*

Evil, then, for the moment, is that force, residing either inside or outside of human beings, that seeks to kill life or liveliness. And goodness is its opposite. Goodness is that which promotes life and liveliness.

I do a lot of speaking and preaching these days. Recently I asked myself what it is I am basically trying to say. In all my talks and sermons, is there a theme, a central message?

There is. Thinking about it, I realized that one way or another, no matter what my topic, I am always trying in whatever way I can to help people take God, Christ, and themselves far more seriously than they generally do.

From the very beginning we are told that God created us in His own image. Are we going to take that seriously? Accept the responsibility that we are godly beings? And that human life is of sacred importance?

Speaking of his relationship to us human beings, Jesus said, "I am come that they might have life, and that they might have it more abundantly."† Abundantly. What a wonderful word! This strange man, who obviously relished weddings and wine, fine oils and good companionship, and yet allowed himself to be killed, was not so concerned with the length of life as with its vitality. He was not interested in human puppets, of whom he once said,

* Erich Fromm, *The Heart of Man: Its Genius for Good and Evil* (Harper & Row, 1964).
† John 10:10.

"Let the dead bury their dead."* Rather, he was interested in the spirit of life, in liveliness. And of Satan, the very spirit of evil, Jesus said, "He was a murderer from the beginning."† Evil has nothing to do with natural death; it is concerned only with unnatural death, with murder of the body or the spirit.

The purpose of this book is to encourage us to take our human life so seriously that we also take human evil far more seriously—seriously enough to study it with all the means at our command, including the methods of science. It is my intention to encourage us to recognize evil for what it is, in all its ghastly reality. There is nothing morbid about my purpose. To the contrary, it is in dedication to "life . . . more abundantly." The only valid reason to recognize human evil is to heal it wherever we can, and (as is currently most often the case) when we cannot, to study it further that we might discover how to heal it in specific instances and eventually wipe its ugliness off the face of the earth.

It is presumably clear, then, that in encouraging us toward the development of a psychology of evil, I am talking of neither a study of evil in the abstract nor of an abstract psychology divorced from the values of life and liveliness. One cannot study a disease without the intention to heal it, unless one is some kind of a Nazi. A psychology of evil must be a healing psychology.

Healing is the result of love. It is a function of love. Wherever there is love there is healing. And wherever there is no love there is precious little—if any—healing. Paradoxically, a psychology of evil must be a loving psychology. It must be brimful of the love of life. Every step of the way its methodology must be submitted not only to the love of truth but also to the love of life: of warmth and light and laughter, and spontaneity and joy, and service and human caring.

Perhaps I am thus already contaminating science. Let me "contaminate" it further. The scientific psychology I am suggesting—if it is to be anything other than sterile and dead and evil itself—if it is to be rich and fertile and humanely productive—must succeed in integrating much that is not currently or generally considered "scientific." It must, for instance, pay serious attention to literature, particularly mythology. As human beings battled against evil throughout the ages, they consciously or uncon-

* Matthew 8:22.
† John 8:44.

sciously incorporated the lessons they learned into mythic stories. The body of mythology is a vast storehouse of such lessons—to which we are still adding. The character of the Gollum, for instance, in Tolkien's recently popular *The Hobbit* and *The Lord of the Rings* trilogy, is perhaps the finest depiction of evil ever written.* Its author, J. R. R. Tolkien, a professor of literature, clearly knew at least as much about human evil as any psychiatrist or psychologist.

At the other end of the spectrum, the methods of "hard" science also need to be applied to the study of evil: not merely Rorschachs but the most advanced biochemical procedures and sophisticated statistical analyses of hereditary patterns. One editor who reviewed a primitive manuscript version of this work exclaimed, "Surely, Scotty, you don't mean to imply that evil might be genetic or biochemical or *physical* in some way!" Yet this same editor well knew that we are coming to learn that almost all diseases have both physical and emotional roots. Good science, good psychology, cannot be narrow-minded. All avenues should be explored, all stones turned.

Finally, of course, a psychology of evil must be a religious psychology. By this I do not mean it must embrace a specific theology. I do mean, however, that it must not only embrace valid insights from all religious traditions but must also recognize the reality of the "supernatural." And, as I have said, it must be a science in submission to love and the sacredness of life. It cannot be a purely secular psychology.

There are a number of different theological models of evil. Perhaps the one thing they all have in common is a failure to adequately distinguish between human evil, such as murder, and natural evil, such as the death and destruction resulting from fire, flood, and earthquake. Knowing I was writing a book on evil, a friend said, "Maybe you will help me to understand my son's cerebral palsy." I cannot. Rabbi Harold S. Kushner's book *When Bad Things Happen to Good People* deals as well as possible with the problem of natural evil.† This book will concern itself solely with the subject of human evil, and its primary focus will be on "bad" people.

Nor is this book intended to be an exhaustive survey of the

* Ballantine Books, 1965.
† Schocken Books, 1981.

subject. My desire is not to be scholarly or thorough but to strike as well as I can at the heart of the matter, so as to encourage us toward scientific scholarship and thoroughness. While other religious traditions have much to offer a psychology of evil, in moving toward that psychology I shall be speaking with my specifically Christian voice.*

Similarly, it is not my intention to review all the extant psychological theories on the subject. Suffice it to acknowledge that although we do not yet have a body of scientific knowledge about human evil worthy of being dignified by the term "psychology," behavioral scientists have laid a foundation that makes the development of such a psychology possible. Freud's discovery of the unconscious and Jung's concept of the Shadow are both basic.

The work of one psychologist, however, requires greater mention. Having fled the Jewish persecution of the Hitler regime, the psychoanalyst Erich Fromm spent much of the rest of his life studying the evil of Naziism. He was the first and only scientist to clearly identify an evil personality type, to attempt to examine evil people in depth, and to suggest that they be studied still further.†

---

* There are three major, different, "living" theological models of evil. One is the nondualism of Hinduism and Buddhism, in which evil is envisioned simply as the other side of the coin. For life there must be death; for growth, decay; for creation, destruction. Consequently the distinction of evil from goodness is regarded by nondualism as an illusion. This attitude has found its way into supposedly Christian sects such as Christian Science and the recently popular Course in Miracles, but it is considered heresy by Christian theologians. A second model would hold that evil is distinct from good but is nonetheless of God's creation. To endow us with free will (essential for creating us in His image) God has to permit us the option of the wrong choice and hence, at the very least, to "allow" evil. This model, which I term "integrated dualism," was the one espoused by Martin Buber, who referred to evil as " 'the yeast in the dough,' the ferment placed in the soul by God, without which the human dough does not rise" (*Good and Evil*, Charles Scribner's Sons, New York, 1953, p. 94). The final major model, that of traditional Christianity, I label "diabolic dualism." Here evil is regarded as being not of God's creation but a ghastly cancer beyond His control. While this model (which will be supported in Chapter 6) has its own pitfalls, it is the only one of the three that deals adequately with the issue of murder and the murderer.

† *The Heart of Man: Its Genius for Good and Evil;* see also his *The Anatomy of Human Destructiveness* (Holt, Rinehart & Winston, 1973), a more elaborate but less seminal work.

Fromm's work is based on his study of certain of the Nazi leaders of the Third Reich and the Holocaust. It has the advantage over my own in that his subjects can surely be certified as evil by the judgment of history. But his work is weakened for the same reason. Because he never actually met his subjects, because they were all men in positions of high political power in a particular regime of a particular culture at a particular time, one is left with the impression that truly evil human beings were "over there" and "back then." The reader is led to believe that real evil does not have anything to do with the mother of three next door or the deacon in the church down the street. My own experience, however, is that evil human beings are quite common and usually appear quite ordinary to the superficial observer.

The great Jewish theologian Martin Buber distinguished between two types of myths about evil. One type concerns people in the process of "sliding" into evil. The other concerns those who have already slid, "fallen victim" to and been taken over by "radical" evil.*

In George we have a real-life story that corresponds to the first type of myth. He had not yet become evil, but he was at the point of doing so. His dealing with the devil represented the moral turning point of his life. Had he not renounced the pact, he would have eventually become evil. But he was not yet evil and, blessed by guilt, he managed to turn away from it.

Let us now consider a couple who, like Fromm's subjects, conform to the second type of myth—people who have crossed the line and descended into "radical," likely inescapable, evil.

## THE CASE OF BOBBY AND HIS PARENTS

It was February in the middle of my first year of psychiatric training. I was working on the inpatient service. Bobby, a fifteen-year-old boy, had been admitted the night before from the emergency room with a diagnosis of depression. Before seeing Bobby for the first time I read the note written in his chart by the admitting psychiatrist:

* *Good and Evil*, pp. 139–140.

Bobby's older brother, Stuart, 16, committed suicide this past June, shooting himself in the head with his .22 caliber rifle. Bobby initially seemed to handle his only sibling's death rather well. But from the beginning of school in September, his academic performance has been poor. Once a B student, he is now failing all his courses. By Thanksgiving he had become obviously depressed. His parents, who seem very concerned, tried to talk to him, but he has become more and more uncommunicative, particularly since Christmas. Although there is no previous history of antisocial behavior, yesterday Bobby stole a car by himself, crashed it (he had never driven before), and was apprehended by the police. His court date is set for March 24th. Because of his age he was released into his parents' custody, and they were advised to seek immediate psychiatric evaluation for him.

The aide brought Bobby into my office. He had that typical body type of fifteen-year-old boys who have just undergone their early adolescent growth spurt: long, spindly arms and legs, like sticks, and a skinny torso that had not yet begun to fill out. His badly fitting clothes were nondescript. His slightly long, unwashed hair fell forward over his eyes so that it was difficult to see his face, particularly as he kept his gaze riveted on the floor. I shook his limp hand and motioned him to sit down. "I'm Dr. Peck, Bobby," I said. "I'm going to be your doctor. How are you feeling?"

Bobby did not answer. He simply sat staring at the floor.

"Did you have a good night's sleep?" I asked.

"Okay, I guess," Bobby mumbled. He started picking at a small sore on the back of his hand. I noticed that there were a number of such sores on both his forearms and hands.

"Are you nervous being here in the hospital?"

No answer. Bobby was really digging into that sore. Inwardly I winced at the damage he was doing to his flesh. "Pretty much everyone's nervous when they first come to the hospital," I commented, "but you'll find that it's a safe place. Can you tell me how you happened to come here?"

"My parents brought me."

"Why did they do that?"

"Because I stole a car and the police said I had to come here."

"I don't think the police said you had to come to the hospital,"

I explained. "They just wanted you to see a doctor. Then the doctor who saw you last night thought you were so depressed, it would be better for you to be in the hospital. How did you happen to steal the car?"

"I don't know."

"It's a pretty scary thing to steal a car, especially when you're alone and when you're not used to driving and don't even have a driver's license. Something very strong had to be pushing you to do it. Do you know what that something was?"

No answer. I didn't really expect one. Fifteen-year-old boys who are in trouble and seeing a psychiatrist for the first time aren't likely to be very verbal—particularly when they're depressed, and Bobby was clearly very depressed. By this time I had had a chance to catch several quick glimpses of his face when he inadvertently raised his gaze from the floor. It was dull, expressionless. There was no life in his eyes or mouth. It was the kind of face I had seen in the movies of concentration camp survivors or victims of natural disasters who had seen their homes destroyed and their families wiped out: dazed, apathetic, hopeless.

"Do you feel sad?" I asked.

"I don't know."

Probably he didn't, I thought. Young adolescents are just beginning to learn how to identify their feelings. The stronger the feelings, the more overwhelmed they will be by them and the less able to name them. "I suspect you have some very good reasons to feel sad," I told him. "I know that your brother, Stuart, committed suicide last summer. Were you close to him?"

"Yes."

"Tell me about the two of you."

"There's nothing to tell."

"His death must have made you hurt and confused," I said.

No reaction. Except that maybe he dug a little deeper into one of the sores on his forearm. He was clearly not able to talk yet in this first session about his brother's suicide. I decided to drop the issue for the present. "How about your parents?" I asked. "What can you tell me about them?"

"They're good to me."

"That's nice. How are they good to you?"

"They drive me to scout meetings."

"Yes, that's good," I commented. "Of course that's the kind of thing parents are supposed to do when they can. How do you get along with them?"

"Okay."

"No problems?"

"Sometimes I'm mean to them."

"Oh, like how?"

"I hurt them."

"How do you hurt them, Bobby?" I asked.

"Like when I stole the car, that hurt them," Bobby said, not with triumph but with a dreary, hopeless heaviness.

"Do you think maybe that's why you stole the car—to hurt them?"

"No."

"I guess you didn't want to hurt them. Can you think of any other ways you've hurt your parents?"

Bobby didn't answer. After a long pause I said, "Well?"

"I just know I hurt them."

"But how do you know?" I asked.

"I don't know."

"Do they punish you?"

"No, they're good to me."

"Then how do you know you hurt them?"

"They yell at me."

"Oh? What are some of the things they yell at you for?"

"I don't know."

Bobby was feverishly picking at his sores now and his head had drooped as far as it would go. I felt it would be best if I steered my questions to more neutral subjects. Perhaps then he would open up a bit more and we could begin developing a relationship. "Do you have any pets at home?" I asked.

"A dog."

"What kind of dog?"

"A German shepherd."

"What's his name?"

"Her name," Bobby corrected me. "Inge."

"That sounds like a German name."

"Yes."

"A German name for a German shepherd," I commented, hoping somehow to get out of my interrogational role. "Do you and Inge do a lot together?"

"No."

"Do you take care of her?"

"Yes."

"But you don't seem very enthusiastic about her."

"She's my father's dog."

"Oh—but you still have to take care of her?"

"Yes."

"That doesn't seem quite fair. Does it make you angry?"

"No."

"Do you have a pet of your own?"

"No."

We clearly weren't getting very far on the topic of pets, so I decided to switch to another topic, which often elicits some enthusiasm from young people. "It's not long since Christmas," I said. "What did you get for Christmas?"

"Nothing much."

"Your parents must have given you something. What did they give you?"

"A gun."

"A gun?" I repeated stupidly.

"Yes."

"What kind of gun?" I asked slowly.

"A twenty-two."

"A twenty-two pistol?"

"No, a twenty-two rifle."

There was a long moment of silence. I felt as if I had lost my bearings. I wanted to stop the interview. I wanted to go home. Finally I pushed myself to say what had to be said. "I understand that it was with a twenty-two rifle that your brother killed himself."

"Yes."

"Was that what you asked for for Christmas?"

"No."

"What did you ask for?"

"A tennis racket."

"But you got the gun instead?"

"Yes."

"How did you feel, getting the same kind of gun that your brother had?"

"It wasn't the same kind of gun."

I began to feel better. Maybe I was just confused. "I'm sorry," I said. "I thought they were the same kind of gun."

"It wasn't the same kind of gun," Bobby replied. "It was the gun."

"The gun?"

"Yes."

"You mean, it was your brother's gun?" I wanted to go home very badly now.

"Yes."

"You mean your parents gave you your brother's gun for Christmas, the one he shot himself with?"

"Yes."

"How did it make you feel getting your brother's gun for Christmas?" I asked.

"I don't know."

I almost regretted the question. How could he know? How could he answer such a thing? I looked at him. There had been no change in his appearance as we had talked about the gun. He had continued to pick away at his sores. Otherwise it was as if he were already dead—dull-eyed, listless, apathetic to the point of lifelessness, beyond terror. "No, I don't expect you could know," I said. "Tell me, do you ever see your grandparents?"

"No, they live in South Dakota."

"Do you have any relatives that you see?"

"Some."

"Any that you like?"

"I like my aunt Helen."

I thought perhaps I detected a faint sign of enthusiasm in his reply. "Would you like it if your aunt Helen came to visit you here while you're in the hospital?" I asked.

"She lives quite far away."

"But if she came anyway?"

"If she wanted to."

Again I felt in him the faintest glimmer of hope—and in myself. I would be getting in touch with Aunt Helen. Now I had to end the interview. I couldn't tolerate any more. I told Bobby about the hospital routines and explained that I would see him the next day, that the nurses would be watching him quite closely and that they'd give him a sleeping pill at bedtime. Then I took him back to the nurses' station. After writing his orders I walked out of the building into the courtyard. It was snowing. I was glad of that. I just let it snow on me for a few minutes. Then I went back to my office and became very busy with dull, routine paper work. I was glad of that also.

The next day I saw Bobby's parents. They were, they told me, hard-working people. He was a tool-and-diemaker, an expert machinist who took pride in the great precision of his craft. She had a job as a secretary in an insurance company, and took pride in the neatness of their home. They went to the Lutheran church every Sunday. He drank beer in moderation on the weekends. She belonged to a Thursday-night women's bowling league. Of average stature, neither handsome nor ugly, they were the upper crust of the blue-collar class—quiet, orderly, solid. There seemed to be no rhyme or reason to the tragedy that had befallen them. First Stuart and now Bobby.

"I've cried myself out, Doctor," the mother said.

"Stuart's suicide was a surprise to you?" I asked.

"Totally. A complete shock," the father answered. "He was such a well-adjusted boy. He did well in school. He was into scouting. He liked to hunt woodchucks in the fields behind the house. He was a quiet boy, but everyone liked him."

"Had he seemed depressed before he killed himself?"

"No, not at all. He seemed just like his old self. Of course, he was quiet and didn't tell us much of what was on his mind."

"Did he leave a note?"

"No."

"Have any of your relatives on either side had a mental illness or serious depression or killed themselves?"

"Nobody in my family," the father responded. "My parents emigrated from Germany, so I have quite a few relatives over there I don't know much about, and I can't tell you about them."

"My grandmother became senile and had to be put in a hospital, but no one else had any mental difficulty," the mother added. "Certainly no one committed suicide. Oh, Doctor, you don't think that there's any chance that Bobby might . . . might also do something to himself, do you?"

"Yes," I replied. "I think there's a very significant chance."

"O God, I don't think I could bear it," the mother wailed softly. "Does this sort of thing—I mean, hurting yourself—does it run in families?"

"Definitely. Statistically, the highest risk of suicide exists in people who have a brother or sister who's committed suicide."

"O God," the mother wailed again. "You mean Bobby might really do it too?"

"You hadn't thought of Bobby being in danger?" I asked.

"No, not until now," the father replied.

"But I understand that Bobby's been depressed for some time," I remarked. "Didn't that worry you?"

"Well, it worried us, of course," the father responded. "But we thought it was natural, what with his brother's death and all. We thought he'd get over it in time."

"You didn't think of taking him to see someone like a psychiatrist?" I continued.

"No, of course not," the father replied again, this time with an edge of annoyance. "We told you we thought he would get over it. We had no idea that it might be this serious."

"I understand that Bobby's grades have gone way down in school," I remarked.

"Yes. It's a shame," the mother responded. "He used to be such a good student."

"The school must have been a bit concerned about him," I commented. "Did they get in touch with you about the problem?"

The mother looked slightly uncomfortable. "Yes, they did. And of course I was concerned too. I even took time off from my job to go in for a conference."

"I'd like to have your permission for me to communicate with the school about Bobby if it seems necessary. It might be quite helpful."

"Of course."

"In that conference you had," I asked, "did anyone from the school suggest that Bobby see a psychiatrist?"

"No," the mother answered. She seemed to have so rapidly regained her composure, I wasn't sure she'd ever lost it. "They did suggest he might get some counseling. But not a psychiatrist. Of course if they had suggested a psychiatrist, we would have done something about it."

"Yes. Then we would have known it was something serious," the father added. "But because they said counseling, we thought they were just concerned about his grades. Not that we weren't concerned about his grades too. But we've never been ones to push the children unless we had to. It's not good to push children too hard, is it, Doctor?"

"I'm not sure that taking Bobby to a counselor would have been the same as pushing him," I commented.

"Well, that's another thing, Doctor," the mother continued, more on the offensive than the defensive. "It's not that easy for us to take Bobby here or there during weekdays. We're both working people, you know. And these counseling people, they don't work on weekends. We can't be just taking off from our jobs every day. We've got a living to make, you know."

It didn't seem as if it would be fruitful for me to engage Bobby's parents in an argument over whether they could or could not have discovered available counseling services in the evenings or on weekends. I decided to raise the issue of Aunt Helen. "You know," I said, "it's possible that my supervisors and I may decide that Bobby will need more than a brief hospitalization—that he may need a complete change of scene for a good while. Do you have any relatives with whom he might stay?"

"I'm afraid not," the father responded immediately. "I don't think any of them would be interested in having an adolescent boy on their hands. They've all got their lives to live."

"Bobby mentioned to me his aunt Helen," I suggested. "Perhaps she might be willing to take him."

The mother jumped in. "Did Bobby tell you he doesn't want to live with us?" she demanded.

"No, we haven't even talked about the subject yet," I replied. "I'm only seeing what all the options are. Who is Aunt Helen?"

"She's my sister," the mother answered. "But she'd be out of the question. She lives at least several hundred miles away."

"That's not far," I responded. "And I'm thinking in terms of a change of scene for Bobby. That distance might be just right. It's close enough so that he could visit you but far enough so that he'd be away from where his brother committed suicide and perhaps away from some of the other pressures that he's experiencing."

"I just don't think it would work out," the mother said.

"Oh?"

"Well, Helen and I aren't close. No, not close at all."

"Why is that?"

"We've just never gotten along well together. She's stuck up, that's what she is. Although what she's got to be so stuck up about, I don't know. All she is is a cleaning lady. She and her husband—he's not very bright, you know—all they have is a little house-cleaning service. I don't know what makes them think they can go around acting superior all the time."

"I can understand that you and she don't get on too well together," I acknowledged. "Are there any other relatives with whom it would be better for Bobby to live?"

"No."

"Even though you don't like your sister, Bobby seems to have some positive feeling for her, and that's important."

"Look, Doctor," the father interjected, "I don't know what you're insinuating. You're asking all these questions like you were a policeman or something. We haven't done anything wrong. You don't have any right to take a boy from his parents, if that's what you're thinking of. We've worked hard for that boy. We've been good parents."

My stomach was feeling queasier moment by moment. "I'm concerned about the Christmas present you gave Bobby," I said.

"Christmas present?" The parents seemed confused.

"Yes. I understand you gave him a gun."

"That's right."

"Was that what he asked for?"

"How should I know what he asked for?" the father demanded belligerently. Then immediately his manner turned plaintive. "I can't remember what he asked for. A lot's happened to us, you know. This has been a difficult year for us."

"I can believe it has been," I said, "but why did you give him a gun?"

"Why? Why not? It's a good present for a boy his age. Most boys his age would give their eyeteeth for a gun."

"I should think," I said slowly, "that since your only other child has killed himself with a gun that you wouldn't feel so kindly toward guns."

"You're one of these antigun people, are you?" the father asked me, faintly belligerent again. "Well, that's all right. You can be that way. I'm no gun nut myself, but it does seem to me that guns aren't the problem; it's the people who use them."

"To an extent, I agree with you," I said. "Stuart didn't kill himself simply because he had a gun. There must have been some other reason more important. Do you know what that reason might have been?"

"No. We've already told you we didn't even know that Stuart was depressed."

"That's right. Stuart was depressed. People don't commit suicide unless they're depressed. Since you didn't know Stuart was depressed, there was perhaps no reason for you to worry about him having a gun. But you did know Bobby was depressed. You knew he was depressed well before Christmas, well before you gave him the gun."

"Please, Doctor, you don't seem to understand," the mother said ingratiatingly, taking over from her husband. "We really didn't know it was this serious. We just thought he was upset over his brother."

"So you gave him his brother's suicide weapon. Not any gun. That particular gun."

The father took the lead again. "We couldn't afford to get him a new gun. I don't know why you're picking on us. We gave him the best present we could. Money doesn't grow on trees, you know. We're just ordinary working people. We could have sold the gun and made money. But we didn't. We kept it so we could give Bobby a good present."

"Did you think how that present might seem to Bobby?" I asked.

"What do you mean?"

"I mean that giving him his brother's suicide weapon was like telling him to walk in his brother's shoes, like telling him to go out and kill himself too."

"We didn't tell him anything of the sort."

"Of course not. But did you think that it might possibly seem that way to Bobby?"

"No, we didn't think about that. We're not educated people like you. We haven't been to college and learned all kinds of fancy ways of thinking. We're just simple working people. We can't be expected to think of all these things."

"Perhaps not," I said. "But that's what worries me. Because these things need to be thought of."

We stared at each other for a long moment. How did they feel, I wondered. Certainly they didn't seem to feel guilty.

Angry? Frightened? Victimized? I didn't know. I didn't feel any empathy for them. I only knew how I felt. I felt repelled by them. And I felt very tired.

"I would like you to sign permission for me to communicate with your sister Helen about Bobby and his situation." I said, turning to the mother. "And yours also," turning back to the father.

"Well, you'll not have mine," he said. "I'll not have you taking this out of the family, you acting so superior, like you're some kind of judge or something."

"To the contrary," I explained with cold rationality. "What I am trying to do is my best to keep it in the family as far as possible. Right now you and Bobby and I are the only people involved. I feel it is necessary to involve Bobby's aunt, at least to the extent necessary to find out if she can be of help. If you tie my hands in doing so, then I will have to discuss the issues thoroughly with my supervisors. I suspect we would conclude we have an obligation to refer Bobby's case to the State Childrens' Protective Agency. If we do that, then you'll have a real judge on your hands. We may have to do it anyway. It seems to me, however, if she is able to help, that approaching Helen is a way that we can avoid notifying the state. But it's up to you. It's completely your choice whether you want to give me permission to communicate with Helen."

"Oh, my husband's just being silly, Doctor," Bobby's mother exclaimed with a gay, charming smile. "It's just been very upsetting to him to have to see our son in a mental hospital, and we're not used to talking to highly educated people like yourself. Of course we'll sign permission. I have no objection whatsoever to my sister being involved. We want to do whatever we can to help. All we care about is what's best for Bobby."

They signed permission and left. That night my wife and I went to a staff party. I drank a bit more than I ordinarily do.

The next day I got in touch with Aunt Helen. She and her husband came to see me right away. They understood the situation quickly and seemed quite caring. They too were working people but were willing to have Bobby live with them as long as his psychiatric care could be paid for. Fortunately, through their employment Bobby's parents had insurance coverage with unusually good psychiatric benefits. I contacted a most competent psychiatrist in Helen's town, who agreed to take on Bobby's case for long-term outpatient psychotherapy. Bobby himself had no understanding of why it was necessary for him to live with his aunt and uncle, and I didn't feel he was ready to deal with any real explanation. I simply told him it would be better for him that way.

Within a couple of days Bobby was quite amenable to the change. Indeed, he improved rapidly with several visits from Helen, the prospect of a new living situation, and the care he received from the aides and nurses. By the time he was discharged to Helen's care, three weeks after his admission to the hospital, the sores on his arms and hands were only scars, and he was able to joke with the staff. Six months later I heard from Helen that he seemed to be doing well and that his grades had come up again. From his psychiatrist I heard that he had developed a trusting therapeutic relationship but was only barely beginning to approach facing the psychological reality of his parents and their treatment of him. After that I had no more follow-up. As to Bobby's parents, I saw them only twice more after that initial meeting, and then only for a couple of minutes each time, while Bobby was still in the hospital. That was all that seemed necessary.

Whenever a child is brought for psychiatric treatment, it is customary to refer to her or him as the "identified patient." By this term we psychotherapists mean that the parents—or other identifiers—have labeled the child as a patient—namely, someone who has something wrong and is in need of treatment. The reason we use the term is that we have learned to become skeptical of the validity of this identification process. More often than not, as we proceed with the evaluation of the problem, we discover that the source of the problem lies not in the child but rather in his or her parents, family, school, or society. Put most simply, we usually find that the child is not as sick as its parents. Although the parents have identified the child as the one requiring correction, it is usually they, the identifiers, who are themselves most in need of correction. They are the ones who should be the patients.

This was exemplified in the case of Bobby. Although he was seriously depressed and desperately in need of help, the source, the cause of his depression, lay not in him but in his parents' behavior toward him. Although depressed, there was nothing sick about his depression. Any fifteen-year-old boy would have been depressed in his circumstances. The essential sickness of the situation lay not in his depression but in the family environment to which his depression was a natural enough response.

To children—even adolescents—their parents are like gods. The way their parents do things seems the way they *should* be done. Children are seldom able to objectively compare their parents to other parents. They are not able to make realistic assessments of their parents' behavior. Treated badly by its parents, a child will usually assume that it is bad. If treated as an ugly, stupid second-class citizen, it will grow up with an image of itself as ugly, stupid and second-class. Raised without love, children come to believe themselves unlovable. We may express this as a general law of child development: *Whenever there is a major deficit in parental love, the child will, in all likelihood, respond to that deficit by assuming itself to be the cause of the deficit, thereby developing an unrealistically negative self-image.*

Bobby, when he first came to the hospital, was literally gouging holes in himself, destroying the surface of himself piece by piece. It was as if he felt there was something bad, something evil, inside him underneath the surface of his skin, and he was digging at himself in order to get it out. Why?

If it happens that someone close to us commits suicide, our first response after the initial shock—if we are normally human, with a normal human conscience—will be to wonder what we did wrong. So it must have been for Bobby. In the days immediately following Stuart's death he would have remembered all manner of little incidents: that only a week before he had called his brother a stupid slob; that a month before he had kicked him in the midst of a fight; that when Stuart picked on him, he often wished that his brother would somehow be removed from the face of the earth. Bobby felt responsible, at least to some degree, for Stuart's death.

What should have happened at this point—and what would have happened in a healthy home—would have been for his parents to begin reassuring him. They should have talked with him about Stuart's suicide. They should have explained that even though they themselves did not realize it, Stuart must have been mentally ill. They should have told him that people don't commit suicide because of everyday squabbles or sibling rivalry. They ought to have said that if anyone was responsible, it was they, the parents, the ones who had had the biggest influence on Stuart's life. But as far as I could ascertain, Bobby had been given none of this reassurance.

When the reassurance he needed was not forthcoming, Bobby became visibly depressed. His grades fell. At this point his parents should have rectified the situation or, lacking the insight to do so themselves, should have sought professional help. But they failed to do so, despite its actually having been suggested to them by the school. It was likely that Bobby even interpreted the lack of attention his depression was receiving as a confirmation of his guilt. Of course no one was concerned about his depression, he felt; he deserved it. He deserved to feel miserable. It was appropriate that he should feel guilty.

Consequently by Christmas Bobby was already judging himself to be an evil criminal. Then, unsolicited, he was given his brother's "murder" weapon. How was he to understand the meaning of this "gift"? Was he to think: My parents are evil people, and out of their evil, desire my destruction, just as they probably destroyed my brother? Hardly. Nor could he, even with his fifteen-year-old mind, think to himself: My parents gave me the gun out of a mixture of laziness, thoughtlessness, and cheapness. So they don't love me very well—so what? Since he already believed himself to be evil and lacked the maturity to see his parents with any clarity, there was but one interpretation open to him: to believe the gun an appropriate message telling him: "Take your brother's suicide weapon and do likewise. You deserve to die."

Fortunately Bobby did not immediately do likewise. He chose what was probably his only other psychological option: to publicly label himself a criminal so that he might be punished for his evil and society might be protected from him by means of his imprisonment. He stole a car. In a very real sense he stole it that he might live.

All this has been supposition. I had no way of knowing precisely what had occurred in Bobby's mind. First of all, adolescents are the most private people. They are not apt to confide the inner workings of their minds to anyone, much less a strange, frightening white-coated adult. But even if he had been willing and able to confide in me, Bobby still would not have been able to tell me such things, for his own awareness of them would have been dim indeed. When we are adults, the greater part of our "thought life" proceeds on an unconscious level. For children and young adolescents, almost all mental activity is unconscious. They feel, they conclude, and they act with precious little awareness of what they are about. So we must deduce from their behavior what is going on. Yet we have learned enough to know that such deductions can be remarkably accurate.

From such deductions we can arrive at another law of child development, this one specific to the problem of evil: *When a child is grossly confronted by significant evil in its parents, it will most likely misinterpret the situation and believe that the evil resides in itself.*

When confronted by evil, the wisest and most secure adult will usually experience confusion. Imagine, then, what it must be like for a naïve child who encounters evil in the ones it most loves and upon whom it depends. Add to this the fact that evil people, refusing to acknowledge their own failures, actually desire to project their evil onto others, and it is no wonder that children will misinterpret the process by hating themselves. And no wonder that Bobby was gouging holes in himself.

We can see, then, that Bobby, the identified patient, was not himself so much sick as he was responding, in the way that most children would, in a predictable fashion, to the peculiar, evil "sickness" of his parents. Although identified as the one who had something wrong with him, the locus of evil in the total situation lay not in him but elsewhere. This is why his most immediate need was not so much for treatment as for protection. Real treatment would come later, and would be long and difficult, as it always is for the reversal of a self-image that does not correspond to reality.

Let us turn now from the identified patient to the parents, the true source of the problem. Appropriately, they should have been formally identified as the sick ones. They should have been the ones to receive treatment. Yet they did not. Why not? There are three reasons.

The first, and perhaps most compelling, is that they did not want it. To receive treatment one must want it, at least on some level. And to want it one must consider oneself to be in need of it. One must, at least on some level, acknowledge his or her imperfection. There are an enormous number of people in this world with serious and identifiable psychiatric problems who, in a psychiatrist's eyes, are quite desperately in need of treatment but who fail to recognize this need. So they don't get treatment, even when it is offered on a silver platter. Not all such people are evil. In fact, the vast majority are not. But it is into this cate-ᵣory of persons most intensely resistant to psychiatric treatment that the thoroughly evil fall.

Bobby's parents gave many indications that they would have rejected any type of therapy I might have offered them. They did not even pretend to demonstrate any guilt over Stuart's suicide. They reacted only with rationalization and belligerence to my intimations that they had been remiss in not earlier seeking professional help for Bobby and that their judgment had been poor, at best, in their choice of his Christmas present. Although I sensed in them no genuine desire to care for Bobby, the idea that it would be better for him to live elsewhere was anathema to them because of its implied criticism of their ability as parents. Rather than acknowledging any deficit, they refused to assume any blame on the grounds that they were "working people."

Still, I might at least have offered them therapy. Just because in all probability they would have rejected the offer, this was insufficient reason not to make it—not to at least make the attempt to help them grow toward understanding and compassion. But I sensed that even if by some miracle they had been willing to undergo psychotherapy, in their case it would have failed.

It is a sad state of affairs, but the fact of the matter is that the healthiest people—the most honest, whose patterns of thinking are least distorted—are the very ones easiest to treat with psychotherapy and most likely to benefit from it. Conversely, the sicker the patients—the more dishonest in their behavior and distorted in their thinking—the less able we are to help them with any degree of success. When they are very distorted and dishonest, it seems impossible. Among themselves therapists will not infrequently refer to a patient's psychopathology as being "overwhelming." We mean this literally. We literally feel overwhelmed by the labyrinthine mass of lies and twisted motives and distorted communication into which we will be drawn if we attempt to work with such people in the intimate relationship of psychotherapy. We feel, usually quite accurately, that not only will we fail in our attempts to pull them out of the morass of their sickness but that we may also be pulled down into it ourselves. We are too weak to help such patients—too blind to see an end to the twisted corridors into which we will be led, too small to maintain our love in the face of their hatred. This was the case in dealing with Bobby's parents. I felt overwhelmed by the sickness I sensed in them. Not only would they likely reject any offer I made to help them but I also knew I lacked the power to succeed in any attempt at healing.

There is one other reason I didn't try to work with Bobby's parents. I simply didn't like them. It was even more than that; they revolted me. To help people in psychotherapy it is necessary to have at least a germ of positive feeling for them, a touch of sympathy for their predicaments, a smidgen of empathy for their sufferings, a certain regard for their personhood and hope for their potentials as human beings. I didn't feel these things. I could not envision sitting with Bobby's parents hour after hour, week after week, month after month, dedicating myself to their care. To the contrary, I could hardly stand being in the same room with them. I felt unclean in their presence. I couldn't get them out of my office fast enough. From time to time I will attempt to work with someone whose case I suspect to be hopeless on the off chance that my judgment is wrong, and for the learning value to me, if nothing else. But not Bobby's parents. Not only would they have rejected my therapy; I rejected them.

People have feelings about each other. When psychotherapists have feelings about their patients, they label those feelings "countertransference." Countertransference can run the whole gamut of human emotions from the most intense love to the most intense hatred. Volumes have been written on the subject of countertransference; it can be either extremely helpful or extremely hurtful to therapeutic relationships. If therapists' feelings are inappropriate, the countertransference will distort, confuse, and sidetrack the healing process. Should the countertransference be an appropriate one, however, it can be the most useful tool there is to understand a patient's problem.

A crucial task of any psychotherapist is to recognize whether the countertransference is or is not appropriate. To fulfill this task therapists must continually analyze themselves as well as their patients. If the countertransference is inappropriate, it is the therapist's responsibility to either heal himself/herself or refer the patient to another therapist, one capable of being more objective in that particular case.

The feeling that a healthy person often experiences in a relationship with an evil one is revulsion. The feeling of revulsion may be almost instant if the evil encountered is blatant. If the evil is more subtle, the revulsion may develop only gradually as the relationship with the evil one slowly deepens.

The feeling of revulsion can be extremely useful to a therapist. It can be a diagnostic tool par excellence. It can signify more truly and rapidly than anything else that the therapist is in the presence of an evil human being. Yet, like a sharp scalpel, it is a tool that must be used with the greatest care. Should the revulsion result not from something in the patient but from some sickness in the therapist, all manner of harm will likely be done unless the therapist is humble enough to recognize it as his or her own problem.

But what would make revulsion a healthy response? Why might it be an appropriate countertransference for an emotionally healthy therapist? Revulsion is a powerful emotion that causes us to immediately want to avoid, to escape, the revolting presence. And that is exactly the most appropriate thing for a healthy person to do under ordinary circumstances when confronted with an evil presence: to get away from it. Evil is revolting because it is dangerous. It will contaminate or otherwise destroy a person who remains too long in its presence. Unless you know very well what you are doing, the best thing you can do when faced with evil is to run the other way. The revulsion countertransference is an instinctive or, if you will, God-given and saving early-warning radar system.*

Despite the volume of professional literature on the subject of

---

* The question arises as to whether one evil person would experience revulsion in the presence of another. I do not know. It is a fascinating question for research, because its answer might reveal much about the nature and genesis of evil in human beings. Theoretically, if a person becomes evil by being raised in an evil home, its parents would appear so normal to the

countertransference, I have never read anything in it specifically about revulsion. There are several reasons for this absence. The revulsion countertransference is so specific to evil, it is hardly possible to write about one without the other; and since evil has been generally thus far off-limits to psychiatric investigation, so has this specific countertransference.* Moreover, psychotherapists are usually kindly people, and such a dramatically negative reaction on their part would be rather threatening to their self-image. Then, because of the intense negativity of the reaction, there is a profound tendency for psychotherapists to avoid sustaining relationships with evil clients. Finally, as I have mentioned, very few evil people are willing to be psychotherapy clients in the first place. Except under extraordinary circumstances, they will do everything possible to flee the light-shedding process of therapy. So it has been difficult for psychotherapists to get together with evil people long enough to study them or their own reactions.

There is another reaction that the evil frequently engender in us: confusion. Describing an encounter with an evil person, one woman wrote, it was "as if I'd suddenly lost my ability to think."† Once again, this reaction is quite appropriate. Lies confuse. The evil are "the people of the lie," deceiving others as they also build layer upon layer of self-deception. If confused in response to a patient, the therapist must wonder if this is not the result of her or his own ignorance. But it also behooves the therapist to question: "Could the patient be doing something to confuse me?" My work with the case described in Chapter 4 was ineffective for months because I failed to ask this question.

I have stated that the revulsion countertransference is an appropriate—even saving—response to evil people. There is one

---

child as to prevent its development of the early-warning radar system. Or else the enforced and longstanding proximity to its evil parents required by childhood would be sufficient to destroy over time any such preexisting saving response mechanism.

* Revulsion may be experienced in the presence of physical disease. It was, for instance, the common response to lepers, and it has been studied in relation to people's reactions to amputees and those with other deformities. While psychiatrists are aware of such reactions, they have not written about the problem within sustained therapeutic relationships.

† *The New Yorker*, July 3, 1978, p. 19.

exception. If the confusion can be penetrated—if the diagnosis of evil can be made, and if the therapist, knowing with what he or she is dealing, decides to attempt to relate with the evil person in a healing manner—then, and only then, the revulsion counter-transference can and should be set aside. That is a lot of ifs. The attempt to heal the evil should not be lightly undertaken. It must be done from a position of remarkable psychological and spiritual strength.

The only reason that it can be done at all is that a therapist who is in a position of such strength will know that while the evil people are still to be feared, they are also to be pitied. Forever fleeing the light of self-exposure and the voice of their own conscience, they are the most frightened of human beings. They live their lives in sheer terror. They need not be consigned to any hell; they are already in it.*

It is therefore not only for the sake of society but also for their own sakes that the attempt should be made to rescue the evil from their living hell. Knowing so little about the nature of evil, we currently lack the skill to heal it. Our therapeutic ineptness is hardly remarkable, however, in view of the fact that we have not even yet discerned evil as a specific disease. It is a thesis of this book that evil can be defined as a specific form of mental illness and should be subject to at least the same intensity of scientific investigation that we would devote to some other major psychiatric disease.

It is natural and wise that under ordinary circumstances we should steer clear of the viper's den. Yet it is also proper that the scientist—the experienced herpetologist—should approach that very same place in order to learn, to obtain venom for the development of an antitoxin that will serve to protect humankind, and perhaps even to assist the serpent in its evolution. Serpents can grow wings to become dragons, and dragons can be tamed to

---

* God does not punish us; we punish ourselves. Those who are in hell are there by their own choice. Indeed, they could walk right out of it if they so chose, except that their values are such as to make the path out of hell appear overwhelmingly dangerous, frighteningly painful, and impossibly difficult. So they remain in hell because it seems safe and easy to them. They prefer it that way. This situation and the psychodynamics involved were the subject of C. S. Lewis' fine book *The Great Divorce*. The notion that people are in hell by their own choice is not widely familiar, but the fact is that it is both good psychology and good theology.

become simultaneously fierce and gentle servants of God. If we can see the evil as ill and pitiable—albeit still dangerous—and if we know what we are doing, it is appropriate that we should transform our revulsion into careful compassion so as to approach them in healing.

As I review the case of Bobby and his parents after a span of twenty years, I doubt that I would today, with all my additional experience, handle the case much differently. I would still envision it as my initial task to rescue Bobby from his parents, and I would still resort, as I did then, to the use of temporal power to accomplish that task. I have learned nothing in twenty years that would suggest that evil people can be rapidly influenced by any means other than raw power. They do not respond, at least in the short run, to either gentle kindness or any form of spiritual persuasion with which I am familiar. But one thing has changed in twenty years. I know now that Bobby's parents were evil. I did not know it then. I felt their evil but had no name for it. My supervisors were not able to help me name what I was facing. The name did not exist in our professional vocabulary. As scientists rather than priests, we were not supposed to think in such terms.

To name something correctly gives us a certain amount of power over it.* At the time I saw Bobby's parents I did not know the nature of the force with which I was dealing. I was revolted by it but not curious about it. I avoided dealing with them not simply out of a healthy respect for that force but also because I was afraid of it—unknowingly afraid. Today I am afraid of it still, but it is not a blind fear. Knowing its name, I know something of the dimensions of that force. Because I have that much of safe ground on which to stand, I can afford to be curious as to its nature. I can afford to move toward it. So I would do something differently today. Having succeeded in getting Bobby out of his parents' home, I would, if I had the opportunity today, attempt to gently tell them in the vaguest of terms that they were possessed by a kind of force destructive not only to their children but also to themselves. And if I happened to have the available time and energy, I would offer to work with them in an attempt to conquer that force. If by some remote chance they agreed, I

* See Ursula Le Guin, *A Wizard of Earthsea* (Parnassus Press, 1968), for a superb account of the power of naming.

would proceed to work with them, not because I would like them better now—not even because I would have significant confidence in my power to heal them—but simply because, knowing the name, I have grown strong enough to do the learning and attempt the work. And it is our task to work the fields that we know.

## EVIL AND SIN

To more fully understand Bobby's parents—and others like them, who will be described in the next chapter—it is necessary that we first draw the distinction between evil and ordinary sin. It is not their sins per se that characterize evil people, rather it is the subtlety and persistence and consistency of their sins. This is because the central defect of the evil is not the sin but the refusal to acknowledge it.*

Bobby's parents and the people described in the next chapter, except for their evil, are most ordinary. They live down the street—on any street. They may be rich or poor, educated or uneducated. There is little that is dramatic about them. They are not designated criminals. More often than not they will be "solid citizens"—Sunday school teachers, policemen, or bankers, and active in the PTA.

How can this be? How can they be evil and not designated as criminals? The key lies in the word "designated." They are criminals in that they commit "crimes" against life and liveliness. But except in rare instances—such as the case of a Hitler—when they might achieve extraordinary degrees of political power that remove them from ordinary restraints, their "crimes" are so subtle and covert that they cannot clearly be designated as crimes. The theme of hiding and covertness will occur again and again throughout the rest of the book. It is the basis for the title *People of the Lie*.

I have spent a good deal of time working in prisons with designated criminals. Almost never have I experienced them as evil people. Obviously they are destructive, and usually repetitively so. But there is a kind of randomness to their destructiveness. Moreover, although to the authorities they generally deny re-

---

* Jung correctly ascribed evil to the failure to "meet" the Shadow.

sponsibility for their evil deeds, there is still a quality of openness to their wickedness. They themselves are quick to point this out, claiming that they have been caught precisely because they are the "honest criminals." The truly evil, they will tell you, always reside outside of jail. Clearly these proclamations are self-justifying. They are also, I believe, generally accurate.

People in jail can almost always be assigned a standard psychiatric diagnosis of one kind or another. The diagnoses range all over the map and correspond, in layman's terms, to such qualities as craziness or impulsiveness or aggressiveness or lack of conscience. The men and women I shall be talking about such as Bobby's parents have no such obvious defects and do not fall clearly into our routine psychiatric pigeonholes. This is not because the evil are healthy. It is simply because we have not yet developed a definition for their disease.

Since I distinguish between evil people and ordinary criminals, I also obviously make the distinction between evil as a personality characteristic and evil deeds. In other words, evil deeds do not an evil person make. Otherwise we should all be evil, because we all do evil things.

Sinning is most broadly defined as "missing the mark." This means that we sin every time we fail to hit the bull's-eye. Sin is nothing more and nothing less than a failure to be continually perfect. Because it is impossible for us to be continually perfect, we are all sinners. We routinely fail to do the very best of which we are capable, and with each failure we commit a crime of sorts—against God, our neighbors, or ourselves, if not frankly against the law.

Of course there are crimes of greater and lesser magnitude. It is a mistake, however, to think of sin or evil as a matter of degree. It may seem less odious to cheat the rich than the poor, but it is still cheating. There are differences before the law between defrauding a business, claiming a false deduction on your income tax, using a crib sheet in an examination, telling your wife that you have to work late when you are unfaithful, or telling your husband (or yourself) that you didn't have time to pick up his clothes at the cleaner, when you spent an hour on the phone with your neighbor. Surely one is more excusable than the other—and perhaps all the more so under certain circumstances—but the fact remains that they are all lies and betrayals. If you are sufficiently

scrupulous not to have done any such thing recently, then ask
whether there is any way in which you have lied to yourself. Or
have kidded yourself. Or have been less than you could be—which
is a self-betrayal. Be perfectly honest with yourself, and you will
realize that you sin. If you do not realize it, then you are not perfectly honest with yourself, which is itself a sin. It is inescapable:
we are all sinners.*

If evil people cannot be defined by the illegality of their deeds
or the magnitude of their sins, then how are we to define them?
The answer is by the consistency of their sins. While usually
subtle, their destructiveness is remarkably consistent. This is because those who have "crossed over the line" are characterized by
their *absolute* refusal to tolerate the sense of their own sinfulness.

I commented that George, *blessed by guilt*, managed to turn
away from becoming evil. Because he was willing—at least to a
rudimentary degree—to tolerate the sense of his own sinfulness,
he was able to reject his pact with the devil. Had he not borne
the pain of "the guilties" he experienced over the pact, his moral
deterioration would have continued. More than anything else, it
is the sense of our own sinfulness that prevents any of us from
undergoing a similar deterioration. As I have written elsewhere:

> "Blessed are the poor in spirit," Jesus began when the time
> came for him to address the multitudes. What did he mean by
> this opener? . . . What is so great about feeling down on

* Although so frequently and even evilly abused, perhaps the greatest
beauty of Christian doctrine is its understanding approach to sin. It is a
two-pronged approach. On the one hand, it insists upon our sinful human
nature. Any genuine Christian, therefore, will consider himself or herself
to be a sinner. The fact that many nominal and overtly devout "Christians"
do not in their hearts consider themselves sinners should not be perceived
as a failure of the doctrine but only a failure of the individual to begin to
live up to it. More will be said later about evil in Christian guise. On the
other hand, Christian doctrine also insists that we are forgiven our sins—at
least as long as we experience contrition for them. Fully realizing the extent
of our sinfulness, we are likely to feel almost overwhelmed by hopelessness
if we do not simultaneously believe in the merciful and forgiving nature of
the Christian God. Thus the Church, when in its right mind, will also insist
that to endlessly dwell on each and every smallest sin one has committed
(a process known as "excessive scrupulosity") is itself a sin. Since God
forgives us, to fail to forgive ourselves is to hold ourselves higher than
God—thereby indulging in the sin of a perverted form of pride.

yourself—about having this sense of personal sin? If you ask that, it might help to remember the Pharisees. They were the fat cats of Jesus' day. They didn't feel poor in spirit. They felt they had it all together, that they were the ones who knew the score, who deserved to be the culture leaders in Jerusalem and Palestine. And they were the ones who murdered Jesus.

The poor in spirit do not commit evil. Evil is not committed by people who feel uncertain about their righteousness, who question their own motives, who worry about betraying themselves. The evil in this world is committed by the spiritual fat cats, by the Pharisees of our own day, the self-righteous who think they are without sin because they are unwilling to suffer the discomfort of significant self-examination.

Unpleasant though it may be, the sense of personal sin is precisely that which keeps our sin from getting out of hand. It is quite painful at times, but it is a very great blessing because it is our one and only effective safeguard against our own proclivity for evil. Saint Thérèse of Lisieux put it so nicely in her gentle way: "If you are willing to serenely bear the trial of being displeasing to yourself, then you will be for Jesus a pleasant place of shelter."*

The evil do not serenely bear the trial of being displeasing to themselves. In fact, they don't bear it at all. I could not, for instance, detect a hint of self-recrimination in Bobby's parents. And it is out of their failure to put themselves on trial that their evil arises.

The varieties of people's wickedness are manifold. As a result of their refusal to tolerate the sense of their own sinfulness, the evil ones become uncorrectable grab bags of sin. They are, for instance, in my experience, remarkably greedy people. Thus they are cheap—so cheap that their "gifts" may be murderous. In *The Road Less Traveled*, I suggested the most basic sin is laziness. In the next subsection I suggest it may be pride—because all sins are reparable except the sin of believing one is without sin. But perhaps the question of which sin is the greatest is, on a certain level, a moot issue. All sins betray—and isolate us from—both the divine and our fellow creatures. As one deep religious thinker put it, any sin "can harden into hell":

* Marilyn von Waldener and M. Scott Peck, "What Return Can I Make?" (awaiting publication).

... There can be a state of soul against which Love itself is powerless because it has hardened itself against Love. Hell is essentially a state of being which we fashion for ourselves: a state of final separateness from God which is the result not of God's repudiation of man, but of man's repudiation of God, and a repudiation which is eternal precisely because it has become, in itself, immovable. There are analogies in human experience: the hate which is so blind, so dark, that Love only makes it the more violent; the pride which is so stony that humility only makes it more scornful; the inertia—last but not least the inertia—which has so taken possession of the personality that no crisis, no appeal, no inducement whatsoever, can stir it into activity, but on the contrary makes it bury itself the more deeply in its immobility. So with the soul and God; pride can become hardened into hell, hatred can become hardened into hell, any of the seven root forms of wrongdoing can harden into hell, and not least that sloth which is boredom with divine things, the inertia that cannot be troubled to repent, even though it sees the abyss into which the soul is falling, because for so long, in little ways perhaps, it has accustomed itself to refuse whatever might cost it an effort. May God in his mercy save us from that.*

A predominant characteristic, however, of the behavior of those I call evil is scapegoating. Because in their hearts they consider themselves above reproach, they must lash out at anyone who does reproach them. They sacrifice others to preserve their self-image of perfection. Take a simple example of a six-year-old boy who asks his father, "Daddy, why did you call Grandmommy a bitch?" "I told you to stop bothering me," the father roars. "Now you're going to get it. I'm going to teach you not to use such filthy language, I'm going to wash your mouth out with soap. Maybe that will teach you to clean up what you say and keep your mouth shut when you're told." Dragging the boy upstairs to the soap dish, the father inflicts this punishment on him. In the name of "proper discipline" evil has been committed.

Scapegoating works through a mechanism psychiatrists call projection. Since the evil, deep down, feel themselves to be faultless, it is inevitable that when they are in conflict with the world they

* Gerald Vann, *The Pain of Christ and the Sorrow of God* (Temple Gate Publishers, Springfield, Illinois, copyright by Aquin Press, 1947, pp. 54–55).

will invariably perceive the conflict as the world's fault. Since they must deny their own badness, they must perceive others as bad. They *project* their own evil onto the world. They never think of themselves as evil; on the other hand, they consequently see much evil in others. The father perceived the profanity and uncleanliness as existing in his son and took action to cleanse his son's "filthiness." Yet we know it was the father who was profane and unclean. The father projected his own filth onto his son and then assaulted his son in the name of good parenting.

Evil, then, is most often committed in order to scapegoat, and the people I label as evil are chronic scapegoaters. In *The Road Less Traveled* I defined evil "as the exercise of political power—that is, the imposition of one's will upon others by overt or covert coercion—in order to avoid . . . spiritual growth" (p. 279). In other words, the evil attack others instead of facing their own failures. Spiritual growth requires the acknowledgment of one's need to grow. If we cannot make that acknowledgment, we have no option except to attempt to eradicate the evidence of our imperfection.*

Strangely enough, evil people are often destructive because they are attempting to destroy evil. The problem is that they misplace the locus of the evil. Instead of destroying others they should be destroying the sickness within themselves. As life often threatens their self-image of perfection, they are often busily engaged in hating and destroying that life—usually in the name of righteousness. The fault, however, may not be so much that they

* Ernest Becker, in his final work, *Escape from Evil* (Macmillan, 1965), pointed out the essential role of scapegoating in the genesis of human evil. He erred, I believe, in focusing exclusively on the fear of death as the sole motive for such scapegoating. Indeed, I think the fear of self-criticism is the more potent motive. Although Becker did not make the point, he might have equated the fear of self-criticism with the fear of death. Self-criticism is a call to personality change. As soon as I criticize a part of myself I incur an obligation to change that part. But the process of personality change is a painful one. It is like a death. The old personality pattern must die for a new pattern to take its place. The evil are pathologically attached to the status quo of their personalities, which in their narcissism they consciously regard as perfect. I think it is quite possible that the evil may perceive even a small degree of change in their beloved selves as representing total annihilation. In this sense, the threat of self-criticism may feel to one who is evil synonymous with the threat of extinction. How this is so will become clear as we go more deeply into the subject of narcissism.

hate life as that they do *not* hate the sinful part of themselves. I doubt that Bobby's parents deliberately wanted to kill Stuart or him. I suspect if I had gotten to know them well enough, I would have found their murderous behavior totally dictated by an extreme form of self-protectiveness which invariably sacrificed others rather than themselves.

What is the cause of this failure of self-hatred, this failure to be displeasing to oneself, which seems to be the central sin at the root of the scapegoating behavior of those I call evil? The cause is not, I believe, an absent conscience. There are people, both in and out of jail, who seem utterly lacking in conscience or superego. Pyschiatrists call them psychopaths or sociopaths. Guiltless, they not only commit crimes but may often do so with a kind of reckless abandon. There is little pattern or meaning to their criminality; it is not particularly characterized by scapegoating. Conscienceless, psychopaths appear to be bothered or worried by very little—including their own criminality. They seem to be about as happy inside a jail as out. They do attempt to hide their crimes, but their efforts to do so are often feeble and careless and poorly planned. They have sometimes been referred to as "moral imbeciles," and there is almost a quality of innocence to their lack of worry and concern.

This is hardly the case with those I call evil. Utterly dedicated to preserving their self-image of perfection, they are unceasingly engaged in the effort to maintain the appearance of moral purity. They worry about this a great deal. They are acutely sensitive to social norms and what others might think of them. Like Bobby's parents, they dress well, go to work on time, pay their taxes, and outwardly seem to live lives that are above reproach.

The words "image," "appearance," and "outwardly" are crucial to understanding the morality of the evil. While they seem to lack any motivation to *be* good, they intensely desire to appear good. Their "goodness" is all on a level of pretense. It is, in effect, a lie. This is why they are the "people of the lie."

Actually, the lie is designed not so much to deceive others as to deceive themselves. They cannot or will not tolerate the pain of self-reproach. The decorum with which they lead their lives is maintained as a mirror in which they can see themselves reflected righteously. Yet the self-deceit would be unnecessary if the evil had no sense of right and wrong. We lie only when we are attempting to cover up something we know to be illicit. Some rudimentary form of conscience must precede the act of lying. There is no need to hide unless we first feel that something needs to be hidden.

We come now to a sort of paradox. I have said that evil people feel themselves to be perfect. At the same time, however, I think they have an unacknowledged sense of their own evil nature. Indeed, it is this very sense from which they are frantically trying to flee. The essential component of evil is not the absence of a sense of sin or imperfection but the unwillingness to tolerate that sense. At one and the same time, the evil are aware of their evil and desperately trying to avoid the awareness. Rather than blissfully lacking a sense of morality, like the psychopath, they are continually engaged in sweeping the evidence of their evil under the rug of their own consciousness. For everything they did, Bobby's parents had a rationalization—a whitewash good enough for themselves even if not for me. The problem is not a defect of conscience but the effort to deny the conscience its due. We become evil by attempting to hide from ourselves. The wickedness of the evil is not committed directly, but indirectly as a part of this cover-up process. Evil originates not in the absence of guilt but in the effort to escape it.

It often happens, then, that the evil may be recognized by its very disguise. The lie can be perceived before the misdeed it is designed to hide—the cover-up before the fact. We see the smile that hides the hatred, the smooth and oily manner that masks the fury, the velvet glove that covers the fist. Because they are such experts at disguise, it is seldom possible to pinpoint the maliciousness of the evil. The disguise is usually impenetrable. But what we can catch are glimpses of "The uncanny game of hide-and-seek in the obscurity of the soul, in which it, the single human soul, evades itself, avoids itself, hides from itself.*

In *The Road Less Traveled* I suggested that laziness or the de-

---

* Buber, *Good and Evil*, p. 111. Since the primary motive of the evil is disguise, one of the places evil people are most likely to be found is within the church. What better way to conceal one's evil from oneself, as well as from others, than to be a deacon or some other highly visible form of Christian within our culture? In India I would suppose that the evil would demonstrate a similar tendency to be "good" Hindus or "good" Moslems. I do not mean to imply that the evil are anything other than a small mi-

sire to escape "legitimate suffering" lies at the root of all mental illness. Here we are also talking about avoidance and evasion of pain. What distinguishes the evil, however, from the rest of us mentally ill sinners is the specific type of pain they are running away from. They are not pain avoiders or lazy people in general. To the contrary, they are likely to exert themselves more than most in their continuing effort to obtain and maintain an image of high respectability. They may willingly, even eagerly, undergo great hardships in their search for status. It is only one particular kind of pain they cannot tolerate: the pain of their own conscience, the pain of the realization of their own sinfulness and imperfection.

Since they will do almost anything to avoid the particular pain that comes from self-examination, under ordinary circumstances the evil are the last people who would ever come to psychotherapy. The evil hate the light—the light of goodness that shows them up, the light of scrutiny that exposes them, the light of truth that penetrates their deception. Psychotherapy is a light-shedding process par excellence. Except for the most twisted motives, an evil person would be more likely to choose any other conceivable route than the psychiatrist's couch. The submission to the discipline of self-observation required by psychoanalysis does, in fact, seem to them like suicide. The most significant reason we know so little scientifically about human evil is simply that the evil are so extremely reluctant to be studied.

If the central defect of the evil is not one of conscience, then where does it reside? The essential psychological problem of human evil, I believe, is a particular variety of narcissism.

## NARCISSISM AND WILL

Narcissism, or self-absorption, takes many forms. Some are normal. Some are normal in childhood but not in adulthood. Some are more distinctly pathological than others. The subject is as

---

nority among the religious or that the religious motives of most people are in any way spurious. I mean only that evil people tend to gravitate toward piety for the disguise and concealment it can offer them.

complex as it is important. It is not the purpose of this book, however, to give a balanced view of the whole topic, so we will proceed immediately to that particular pathologic variant that Erich Fromm called "malignant narcissism."

Malignant narcissism is characterized by an unsubmitted will. All adults who are mentally healthy submit themselves one way or another to something higher than themselves, be it God or truth or love or some other ideal. They do what God wants them to do rather than what they would desire. "Thy will, not mine, be done," the God-submitted person says. They believe in what is true rather than what they would like to be true. Unlike Bobby's parents, what their beloved needs becomes more important to them than their own gratification. In summary, to a greater or lesser degree, all mentally healthy individuals submit themselves to the demands of their own conscience. Not so the evil, however. In the conflict between their guilt and their will, it is the guilt that must go and the will that must win.

The reader will be struck by the extraordinary willfulness of evil people. They are men and women of obviously strong will, determined to have their own way. There is a remarkable power in the manner in which they attempt to control others.*

Theologians speak of evil being a consequence of free will. When God, creating us in His own image, gave us free will, He had to allow us humans the option of evil. The problem can also be envisioned in the secular terms of evolution theory. The "will" of less evolved creatures seems largely under the control of their instincts. When humans evolved from the apes, however, they

---

* The overcontrollingness of evil is well expressed through the Mormon myth in which Christ and Satan were each required to present God with his own plan for dealing with the infant human race. Satan's plan was simple (of the sort that most business and military leaders today would come up with): God had armies of angels at His command; just assign an angel with punitive power to each human, and He would have no trouble keeping them in line. Christ's plan was radically different and more imaginative (and biophilic): "Let them have free will and go their own way," he proposed, "but allow me to live and die as one of them, both as an example of how to live and of how much You care for them." God, of course, chose Christ's plan as the more creative, and Satan rebelled at the choice. The controlling nature of evil is also treated at length by Marguerite Shuster in her unpublished dissertation, "Power, Pathology and Paradox" (Fuller Theological Seminary, 1977).

largely evolved out from under such instinctual controls and hence into free will. This evolution leaves humans in the position of being either totally willful or having to seek new ways of self-control through submission to higher principles. But this still leaves us with the question of why some human beings are able to achieve such submission while others are not.

Indeed, it is almost tempting to think that the problem of evil lies in the will itself. Perhaps the evil are born so inherently strong-willed that it is impossible for them ever to submit their will. Yet I think it is characteristic of all "great" people that they are extremely strong-willed—whether their greatness be for good or for evil. The strong will—the power and authority—of Jesus radiates from the Gospels, just as Hitler's did from *Mein Kampf*. But Jesus' will was that of his Father, and Hitler's that of his own. The crucial distinction is between "willingness and willfulness."*

This willful failure of submission that characterizes malignant narcissism is depicted in both the stories of Satan and of Cain and Abel. Satan refused to submit to God's judgment that Christ was superior to him. For Christ to be preferred meant that Satan was not. Satan was less than Christ in God's eyes. For Satan to have accepted God's judgment, he would have had to accept his own imperfection. This he could not or would not do. It was unthinkable that he was imperfect. Consequently submission was impossible and both the rebellion and fall inevitable. So also God's acceptance of Abel's sacrifice implied a criticism of Cain: Cain was less than Abel in God's eyes. Since he refused to acknowledge his imperfection, it was inevitable that Cain, like Satan, should take the law into his own hands and commit murder. In some similar, although usually more subtle fashion, all who are evil also take the law into their own hands, to destroy life or liveliness in defense of their narcissistic self-image.

"Pride goeth before the fall," it is said, and of course laymen simply call pride what we have labeled with the fancy psychiatric term of "malignant narcissism." Being at the very root of evil, it is no accident that Church authorities have generally considered pride first among the sins. By the sin of pride they do not generally mean the sense of legitimate achievement one might

---

* Gerald G. May, M.D., *Will and Spirit* (Harper & Row, 1982).

enjoy after a job well done. While such pride, like normal narcissism, may have its pitfalls, it is also part of healthy self-confidence and a realistic sense of self-worth. What is meant is, rather, a kind of pride that unrealistically denies our inherent sinfulness and imperfection—a kind of overweening pride or arrogance that prompts people to reject and even attack the judgment implied by the day-to-day evidence of their own inadequacy. Despite its fruits, Bobby's parents saw no fault in their child care. In Buber's words, the malignantly narcissistic insist upon "affirmation independent of all findings."*

What is the cause of this overweening pride, this arrogant self-image of perfection, this particularly malignant type of narcissism? Why does it afflict a few when most seem to escape its clutches? We do not know. In the past fifteen years psychiatrists have begun to pay increasing attention to the phenomenon of narcissism, but our understanding of the subject is still in its infancy. We have not yet succeeded, for instance, in distinguishing the different types of excessive self-absorption. There are many who are clearly—even grossly—narcissistic in one way or another but are not evil. All I can say at this point is that the particular brand of narcissism that characterizes evil people seems to be one that particularly afflicts the will. Why a person should be a victim of this type and not another or none at all, I can only vaguely surmise.

It is my experience that evil seems to run in families. The person to be described in Chapter 4 had evil parents. But the familial pattern, if accurate, does nothing to resolve the old "nature versus nurture" controversy. Does evil run in families because it is genetic and inherited? Or because it is learned by the child in imitation of its parents? Or even as a defense against its parents? And how are we to explain the fact that many of the children of evil parents, although usually scarred, are not evil? We do not know, and we will not know until an enormous amount of painstaking scientific work has been accomplished.

Nonetheless, a leading theory of the genesis of pathological narcissism is that it is a defensive phenomenon. Since almost all young children demonstrate a formidable array of narcissistic characteristics, it is assumed that narcissism is something we gen-

* *Good and Evil,* p. 136.

erally "grow out of" in the course of normal development, through a stable childhood, under the care of loving and understanding parents. If the parents are cruel and unloving, however, or the childhood otherwise traumatic, it is believed that the infantile narcissism will be preserved as a kind of psychological fortress to protect the child against the vicissitudes of its intolerable life. This theory might well apply to the genesis of human evil. The builders of the medieval cathedrals placed upon their buttresses the figures of gargoyles—themselves symbols of evil—in order to ward off the spirits of greater evil. Thus children may become evil in order to defend themselves against the onslaughts of parents who are evil. It is possible, therefore, to think of human evil—or some of it—as a kind of psychological gargoylism.

There are other ways, however, to look at the genesis of human evil. The fact of the matter is that some of us are very good and some of us very evil, and most of us are somewhere in between. We might therefore think of human good and evil as a kind of continuum. As individuals we can move ourselves one way or another along the continuum. Just as there is a tendency for the rich to get richer, however, and the poor to get poorer, so there seems to be a tendency for the good to get better and the bad to get worse. Erich Fromm spoke of these matters at some length:

> Our capacity to choose changes constantly with our practice of life. The longer we continue to make the wrong decisions, the more our heart hardens; the more often we make the right decision, the more our heart softens—or better perhaps, comes alive. . . . Each step in life which increases my self-confidence, my integrity, my courage, my conviction also increases my capacity to choose the desirable alternative, until eventually it becomes more difficult for me to choose the undesirable rather than the desirable action. On the other hand, each act of surrender and cowardice weakens me, opens the path for more acts of surrender, and eventually freedom is lost. Between the extreme when I can no longer do a wrong act and the extreme when I have lost my freedom to right action, there are innumerable degrees of freedom of choice. In the practice of life the degree of freedom to choose is different at any given moment. If the degree of freedom to choose the good is great, it needs less effort to choose the good. If it is small, it takes a great effort, help from others, and favorable circumstances. . . . Most peo-

ple fail in the art of living not because they are inherently bad
or so without will that they cannot lead a better life; they fail
because they do not wake up and see when they stand at a fork
in the road and have to decide. They are not aware when life
asks them a question, and when they still have alternative answers. Then with each step along the wrong road it becomes
increasingly difficult for them to admit that they *are* on the
wrong road, often only because they have to admit that they
must go back to the first wrong turn, and must accept the fact
that they have wasted energy and time.*

Fromm saw the genesis of human evil as a developmental process: we are not created evil or forced to be evil, but we become
evil slowly over time through a long series of choices. I applaud
his view—particularly its emphasis upon choice and will. I think
it is correct as far as it goes. But I do not think it is the whole
truth of the matter. On the one hand, it does not take into account the tremendous forces that tend to shape the being of a
young child before it has much opportunity to exercise its will
in true freedom of choice. On the other hand, it perhaps under-
estimates the very power of the will itself.

I have seen cases in which an individual made an evil choice for
no apparent reason other than the pure desire to exercise the freedom of his or her will. It is as if such people say to themselves, "I
know what is supposed to be the right action in this situation, but
I am damned if I am going to be bound to notions of morality or
even to my own conscience. Were I to do the good thing, it
would be because it is good. But if I do the bad thing, it will be
solely because I want to. Therefore I shall do the bad, because it
is my freedom to do so."

Malachi Martin, depicting the struggle of a man to free himself from possession, gives the best description I know of the free
human will in action:

All at once he knew what that strength was. It was his will. His
autonomous will. He himself as a freely-choosing being. With a
sidelong glance of his mind, he dismissed once and for all that
fabric of mental illusions about psychological motivations, behavioral stimulations, rationales, mentalistic hedges, situational
ethics, social loyalties and communal shibboleths. All was dross
and already eaten up and disintegrated in the flames of this ex-

* *The Heart of Man: Its Genius for Good and Evil*, pp. 173–178.

perience which still might consume him. Only his will remained. Only his freedom of spirit to choose held firm. Only the agony of free choice remained . . . afterwards he wondered for a long time how many real choices he had made freely in his life before that night. For it was that agony of choosing freely— totally freely—that was now his. Just for the sake of choosing. Without any outside stimuli. Without any background in memory. Without any push from acquired tastes and persuasions. Without any reason or cause or motive deciding his choice. Without any gravamen from a desire to live or die—for at this moment he was indifferent to both. He was, in a sense, like the donkey medieval philosophers had fantasized as helpless, immobilized, and destined to starve because it stood equidistant from two equivalent bales of hay and could not decide which one to approach and eat. Totally free choice . . . He had to choose. The freedom to accept or reject. A proposed step into a darkness . . . All seemed waiting on his next step. His own. Only his.*

In my own view, the issue of free will, like so many great truths, is a paradox. On the one hand, free will is a reality. We *can* be free to choose without "shibboleths" or conditioning or many other factors. On the other hand, we cannot choose freedom. There are only two states of being: submission to God and goodness or the refusal to submit to anything beyond one's own will—which refusal automatically enslaves one to the forces of evil. We must ultimately belong either to God or the devil. This paradox was, of course, expressed by Christ when he said, "Whosoever will save his life shall lose it. And whosoever shall lose his life, for my sake, shall find it."† It was also expressed by the hero, Dysert, in the final lines of Peter Shaffer's play *Equus:* "I cannot call it ordained of God: I can't get that far. I will, however, pay it so much homage. There is now in my mouth this sharp chain. And it no longer comes out."‡ As C. S. Lewis put it, "There is no neutral ground in the universe: every square inch, every split second is claimed by God and counterclaimed by Satan."§ I sup-

---

* *"Hostage to the Devil"* (Bantam Books, 1977), pp. 192–193.
† Matthew 10:39, 16:25, Mark 8:35; Luke 9:24.
‡ Avon Books, 1974.
§ *Christianity and Culture* contained in *Christian Reflections,* edited by Walter Hooper, Wm. B. Eerdmans Publishing Co., Grand Rapids, 1967, p. 33.

pose the only true state of freedom is to stand exactly halfway between God and the devil, uncommitted either to goodness or to utter selfishness. But that freedom is to be torn apart. It is intolerable. As Martin indicates, we must choose. One enslavement or the other.

It is fitting that at the conclusion of this section dealing with concepts from the science of psychology we should be left face-to-face with the notion of will. We have considered various possible factors in the genesis of human evil. I do not think we need to pick one as the right one and discard the others. There is a rule in psychiatry that all significant psychological problems are overdetermined—that is, that they have more than one and usually many different causes, just as plants will often have many roots. The problem of evil, I am sure, is no exception. But it is good to remember that among these factors is the mysterious freedom of the human will.

# 3

# THE ENCOUNTER
# WITH EVIL IN
# EVERYDAY LIFE

≛ IN THE CASE OF GEORGE we considered a person who was not evil but was in grave danger of becoming so. Then, in the last chapter, to illustrate some of the principles involved, a couple was described who, for whatever reason, had crossed the line. Now I shall continue to describe others who are frankly evil. I shall also address the issue of healing those who, like Bobby, are their victims.

Since I met the men and women and families I am describing in my practice of psychiatry, I am concerned that the reader will think: Ah, yes, but these are special cases. These people may be evil, but he is not talking about my kind of people—my colleagues, my acquaintances, my friends or relatives. There is a tendency among lay persons to think that people who see a psychiatrist are abnormal, that there is something radically different about them in comparison to the ordinary population. This is not so. Like it or not, the psychiatrist sees as much psychopathology at cocktail parties, conferences, and corporations as in her or his own office. I am not saying there are absolutely no differences between those who visit a psychiatrist and those who do not, but the differences are subtle and, as often as not, reflect unfavorably upon the "normal" population. The process of living is difficult and complex, even under the best of circumstances. We all have problems. Do people see a psychiatrist because their problems are greater than average or because they possess greater courage and wisdom with which to face their problems more directly? Sometimes one reason is the motive, sometimes the other, sometimes both. While the data I am presenting are drawn from my psychiatric practice, most of the time I shall be speaking not so much about psychiatric patients as about human beings anywhere and everywhere.

Indeed, the case of Bobby and his parents was truly unusual in only one respect: its relatively successful outcome. Bobby was fortunate that he did steal a car and attracted attention before he killed himself. It was fortunate that he had a relative who was willing to assume the burden of his care. And it was fortunate that through his parents' insurance there was the money to support his psychotherapy. Most victims of evil are not so lucky.

But in other respects Bobby's case was not unusual. Even in my small practice I see a new set of parents like Bobby's every month or so. It is no different for other psychiatrists. We brush against evil not once or twice in a lifetime but almost routinely as we come in contact with human crises. And it is my contention that the name of evil should have a definite place in our lexicon. It is true that there are very real dangers to such naming, and they will be discussed in the final chapter. But without the name, we will never clearly know what we are doing in such cases. We will remain limited in our capacity to help the victims of evil. And we will have no hope whatsoever of dealing with the evil ones themselves. For how can we heal that which we do not even dare study?

While the reader may acknowledge that there was something evil about Bobby's parents, many lay persons may be inclined to feel that the case was an aberrant one. Just because I say that we brush up against evil with regularity does not make it a fact. After all, there can't be very many parents who give their children suicide weapons for Christmas! Therefore I shall present a case of another fifteen-year-old boy, who was both the identified patient and a victim of evil. The value of this more subtle case may lie precisely in its differences from Bobby's. For here we will be talking about a boy whose parents were well-to-do and who, while they demonstrated no apparent desire to literally kill him, seemed bent, for whatever reason, on killing his spirit.

## THE CASE OF ROGER AND HIS PARENTS

At one point during my career I held an administrative post in the government which generally precluded the practice of ongoing therapy. I did from time to time, however, see people for brief consultations. Often they were high-ranking political figures. One such was Mr. R., a wealthy lawyer on leave of absence from his firm while serving as general counsel to a large federal department. It was June. Mr. R. had consulted me about his son, Roger, who had turned fifteen the month before. Although Roger had been a good scholar in one of the suburban public schools, his marks had declined gradually but steadily throughout the ninth grade. In his end-of-the-year evaluation the school guidance counselor had told Mr. and Mrs. R. that Roger would be promoted to the tenth grade but suggested a psychiatric evaluation to determine the cause of his academic decline.

As was my custom, I saw Roger, the identified patient, first. He looked very much like an upper-class version of Bobby. Wearing a necktie and well-tailored clothes, he still had that gangly, awkward look of late pubescence. He was similarly nonverbal and kept his gaze on the floor. He did not pick at his hands, and I did not sense him to be depressed to the same degree as Bobby had been. But his eyes had the same lifeless quality. Roger was clearly not a happy boy.

As with Bobby, I initially got nowhere talking with Roger. He didn't know why his grades were so poor. He wasn't aware that he was depressed. Everything in his life, he said, was "all right." Finally I decided to play a game I usually reserved for younger children. I picked up an ornamental vase from my desk.

"Supposing this was a magic bottle," I said, "and if you rubbed it, a genie would appear who could grant you any three wishes you might want. Anything in the whole world. What would you ask him for?"

"A stereo, I guess."

"Good," I said. "That was a smart thing to ask for. You've got two choices left. So I want you to think big. Don't worry if it seems impossible. Remember, this genie can do anything. So ask for what you really want the most."

"How about a motorbike?" Roger asked without enthusiasm but with somewhat less apathy than he'd shown up until then. He seemed to like the game, at least more than he'd liked anything thus far.

"Fine," I said. "That's a great choice. But you've got only one left. So remember to think big. Go after what's really important."

"Well, I'd like to go to boarding school."

I stared at Roger, caught by surprise. Suddenly the level had shifted to something real and personal. I mentally crossed my fingers. "That's a very interesting choice," I commented. "Could you tell me more about it?"

"Nothing to tell," Roger mumbled.

"I suppose maybe you want to go away to school because you don't like the school you're in now," I suggested.

"My school's all right," Roger responded.

I tried again. "Maybe you need to get away from home, then. Maybe there's something at home that's bothering you."

"Home's all right," Roger said, but there seemed to be a hint of fear in his voice.

"Have you told your parents you want to go away to boarding school?" I asked.

"Last fall." Roger's voice was almost a whisper.

"I bet that took a bit of courage. What did they say?"

"They said no."

"Oh? Why did they say that?"

"I don't know."

"How did it make you feel when they said no?" I queried.

"It's all right," Roger answered.

I sensed we had gotten as far as we were likely to get in a single session. It would take a long time for Roger to develop sufficient trust in a therapist to really open up. I told him I was going to speak with his parents for a while and afterward I would talk briefly with him again.

Mr. and Mrs. R. were a handsome couple in their early forties—articulate, impeccably dressed, obviously to the manor born.

"You're so kind to see us, Doctor," Mrs. R. said, genteelly removing her white gloves. "You have an excellent reputation. I'm sure you must be very busy."

I asked them to tell me how they perceived Roger's problem.

"Well, that's just why we've come to you, Doctor," Mr. R.

said, smiling urbanely. "We don't know how to perceive the problem. If we knew what was causing it, we could have taken appropriate action and wouldn't have needed to consult you."

Quickly, easily, almost conversationally, fluidly alternating their responses, they outlined the background for me. Roger had had a lovely summer at tennis camp just before the beginning of the school year. There had been no changes in the family. He'd always been a normal child. The pregnancy was normal. The delivery was normal. No feeding problems during infancy. Toilet training was normal. Peer relations were normal. There was little tension in the home. They—the two of them—had a happy marriage. Of course they had an occasional rare argument, but never in front of the children. Roger had a ten-year-old sister, who was doing well in school. The two of them squabbled between themselves of course, but nothing out of the ordinary. Of course it must be difficult for Roger to be the older child, but then that didn't really explain things, did it? No—his fall in grades was a mystery.

It was a pleasure to interview people so intelligent and sophisticated that they answered my questions before I even asked them. Yet I felt vaguely uneasy.

"Although you don't *know* what's bothering Roger," I said, "I'm sure you must have considered some possible explanations."

"We've wondered, of course, whether the school might not be right for him," Mrs. R. responded. "Since he's always done well until now, I hesitate to think so. But after all, children do change, don't they? It may not be what he needs now."

"Yes," Mr. R. contributed. "We've given some thought to putting him in a nearby Catholic parochial school. It's right up the street and remarkably inexpensive."

"Are you Catholics?" I inquired.

"No, Episcopalians," Mr. R. answered. "But we thought that Roger might benefit from the discipline of a parochial school."

"It's got a very fine reputation," Mrs. R. added.

"Tell me," I asked, "have you given any thought to the possibility of sending Roger away to boarding school?"

"No," Mr. R. replied. "Of course we would if it was something you recommended, Doctor. But it would be a costly solution, wouldn't it? It's outrageous what those schools are charging nowadays."

There was a brief moment of silence. "Roger told me he asked you last fall if he could go away to boarding school," I said.

"Did he?" Mr. R. looked blank for a second.

"You remember, dear," Mrs. R. said, jumping in smoothly. "We considered it quite seriously at the time."

"Certainly. That's right," Mr. R. agreed. "When you asked whether we'd given thought to it, Doctor, I assumed you meant recently—since Roger's had this problem with his grades. Back then we gave it considerable thought."

"I gather you decided against it?"

Mrs. R. picked up the ball. "Perhaps we're prejudiced on the subject, but both my husband and I feel that children shouldn't just be sent away from the home at a young age. So many children, I think, go to boarding school just because their parents don't want them. I think children do best when they're in a good, stable home, don't you, Doctor?"

"But perhaps we ought to reconsider it now, dear, if the doctor thinks it is advisable," Mr. R. interjected. "What do you think, Doctor? Do you think that Roger's problem would be solved if we sent him away to school?"

I was torn. I sensed there was something radically wrong with Mr. and Mrs. R. But it was subtle. How could they have forgotten that their son had asked to go away to boarding school? But then they claimed they did remember. It was a lie, I suspected, a cover-up. Yet I couldn't be sure. And so what? Should I build a whole case around such a little lie? I imagined there was something so wrong in the home that Roger desperately needed to get away from it—and this was why he sought boarding school. Still, that was just imagining. Roger wasn't telling me about anything bad at home. On the surface Mr. and Mrs. R. were highly intelligent, concerned, responsible parents. I had a hunch that boarding school would be the healthiest place for Roger. But I had no proof of this. How could I justify it to his parents, particularly when they seemed so cost-conscious despite their wealth? And why were they so cost-conscious? Certainly there was no way I could give them any guarantee that Roger's grades would improve or that he would be any happier if he were away from home. Yet might it not somehow hurt him if I equivocated? I wished I could somehow be somewhere else.

"Well?" asked Mr. R., waiting for my response.

"First of all," I said, "I think Roger's depressed. I don't know why he's depressed. Fifteen-year-olds usually aren't able to tell us why they're depressed, and it customarily takes us a good deal of time and work before we can find out. But his falling grades are a symptom of his depression, and his depression is a sign that something is not right. Some change does need to be made. It's not just going to go away. It's not something he's just going to grow out of. I think that the problem will get worse unless the right thing is done. Any questions so far?"

There were none.

"Next, I think it is quite likely sending Roger away to boarding school would be the right thing—or one of the right things," I continued. "But there is no way at this point I can be sure. Most of what I have to go on is simply his own desire. Yet that's a lot. In my experience, children this age do not make such requests lightly. Moreover, while they may not be able to express their reasons, they often have an instinctive sense of what is right for them. Roger still wants to go to boarding school six months after he first talked to you about it, and I think you should take his desire very seriously and respectfully. Any questions up to this point? Is there anything you don't understand?"

They said they understood.

"If you had to make a decision right at this moment," I concluded, "I would tell you to go ahead and send him to boarding school. But I don't think you have to make that decision immediately. I think there's probably time to take a deeper look. Since I can't give you any firm guarantees at this point that Roger will do better in boarding school, and if you want to be more clear that it's the right thing to do, I suggest you take such a deeper look. As I explained to you over the phone when you first called, I only do brief consultations, so I wouldn't be able to help you further. Besides, I'm not the best person to do so. When we work with young teenagers who aren't in touch with their feelings, one of the best tools we have is psychological testing. What I would like to do is refer you and Roger to Dr. Marshall Levenson. He's a psychologist who not only does testing but specializes in the evaluation and psychotherapy of adolescents."

"Levenson?" Mr. R. queried. "That's a Jewish name, isn't it?"

I looked at him, surprised. "I don't know. I suppose so. Probably half the people in our business are Jewish. Why do you ask?"

"No particular reason," Mr. R. replied. "I'm not prejudiced or anything. I was just curious."

"You say this man is a psychologist?" Mrs. R. asked. "What are his credentials? I'm not sure I would trust Roger to someone who was not a psychiatrist."

"Dr. Levenson's credentials are impeccable," I said. "He is as trustworthy as any psychiatrist. I would be happy to refer you to a psychiatrist if that is what you'd like. But I honestly don't know of one in the area whose judgment I would respect as much in this type of case. Furthermore, any psychiatrist would be likely to want to refer Roger to a psychologist for testing anyway, since only psychologists do testing. Finally," I said, looking at Mr. R., "psychologists' fees are a little less expensive than psychiatrists'."

"Money is no object when it comes to one of our children," Mr. R. responded.

"Oh, I'm sure that your Dr. Levenson is appropriate," Mrs. R. said, beginning to put on her gloves.

I wrote down Marshall Levenson's name and phone number on a prescription blank and gave it to Mr. R. "If there are no more questions, I'll see Roger now," I said.

"Roger?" Mr. R. looked alarmed. "What do you want to see Roger again for?"

"I told him that after I saw you I would meet with him again," I explained. "I do that routinely with all adolescent patients. It gives me a chance to tell them what I've recommended."

Mrs. R. stood up. "I'm afraid we need to go. We hadn't expected this would take so long. You've been very kind, Doctor, to give us so much of your time." She held out her gloved hand for me to shake.

I took her hand. But as I did so I looked her in the eye, saying, "I need to see your son. It will take no more than a couple of minutes."

Mr. R. seemed in no hurry. Still sitting, he said, "I don't see why you need to see Roger again. What business is it of his what you recommend? After all, it's our decision, isn't it? He's just a child."

"It is ultimately your decision," I acknowledged. "You're the parents and you're the ones who pay the bills. But it's his life. He's the one who's most concerned with what goes on in here. I will tell him that my recommendation of boarding school and/or Dr. Levenson is just a recommendation, and that you are the ones who have to make the decision. In fact, I will tell him that you are in a better position to know him and what is best for him than I am. You've spent fifteen years with him and I less than an hour. But he has a right to know what is happening to him, and assuming that you do take him to Dr. Levenson, it is only fair to explain to him what to expect. Not to do so would be rather inhumane, don't you think?"

Mrs. R. looked at her husband. "Let the doctor do what he thinks best, dear. We'll be even later for our engagement if we sit around discussing philosophical issues."

So I did get to talk to Roger again, and I explained to him the gist of my recommendations. I also explained that if he did see Dr. Levenson, he would likely take some psychological tests. I told him that he should not be frightened of these. Almost everyone, I told him, experienced this testing as fun. Roger said it would be "all right." He had no questions. At the end, instinctively, I did something slightly unusual. I gave him my card and told him he could call me if he needed to. He had a wallet, and he put the card in it carefully.

I called Marshall Levenson that night to let him know that I had referred Roger and his parents to him. I told him that I was not sure they would follow through.

A month later I met Marshall at a meeting and asked him about the case. He said that the parents had never gotten in touch with him. I was not terribly surprised. I assumed that I wouldn't hear of Roger again.

I was wrong.

It was at the end of January, seven months later, that Mr. R. called me for a second consultation. "Roger's really done it this time," he said. "The boy's got himself in serious trouble now." He told me that Roger's school principal was sending me a letter about the "incident," which I should receive in a few days. We made an appointment for the following week.

The letter arrived in the next afternoon's mail. It was from Sister Mary Rose, principal of the St. Thomas Aquinas High School in the suburb where the family lived:

Dear Dr. Peck:

When I advised Mr. and Mrs. R. to seek psychiatric consultation for their son, they told me you had treated Roger previously and asked that I send you this report.

Roger came to us this past fall from the local public school where his grades had been declining. He has not done well here academically either, earning only a C— average for the term. His social adjustment, however, has been excellent. He is well liked by both students and faculty. Particularly impressive has been his performance in our community affairs program. As part of his participation in this program, Roger elected to work with retarded children in the area during after-school hours. He not only demonstrated visible enthusiasm about this activity to me, but in their report his supervisors stressed his unusual empathy and dedication in working with the children. In fact they even voted funding for him to attend a mental-retardation conference in New York City over the Christmas holidays.

The incident precipitating this letter occurred January 18th. On that afternoon, Roger and a classmate broke into the room of Father Jerome, an old retired priest who lives at the school, and stole a watch and several other personal belongings. Ordinarily this would be a cause for dismissal from the school, and, indeed, the other boy involved has already been dismissed. The incident, however, seems to us distinctly out of character for Roger. Consequently, despite his serious academic underachievement, at a faculty meeting it was voted to retain Roger in our school subject to confirmation from you that such would be in his best interests. Obviously we like the young man a great deal and feel that we have something to offer him.

One other piece of information may be helpful to you. At the faculty meeting several of his teachers commented that Roger seemed to them quite depressed after returning from his Christmas holidays even before the incident in question.

I am looking forward to hearing of your recommendations. Please do not hesitate to contact me if you desire further information.

Sincerely,
Mary Rose OSC
Principal

When the family came for their appointment I saw Roger first again. As before, he appeared depressed. What was different, however, was a faint hint of hardness. There was a touch of both bitterness and false bravado in his manner. He didn't know why he had broken into the old priest's room.

"Tell me about Father Jerome," I asked.

Roger looked slightly surprised. "There's nothing to tell," he said.

"Is he a nice man or not a nice man?" I pressed. "Do you like him or dislike him?"

"He's okay, I guess," Roger answered, as if he'd never considered the question before. "He used to invite us to his room sometimes for cookies and tea. I suppose I like him."

"I wonder why you would steal from a man you like?"

"I don't know why I did it, I told you."

"Maybe you were looking for some more cookies," I suggested.

"Huh?" Roger appeared embarrassed.

"Perhaps you were looking for some more kindness. Maybe you need as much kindness as you can get."

"Nah," Roger exclaimed toughly. "We were just looking for something to steal."

I switched the subject. "Last time I saw you, Roger, I recommended that you go to a psychologist, Dr. Levenson. Did you ever see him?"

"No."

"Why not?"

"I don't know."

"Did your parents ever talk to you about it?"

"No."

"What do you make of that? Doesn't it seem strange that I recommended it and then you and your parents never mentioned it again?"

"I don't know."

"We'd also been talking the last time about the possibility of you going to boarding school," I said. "Did you and your parents ever talk more about that?"

"No. They just told me I was going to St. Thomas."

"How did that make you feel?"

"It was all right."

"Would you still like to go away to boarding school if you had the chance?"

"No. I want to stay at St. Thomas. Please, Dr. Peck, help me to stay at St. Thomas."

I was surprised and touched by Roger's sudden spontaneity. Clearly the school had become important to him. "Why do you want to stay?" I asked.

Roger looked confused for a moment, then thoughtful. "I don't know," he said after a pause. "They like me. I feel that I'm liked there."

"I think you are, Roger," I responded. "Sister Mary Rose wrote me and said very clearly that they liked you and want you to stay. And since you want to stay, that's probably what I'll recommend to her and to your parents. By the way, Sister Mary Rose said you were doing some fine work with retarded children. How was your trip to New York?"

Roger looked blank. "What trip?"

"Why, the trip to the conference on retardation. Sister Mary Rose told me you'd been funded to go. It seemed to me quite an honor for someone not yet sixteen. How was the conference?"

"I didn't go."

"You didn't go?" I repeated stupidly. Then I began to feel a sense of dread. Intuitively I had an idea of what was coming. "Why didn't you go?"

"My parents wouldn't let me."

"And why was that?"

"They said I didn't keep my room clean at home."

"How did that make you feel?"

Roger appeared numb. "All right," he said.

I allowed a note of outrage in my voice. "All right? You get awarded an exciting trip to New York City, all on your own merits, and then you're not allowed to go, but you tell me it's all right. That's a lot of crap."

Roger looked very unhappy. "My room wasn't clean," he said.

"Do you believe that the punishment fitted the crime? Do you think the fact that you didn't pick up your room was sufficient reason to deny you such an exciting trip—a trip you had earned, a trip that would be educational for you?"

"I don't know." Roger just sat there dumbly.

"Were you disappointed, angry?"

"I don't know."

"Do you think that maybe you were very disappointed and very angry and that maybe that had something to do with your breaking into Father Jerome's room?"

"I don't know."

Of course he didn't know. How could he? It was all uncon-scious. "Do you ever get angry at your parents, Roger?" I asked softly.

He kept his gaze riveted to the floor. "They're all right," he said.

If Roger's depression was unchanged, so was his parents' urbane composure. "We're sorry to have to bother you again, Doctor," Mrs. R. announced as I led them into my office after seeing Roger. She sat down and removed her gloves. "We don't mind being here," she smiled, "but of course we did so hope for Roger's sake that something like this wouldn't be necessary again. You've re-ceived correspondence, I believe, from the principal?"

I acknowledged that I had.

"My wife and I are very worried that the boy is well on the road to becoming a common criminal," Mr. R. said. "Perhaps we should have taken your advice and sent him to that doctor you recommended. What was his name? It was a foreign-sounding name."

"Dr. Levenson."

"Yes. As I said, perhaps we should have sent him to your Dr. Levenson."

"Why didn't you?" I expected the answer would be well pre-pared. Returning to see me, they would have known the issue to be unavoidable. Indeed, they had wasted no time in raising it themselves. But I was curious to hear their response.

"Well, you left us with the impression that it was up to Roger," Mr. R. replied facilely. "I remember your saying that it was his life—or something like that. And then I know you talked to him about it. When he expressed no enthusiasm about it, we assumed he did not want to go see your Dr. Levenson, and we decided it would be better not to press the matter."

"Then we were also concerned with Roger's self-esteem," Mrs. R. contributed. "Since he was already doing badly in school, we were worried what effect his seeing a psychologist would have on his confidence. Self-esteem is so important to young peo-ple, don't you think, Doctor? . . . But perhaps we were wrong," she added with a charming little smile.

It was clever. With a few words the issue of their not following through with my recommendation had become a combination of my own fault and Roger's. There seemed to be no point in arguing the matter with them. "Do you have any idea why Roger might have become involved in this stealing incident?" I asked.

"None at all, Doctor," Mr. R. replied. "We tried to talk with him, of course, but he wouldn't give us anything to go on. No, we're at a total loss."

"Stealing is often an angry act," I said. "Do you have any idea why Roger might have been angry or resentful lately? Angry at the world or angry at the school or angry at you?"

"No reason that we know of, Doctor," Mrs. R. answered.

"Is there any interaction that you can think of that you had with Roger in the month before his stealing that might have made him angry or resentful?"

"No, Doctor," Mrs. R. answered again. "As we told you, we're at a total loss."

"I understand that you wouldn't allow Roger to go on a trip to New York to a mental-retardation conference during the Christmas holidays," I said.

"Oh, is Roger upset about *that?*" Mrs. R. exclaimed. "He didn't seem upset when we told him he couldn't go."

"Roger has great difficulty expressing his anger," I said. "It's a large part of his problem. But tell me, did you think that he would be upset when you wouldn't let him go?"

"How should we know? We can't predict that sort of thing," Mrs. R. responded with faint belligerence. "We're not psychologists, you know. We just did what we thought was right."

A picture flashed before me of the endless strategy sessions Mr. R. attended in the councils of power where politicians made and discussed just such predictions. But again there would be no use in fighting the issue. "Why did you think it was right not to let Roger go on his trip to New York?" I asked.

"Because he won't pick up his room," Mr. R. replied. "Time and again we've told him to keep his room clean, and he just won't do it. So we told him he was not fit to be an ambassador abroad when he couldn't keep his own house in order."

"I'm not sure what being an ambassador abroad has to do with a weekend trip to New York City," I said, becoming exasperated. "I also think your expectations in this regard are unrealistic. Very few fifteen-year-old boys keep their rooms neat. In fact, I would worry about them if they did. It doesn't seem to me an adequate reason to prevent a young man from going on an exciting educational trip that he has earned by his own efforts in a worthy field of endeavor."

"Well, we have some questions about that, Doctor," Mrs. R. said gently, even sweetly. "I'm not at all sure it's right for Roger to be working with those retarded children. After all, some of those children are mentally ill too."

I felt helpless.

"This chitchat is all very nice," Mr. R. pronounced, "but we've got to get on with it. Something's got to be done or the boy will become a common criminal. In the summer we were talking about sending him away to boarding school. Would that still be your recommendation, Doctor?"

"No," I answered. "Back in June I was sufficiently uneasy about it to recommend that Roger ought to see Dr. Levenson before making a definite decision. I don't want to absolutely rule out boarding school, but I'm even more uneasy about it now. Roger likes his new school. He feels cared for there, and I think it would be quite traumatic for him if he were suddenly removed. I see no need for anything to be done precipitately, so once again I would recommend that Roger see Dr. Levenson."

"That just puts us back at square one," Mr. R. exclaimed, obviously annoyed. "Don't you have anything more definitive to recommend, Doctor?"

"Well, I do have one other recommendation," I said.

"What's that?"

"I strongly recommend that the two of you go into treatment. I think Roger needs help very badly. I think that both of you also need it."

There was a moment of deadly silence. Then Mr. R. smiled a slight, amused smile. "That's very interesting, Doctor," he said equably. "I would be very interested as to why you think we need treatment, as you put it."

"I'm glad you're interested," I responded. "I'd thought perhaps you'd be upset. I think the two of you ought to get into psychotherapy yourselves because you really seem to me to lack empathy for Roger, and your own psychotherapy would be the only thing I can think of that might enable you to understand Roger better."

"Really, Doctor," Mr. R. continued equably and urbanely, "I

do find your recommendation intriguing. I'm not boasting, but it seems to me I've been quite successful in my profession. My wife also has been rather successful. We have no problems with our other child. And my wife is very much a community leader, you know. She's a member of the zoning board and highly active in church affairs. I'm intrigued as to why you might consider us mentally ill."

"What you're saying," I paraphrased, "is that Roger's the sick one and the two of you are healthy. It's quite true that Roger is the one whose problems are most visible. But first of all, Roger's problems are your problems. And from my point of view, everything you've done to cope with Roger's problems in the past years has been wrong. Roger wanted to go to boarding school. You refused him without looking into the matter any further. I advised that you take him to see Dr. Levenson. You rejected that advice. And now, when he was rewarded for his own role in community affairs, you refused him his reward without even thinking of the effect it might have on him. I'm not saying that you consciously want to hurt Roger. But I am saying that from a psychological point of view your behavior indicates that on an unconscious level you have a good deal of animosity toward him."

"I'm glad to hear you refer to your point of view, Doctor," Mr. R. said in his smoothest lawyer's manner. "Because it is just your point of view, isn't it? And there might be other points of view, mightn't there? I will admit I am beginning to feel a certain amount of animosity toward Roger now that he seems to be becoming a common criminal. And I know that your psychological point of view might hold us, his parents, to be responsible for every little nasty thing he does. But it's easy for you to point the finger at us. You haven't sweated like we have to give him the very best education and the most stable of homes. No, you haven't sweated at all."

"What my husband's trying to say, Doctor," Mrs. R. said, joining in, "is that there might be some other explanation. My uncle, for instance, was an alcoholic. Isn't it possible that Roger's problem has been inherited, that he's got some kind of defective gene, that he would have turned out bad no matter how we treated him?"

I looked at them with a growing sense of horror. "You mean,

isn't it possible that Roger's incurable—that's what you're saying, isn't it?"

"Well, we'd hate to think that he's incurable. I should hope that there'd be some medicine or something that could help him," Mrs. R. said calmly. "But we certainly can't expect you doctors to have found a cure for everything, can we?"

What could I say? I had to remain scientific, detached. "There are many psychiatric conditions that are wholly or partially inherited and genetic in basis. There is absolutely no evidence, however, to suggest that Roger's difficulties are part of any such condition. My diagnosis in your son's case is that he is suffering from a depression that is not hereditary and not incurable. To the contrary, I believe his difficulties are completely curable if he is helped to understand his feelings and if you can be helped to change the way you respond to him. Now, I cannot guarantee that my diagnosis is correct. It is a best guess based upon my experience and judgment. I would estimate that chances are ninety-eight percent that my diagnosis is accurate. I cannot tell you that it is a hundred percent accurate. If you are distrustful of it, you should get additional consultation from another psychiatrist. I can recommend several others to you or you can seek one on your own. But I must tell you that I do not believe there is much time. While I think his problem is curable with the proper help at present, I'm not sure it will be if he doesn't get that help very soon."

"So it is just your opinion, isn't it, Doctor?" Mr. R. was boring in on me in his best trial-lawyer fashion.

"Yes," I acknowledged, "it's just my opinion."

"And it's not a matter of scientific proof, is it? You think, but you do not *know*, what Roger's problem is. That's right, isn't it?"

"Yes, that's right."

"So it is in fact perfectly possible that Roger has a hereditary, incurable condition that you are not able to diagnose at this time."

"Yes, possible, but hardly likely." I paused to light a cigarette. My hands were shaking. I looked at them. "You know," I said, "what strikes me about all this is that the two of you seem more eager to believe that Roger has an incurable illness—more willing to write him off—than to believe that you yourselves might be in need of treatment."

For a fraction of a second all I could see was fear in their eyes, pure animal fear. But within an instant they had recovered their urbanity.

"All we are trying to do is to get the facts straight, Doctor. You can hardly criticize us for wanting to separate fact from fiction, can you, now?" explained Mr. R.

"Many people are afraid of entering psychotherapy," I commented, feeling as if I were attempting to sell Bibles inside the Kremlin. "It's a natural reluctance. No one is eager to have his or her inner thoughts and feelings examined. But once you get into it, it's not so fearful. If it would make it any easier for you, I would be willing to work with you myself. It would break my rule that I do only consultations, but I would do anything in my power to see that you and Roger get the help you need."

I certainly did not expect that they would take me up on this offer, and one part of me certainly hoped that they wouldn't. But I felt compelled to make it. Much as I found the notion of trying to work with them distasteful, I could not in good conscience automatically refer them to someone else. Now at least, seven years after the case of Bobby, I had some idea of what I would be up against.

"Oh, I'm sure you're right, Doctor," Mrs. R. said amiably, as if we were chatting at a tea party. "It would be pleasant to talk about oneself and have someone to lean on. But it is so terribly time-consuming and so terribly expensive, isn't it? I do wish we were in the upper-income bracket so we could afford it. But we have two children to educate. I'm afraid we simply don't have thousands of dollars to spend year after year on an art form."

"Whether you are in the upper-income bracket, I do not know," I answered her, "but I do know that in all probability you are covered under the federal government insurance program, which offers the best benefits anywhere for outpatient psychotherapy. Probably you would only have to pay a fifth of the cost of treatment yourselves. And if you are still worried about the expense, you might want to consider family therapy, in which the therapist would talk to you and Roger together."

Mr. R. stood up. "This has been a most interesting conversation, Doctor. Yes, most enlightening. But we've taken quite enough of your time. And I must be getting back to my office."

"But what about Roger?" I asked.

"Roger?" Mr. R. looked at me blankly.

"Yes. He's guilty of breaking and entering. He's doing poorly academically. He's depressed. He's frightened. He's in trouble. What's to become of him?"

"Well, we're going to have to give a lot of thought to Roger," Mr. R. replied. "Yes, a lot of thought. And you've given us a lot to think about also, Doctor. You've been most helpful."

"I hope I have," I said, standing up as well. The interview was clearly being terminated whether I liked it or not. "And I do hope you'll give serious thought to what I've recommended."

"Of course, Doctor," Mrs. R. purred. "We'll give everything you've said serious consideration."

As before, Mr. and Mrs. R. attempted to prevent me from talking to Roger again. "He's not a piece of furniture," I insisted. "He has a right to know what's going on."

So I spent a few final moments with Roger. I found out that he still had my card in his wallet. I said I would call Sister Mary Rose and advise that he continue at St. Thomas. I told him I had recommended that he should still see Dr. Levenson. I also told him I had recommended therapy for his parents. "You see, Roger," I said, "I don't think it's all your problem. I think your parents have psychological problems that are at least as big as yours. I don't think they try very well to understand you. And I don't know that they will get the help you all need."

Roger was, as expected, noncommittal when we parted.

Three weeks later I received a check in the mail enclosed with a note from Mrs. R. on her tasteful, personal stationery:

> Dear Dr. Peck:
>     You were so kind to see us again last month at such short notice. My husband and I truly appreciate your concern for Roger. I wanted to let you know that we have followed your advice and have sent Roger to boarding school. It is a military academy in North Carolina, and has an excellent reputation for working with children with behavior problems. I am sure things will be better from now on. Thank you so much for all you have done for us.
>
> Very sincerely yours,
> Mrs. R.

That was ten years ago. I have no idea what happened to Roger. He would be twenty-five now. Occasionally I remember to pray for him.

One respect in which it is difficult to write about evil is its subtlety. I began with the case of Bobby and his parents because
of its obvious clarity. To give a child his older brother's suicide weapon is an act of such gross outrageousness that anyone would think, Yes, that is evil all right. But there was no such
grossly outrageous act committed by Roger's parents; we are
dealing only with trip permissions and school choices—the ordinary kind of decisions that parents routinely make. Simply because the judgment of Roger's parents in these matters differed
from my own may not seem grounds for labeling them evil. Indeed, might I not be guilty of evil myself by so labeling clients
who disagree with my opinions and fail to take my advice? Might
I not be misusing the concept of evil by facilely applying it to
any and all who oppose my judgment?

This problem of the potential misapplication of the concept of
evil is a very real one and will be considered at some length in
the final chapter. Certainly it is my obligation to justify my conclusion that Roger was the victim of evil. It is particularly important for me to do so because, of the two cases, Bobby's and
Roger's, Roger's is the more typical. While evil may manifest
itself obviously, as in the case of Bobby, it rarely does so. More
commonly by far its manifestations are seemingly ordinary, superficially normal, and even apparently rational. As I have said,
those who are evil are masters of disguise; they are not apt to
wittingly disclose their true colors—either to others or to themselves. It is not without reason that the serpent is renowned for his
subtlety.

It is exceedingly rare, therefore, that we can pass judgment on
a person as being evil after observing a single act; instead, our
judgment must be made on the basis of a whole pattern of acts
as well as their manner and style. It is not simply that his parents
chose a school against Roger's wishes or contrary to my advice;
in a period of a year they made three such choices consecutively.
It is not that they disregarded Roger's feelings on a particular
occasion; they did so at every possible opportunity. Their lack
of concern for him as a person was utterly consistent.

Still, is this evil? Might we not say that Mr. and Mrs. R. were
remarkably insensitive people and leave it at that? But the fact is

that they were not insensitive people. Highly intelligent, they were finely tuned to social nuances. We are not talking of poor dirt farmers in Appalachia but of a well-educated, gracious, politically sophisticated couple, quite adept in the committee and at the cocktail party. They could not have been who they were had they lacked sensitivity. Mr. R. would not make an unconsidered legal decision and Mrs. R. would always remember to send flowers on the right occasion. But Roger they would not remember or consider. The fact is that their insensitivity toward him was selective. Conscious or unconscious, it was a choice.

Why? Why should they make such a choice? Was it merely that they did not want to be bothered with Roger and that all their reactions to him were predicated on what would be cheapest and easiest rather than on what he might need? Or did they actually, in some dark way, want to destroy him? I do not know. I never will know. There is, I suspect, something basically incomprehensible about evil. But if not incomprehensible, it is characteristically inscrutable. The evil always hide their motives with lies.

If the reader reviewed my account of the interactions that Mr. and Mrs. R. had with me, she or he would find somewhere between one and two dozen lies. Here again we see this striking consistency. It is not a matter of one lie or two. Roger's parents lied to me repeatedly and routinely. They were people of the lie. The lies were not gross. There was not one they could have been taken to court on. Yet the process was pervasive. Indeed, even their coming to see me at all was a lie.

Why did they seek my services when they neither had any real concern for Roger nor any real interest in my advice? The answer is that it was part of their pretense. They wanted to *appear* as if they were trying to help Roger. Since it had been advised by his school in each instance, they would have seemed remiss had they not sought attention. In case others might ask, "You've taken him to a psychiatrist, haven't you?" Mr. and Mrs. R. made sure they were in a position to respond, "Oh, yes. Several times. But nothing has seemed to help."

For a while I wondered why they had brought Roger back specifically to me the second time when our first meeting had not been exactly pleasant for them and when they knew they would have to face the issue of their failure to follow my recommendations. It seemed like an odd choice. But then I remembered I had been very clear about the fact that I did only very brief consultations. This meant there could be no significant pressure on them to follow through on recommendations. Their escape route was wide open. My schedule fitted the pretense.

Naturally, since it is designed to hide its opposite, the pretense chosen by the evil is most commonly the pretense of love. The message Mr. and Mrs. R. sought to convey was: "Because we are good, loving parents, we are deeply concerned about Roger." As I pointed out in the previous chapter, the pretense of the evil is designed at least as much to deceive themselves as others. I am quite certain that Mr. and Mrs. R. actually believed they were doing everything they could for Roger. And when they would say—as I am sure they would—"We have taken him to a psychiatrist several times, but no one could help him," they would have forgotten the details of which truth is composed.

Any experienced psychotherapist knows that unloving parents abound, and that the vast majority of such parents maintain at least some degree of a loving pretense. Surely they do not all deserve the designation of evil! I suppose not. I suppose that it is a matter of degree, that in consonance with Martin Buber's two types of myths, there are the "falling" and the "fallen." I do not know exactly where to draw the line between them. I do know, however, that Mr. and Mrs. R. had crossed it.

First there is the matter of the degree to which they were willing to sacrifice Roger for the preservation of their narcissistic self-image. There seemed to be no lengths to which they would not go. It bothered them not at all to think of him as a "genetic criminal"—to blandly offer him up to the designation of hopeless, incurable, and malformed as a defense against my suggestion that they themselves needed therapy. I sensed no limit to their willingness to use him as a scapegoat if necessary.

Then there is also the degree—the depth and distortion—of their lying. Mrs. R. wrote: "I wanted to let you know that we have followed your advice and have sent Roger to boarding school." What an extraordinary statement! It says that I advised them to take Roger out of St. Thomas when I specifically advised against such action. It states that they followed my advice when they specifically did not; my primary advice was that they themselves have therapy. Finally, it implies that they did what they did *because* I advised it when, in fact, they considered my advice irrelevant. Not one lie, not even two lies, but three lies, all twisted around each other in a single short sentence. It is, I suppose, a form of genius that one can almost admire for its perversity. I suppose also that Mrs. R. actually believed it herself when she wrote "we have followed your advice." Buber stated it well when he wrote of "the uncanny game of hide and seek in the obscurity of the soul, in which it, the single human soul, evades itself, avoids itself, hides from itself."*

The most typical victim of evil is a child. This is to be expected, because children are not only the weakest and most vulnerable members of our society but also because parents wield a power over the lives of their children that is essentially absolute. The dominion of master over slave is not far different from the dominion of parent over child. The child's immaturity and resulting dependency mandate its parents' possession of great power but do not negate the fact that this power, like all power, is subject to abuse of various degrees of malignancy. Moreover, the relationship between parent and child is one of enforced intimacy. A master could always sell a slave if the relationship was one he found intolerable. But just as children are not free from their parents, so it is not easy for parents to escape from their children and the pressures that their children impose.†

Another typical—and rather intriguing—feature of the cases of Bobby and Roger is the extraordinary unity of their parents. Each set of parents functioned as a team. We cannot say that Bobby's father was evil, but his mother was not, or that his mother was evil and his father was just along for the ride. As far as I could tell, they were both evil. So it was also with Mr. and Mrs. R. Both seemed equally ungenuine; both seemed to participate in the destructive decision-making; both seemed equally

---

* *Good and Evil* (Charles Scribner's Sons, 1953), p. 111.

† If one wants to seek out evil people, the simplest way to do so is to trace them from their victims. The best place to look, then, is among the parents of emotionally disturbed children or adolescents. I do not mean to imply that *all* emotionally disturbed children are victims of evil or that *all* such parents are malignant persons. The configuration of evil is present only in a minority of these cases. It is, however, a substantial minority.

willing to write off Roger as incurable when they were impli-
cated in his problem.*

The victims of evil encountered in everyday psychiatric practice are not, however, always children. Let us turn now to the
case of Hartley and Sarah, a childless couple in their late forties.
I shall describe a single interview that I had with the two of them
together. It will demonstrate that the victimization of an adult by
evil is in some ways radically different from that of a child. It
will also give us a clue to the further understanding of the phenomenon of the "evil couple" which we have just been discussing.
Finally, the case will reveal a new and puzzling dimension to the
problem of the psychiatric classification of human evil.


## THE CASE OF HARTLEY AND SARAH

I first saw them a week after Hartley had been discharged from
the state hospital. A month before, at 11 o'clock on a Saturday
morning, Hartley had cut both sides of his neck with a straightedge razor. Bare-chested, he walked out from the bathroom into
the living room, where Sarah was balancing their checkbook. "I
just tried to kill myself again," he announced.

Sarah turned around to see the blood streaming down his torso.
She called the police, who called the ambulance. Hartley was
taken to the local emergency room. The cuts were relatively
superficial; he had failed to sever either the carotid arteries or the
jugular veins. After the cuts were sutured he was transferred to
the state hospital. It was his third suicide attempt and third admission to the state hospital during the preceding five years.

Because they had recently moved into the area, Hartley was
referred for follow-up care to our clinic after he was discharged
from the hospital. His discharge diagnosis was "involutional de-

* This parental unity will not be surprising to psychiatrists. When we examine cases of child battering, we find it to be the rule that both parents
have been involved in the crime. Even in cases of repetitive father-daughter
incest, we usually find some degree of collusion on the mother's part. Once
again, I do not wish to imply that all battering or incestuous parents are
evil. I cite these phenomena only to illustrate the fact that both parents are
almost always culpable in the creation of psychopathology in their children.
Those who have read *Sybil*, by Flora Schreiber (Warner Books, 1974), will
recall the truth of this principle.

pressive reaction." He was on high doses of antidepressant and tranquilizing medication.

When I went out to the waiting room to greet him, Hartley was sitting silently next to his wife, staring into space with dull eyes—an average-sized gray man who seemed smaller, as if he had been crushed into a very little space. I felt tired looking at him. Lord, I thought, I wish the state hospital would try to get these people a little better before they kick them out. He's still as depressed as the Black Hole of Calcutta. But I tried to look welcoming. "I'm Dr. Peck," I said to him. "Come on into my office."

"Can my wife come too?" Hartley mumbled in a pleading tone.

I looked at Sarah, a thin, angular woman, smaller than her husband, yet seeming considerably larger. "If it's all right with you, Doctor," she responded, smiling sweetly. Her smile did not make me feel any happier. Somehow it was incongruous with the faintly bitter expression conveyed by the tight wrinkles around her mouth. She wore steel-rimmed spectacles and reminded me of a missionary lady.

I led them both into my office. Once we were all seated I looked at Hartley. "Why did you want your wife to come in with you?" I asked.

"I'm more comfortable when she's close to me," he replied flatly. There was no particular warmth in this; it was just a statement of fact.

I must have looked quizzical.

"Hartley's been that way for the longest time, Doctor," Sarah announced, smiling gaily. "He hates to let me out of his sight for a moment."

'Is that because you're jealous?" I asked Hartley.

"No," he said dully.

"Then why?"

"I'm scared."

"Scared of what?" I inquired.

"I don't know. I'm just scared."

"I think it's because of his thoughts, Doctor," Sarah interrupted. "Go on, Hartley, you can tell him about your thoughts," she instructed. Hartley said nothing.

"What thoughts is she talking about?" I asked.

"My thoughts about kill," Hartley replied in his monotone.

"Kill?" I repeated. "You mean you have thoughts about killing?"

"No. Just kill."

"I'm afraid I don't understand," I said lamely.

"It's just a word thought," Hartley explained without emotion. "The word 'kill' comes into my mind. Like someone had said it. It can come any time. But most of the time it's in the morning. When I get up and start shaving and start looking at myself in the mirror, it's just there. 'Kill.' Almost every morning."

"You mean like a hallucination?" I queried. "You hear a voice telling you to kill?"

"No," Hartley answered. "No voice. Just the word in my mind."

"When you're shaving?"

"Yes. I always feel worst in the morning."

"Do you shave with a straightedge razor?" I asked with sudden intuition. Hartley nodded. "It sounds as if you want to kill someone with your razor," I continued.

Hartley looked frightened. It was the first sign of emotion I had seen on his face. "No," he said emphatically. "I don't want to kill anyone. It's not a feeling—just a word."

"Well, you apparently wanted to kill yourself," I commented. "Why was that?"

"I feel so horrible. I'm no good to anyone. I'm nothing but a burden to Sarah." The heaviness of his voice weighed on me. He certainly would not be a joy to be around.

"Is he a burden to you?" I asked Sarah.

"Oh, I don't mind," she replied cheerfully. "I would like to be able to have a little time to myself. And of course we don't have enough money."

"So he is a burden, you feel?"

"The Lord supports me," Sarah answered.

"Why is it you don't have enough money?" I asked.

"Hartley hasn't worked for eight years, he's been so depressed, the poor dear. But we get by on what I make at the telephone company."

"I used to be a salesman," Hartley interjected plaintively.

"He did manage to work the first ten years we were married," Sarah agreed. "But he was never really very aggressive—were you, dear?"

"I made over twenty thousand dollars in commissions alone the year we got married," Hartley objected.

"Yes, but that was in 'fifty-six. That was a boom year for electrical switches," Sarah explained patiently. "Anyone who happened to be selling switches in 'fifty-six would have made that kind of money."

Hartley was silent.

"Why did you stop working?" I asked him.

"My depression. I felt so awful in the mornings. I just couldn't go to work anymore."

"What was making you so depressed?"

Hartley looked puzzled, as if unable to remember something. "It must have been my words," he said finally.

"You mean the words in your mind, like 'kill'?"

He nodded.

"You said words—plural. Are there other words as well?" I asked.

Hartley was silent.

"Go on, dear," Sarah said. "Tell the doctor about the other words."

"Well, sometimes there are other words," he acknowledged reluctantly. "Like 'cut' or 'hammer.' "

"Any others?"

"Sometimes 'blood.' "

"Those are all angry words," I commented. "I don't think they would come into your head unless you were very angry."

"I'm not angry," Hartley insisted dully.

"What do you think?" I asked, turning to Sarah. "Do you think he's angry?"

"Oh, I think Hartley hates me," she answered with her gay little smile, as if she were talking about a cute prank played by a neighbor's child.

I stared at her in amazement. I had begun to suspect the truth of this, but I hardly expected her to be so calmly aware of it. "Aren't you worried that he might hurt you?" I asked.

"Oh, no. Hartley wouldn't hurt a fly—would you, dear?"

Hartley did not respond.

"Seriously," I said to Sarah, "he thinks of kill and blood and hammer. It seems to me that if I were you, I'd be quite frightened living with a husband who hates you and thinks of such things."

"But you don't understand, Doctor," Sarah explained placidly. "He couldn't hurt me. He's such a weakling."

I quickly glanced at Hartley. There was absolutely no expression on his face. I sat there for almost a minute in stunned silence trying to focus on how to proceed. Finally I asked him, "How does it make you feel to hear your wife call you a weakling?"

"She's right. I am weak," he mumbled.

"If she's right," I said, "how does *that* make you feel?"

"I'd like to be stronger," he responded without enthusiasm.

"Hartley can't even drive a car," Sarah interjected. "He can't go out of the house alone without me. He can't go into a supermarket or any crowded place—can you, dear?"

Hartley nodded in dumb assent.

"You seem to agree with your wife about everything," I pointed out.

"She's right. I can't go anywhere without her."

"Why can't you?"

"I'm scared."

"Scared of what, damn it?" I asked, trying to push him.

"I don't know," he replied abjectly. "All I can tell you is I get scared whenever I have to do anything by myself. I get scared when Sarah isn't around to help me."

"You sound like you're a very young child," I commented.

Sarah smiled complacently. "Hartley is a child in some ways," she said. "You aren't very grown up, are you, dear?"

"Maybe you don't want him to grow up," I said quickly, turning to her.

Sarah flashed me a look of sudden hatred. "Want?" she snapped. "When have my wants ever been considered? My wants don't matter. My wants have never mattered to anyone. It isn't a question of what I want or don't want. I only do what I have to do, what the Lord wants me to do. Oh, there's no telling what I would want. Who cares that Hartley's a burden? Who cares that I do all the work, that I do all the driving, that I do all the shopping? But I don't complain. No. What right do I have? No, Sarah doesn't have rights. Sarah doesn't complain. Hartley's depressed. It's not for me to complain. Hartley's a worm of a man. But no one cares about Sarah. I just shoulder the burdens the Lord has given me. Sarah does what she has to do."

I was taken aback by this diatribe and not sure that I wanted to tangle with her again. But I proceeded, more out of curiosity than a sense that there was any way I could help the situation. "I gather the two of you have no children," I said. "Was that a choice you made?"

"Hartley's incapable of producing children," Sarah announced.

"Oh? How do you know that?"

Sarah gave me a look suggesting I was ignorant of the facts of life. "Because I've been examined by the gynecologist," she explained. "He said I was perfectly all right. There's nothing wrong with me."

"Have you also been examined?" I asked Hartley.

He shook his head.

"Why not?"

"Why should I?" Hartley countered, as if I were unable to see the obvious. "There's nothing wrong with Sarah, so it must be my fault."

"Hartley, you're just about the most passive man I've ever met," I said. "You passively assume your wife is telling the truth about her examination. You passively assume that because her examination was normal, yours would be abnormal. There are lots of cases in which both the husband and wife are normal but still don't have children. You may well be perfectly okay. Why don't you check it out?"

"There would be no point to that, Doctor," Sarah answered for him. "We're too old to have children. And we don't have the money for any more tests. You forget that I'm the only one who makes the money. Besides," she said, smiling, "can you imagine Hartley being a father? He can't even make a living."

"But wouldn't it be worth it for Hartley just to know that he's not physically incapable of being a father?"

"Sarah's right," Hartley said, actually coming to the defense of his wife's assumption of his inadequacy. "There'd be no point to it."

By now I was feeling very tired. I had twenty minutes left before my next patient, but I was strongly tempted to terminate the interview. There was no hope for change. There was no possibility of help for Hartley. He was too far gone. But why? Why and how in the name of God did such misery come about, I wondered. "Tell me about your childhood," I directed him.

"There's nothing to tell," Hartley mumbled.

"Well, how far did you go in school?" I asked.

"Hartley went to Yale," Sarah answered for him again. "But then you flunked out, didn't you, dear?"

Hartley nodded.

I felt ill thinking that this worm of a man, as Sarah accurately and callously called him, had once been a bright-eyed college youth. "How did you happen to go to Yale?" I asked.

"My family was wealthy."

"But you also must have been quite bright," I commented.

"It's no good being bright if you don't work," Sarah interjected once more. "Handsome is as handsome does, I always say."

I turned to her. "Are you aware that every single time I try to focus on whatever assets your husband might have, you jump in and castrate him?"

She screeched at me, "Castrate him? Castrate him, do I? All you doctors are alike. Maybe you castrate him, they say. It's all my fault, isn't it? Oh, yes, it's always Sarah's fault. He doesn't work, he doesn't drive, he doesn't do anything, but it's all Sarah's fault. Well, let me tell you, he was castrated before I ever met him. His mother was an alcoholic slob. His father was as weak as he is. He couldn't even make it through college. And then they accused me of marrying him for his money. Hah, what money? His slut of a mother had spent all the money slopping up her booze. I haven't seen any money. Nobody's ever helped me out. Nobody helps Sarah. Sarah does it all. But she castrates him, they accuse. But do you think any of them are ever interested in me? No. No one. They just accuse me."

"I could be interested in you, Sarah," I said gently, adding, "if you'd let me. Why don't you tell me something about your family and your growing up?"

"Oh, so now I'm the patient, am I?" she asked bitterly. "Well, I'm sorry. I'm not going to be your guinea pig. I don't need your help. There's nothing wrong with me. I can get all the help I need from my minister. He understands me. He knows what I go through. God gives me all the strength I require. I brought Hartley here for help. He's the one who needs it. You help him—that is, if you can."

"I'm quite serious, Sarah," I said. "You're quite right that Hartley needs help, and we'll give him whatever help we can. But I think you need help as well. It's a terribly difficult situation that you're in, and I can see you get upset by it. I think you might feel much better if you had someone to talk to or if you let me give you a mild tranquilizer."

But Sarah had pulled herself together. She sat back in her chair and smiled at me as if I were a nice but misguided young man. "Thank you, Doctor, you're very kind," she said, "but I'm afraid I don't get upset. There's very little that upsets me in this world."

"I beg to differ," I countered. "I think you just were upset. Quite upset."

"Perhaps you're right, Doctor," Sarah replied, not about to be shaken again. "Hartley's illness has been a terrible burden on me. It would be much easier for me if he didn't exist."

I winced inwardly. Hartley seemed unaffected; he was already so depressed and downtrodden that he was beyond being affected any further. "Why don't you leave him, then?" I asked. "I think you would be better off without the burden. And in the long run it might also be better for Hartley if he were forced to stand on his own two feet."

"Oh, I'm afraid Hartley needs me too much for that, Doctor," Sarah responded, smiling maternally. She turned to her husband. "You wouldn't be able to make it if I left you, would you, dear?"

Hartley looked terrified.

"It would certainly be very difficult for him," I acknowledged. "But it could perhaps be arranged for Hartley to go into the hospital for an extended period of time. You would know that he'd been well taken care of, and he could be supported there as long as necessary to make the adjustment."

"Do you think you would like that, dear?" Sarah asked him. "Would you like to go back to the hospital and have me leave you?"

"Please," Hartley whined, "please don't."

"Tell the doctor why you don't want me to leave you, dear," Sarah commanded.

"I love you," Hartley whimpered.

"See, Doctor," Sarah explained victoriously. "I couldn't leave him when he loves me."

"But do you love him?" I asked.

"Love?" Sarah asked, almost with amusement. "What is there

to love? No, I think you might best call it duty, Doctor. I have a duty to take care of him."

"I'm not sure how much it's duty and how much it's need," I said, confronting her. "From where I sit it looks as if you have a deep-seated need for the burden that Hartley represents. Perhaps it's because you never had a child of your own. Perhaps you're trying to make Hartley the infant you couldn't have. I don't know. But I do know that for some reason or other you have an overpowering need to dominate Hartley, just as he has an over-powering need to depend on you. Your needs are being fulfilled by this strange marriage just as much as his are."

Sarah laughed oddly, a weird, hollow giggle. "Apples and or-anges, Doctor," she said. "Yes, apples and oranges. You can't compare them. You can't compare Hartley and me; we're like apples and oranges. But you don't know which is which, do you? Am I the apple or am I the orange? Am I crinkly-skinned or smooth-skinned? Or am I thick-skinned?" She gave her odd gig-gle again. "Yes, I guess I'm thick-skinned. We have to be thick-skinned against those who persecute us. You're the pseudoscience persecutors. But it's all right. I know how to handle the orange peelers and apple slicers. The Lord loves me. We have power in heaven. You can think what you think, say what you say. But it's garbage," she spat. "That's where they end up, isn't it? The or-ange peels and the apple slices? In the garbage. And that's where all you pseudoscience persecutors will end up. In the garbage. With all the other fruits," she ended triumphantly.

I became frightened that I had made a mistake in confronting Sarah as I listened to her lose her control. Hartley, with his mis-ery, his suicide attempts, and his pathetic existence, was bad enough; what could be served with both of them ending up in the hospital? She probably felt cornered. I had better give her plenty of exit space so that she might pull herself together again. "We've almost come to the end of our time," I said, "and we've got to decide on a plan of treatment. I gather you don't feel your-self in need of any treatment at this time, Sarah, and certainly you seem to be functioning well. But Hartley definitely seems to require some assistance, don't you think?"

"Yes, poor Hartley is not doing well," Sarah agreed, acting as if the past few minutes had never happened. "We should do whatever we can to help him."

I breathed a silent sigh of relief. My meddling in the marriage, although accomplishing nothing, had apparently done no additional harm. "Do you think you need to stay on your medicine?" I asked Hartley.

He nodded mutely. "Your thoughts get worse when you don't take your pills, don't they, dear?" Sarah said. He nodded again.

"I suspect that's the case," I commented. "How about psychotherapy? Do you think you'd like to spend time with someone talking about yourself in depth?"

Hartley shook his head. "It makes me feel bad," he mumbled.

"His last suicide attempt before this one occurred when they tried to give him psychotherapy," Sarah confirmed.

I wrote out prescriptions for the same medicine Hartley had been on in the hospital at the same dosage and said I would like to see them again in three weeks to determine whether the medication needed adjusting. "But that appointment won't be a long one like this," I explained. "In fact, it will be very brief."

"Of course, Doctor," Sarah said as the three of us stood up. "You've already done so much for Hartley. We can't thank you enough."

Two minutes later, having written a brief note on the chart, I went out for a cup of coffee. Hartley and Sarah had just finished paying the secretary for the visit, and as they were going out the door I overheard Sarah say, "This doctor's so much nicer than the one at the other clinic, don't you think? At least he's American. We couldn't even understand what that other one was saying, could we, dear?"


Perhaps the most interesting aspect of this case is not Sarah's evil but Hartley's relationship to it. Hartley was in thrall to Sarah. The theme of thralldom is not infrequent in fairy tales and myths in which princes and princesses and other beings have become captive to the evil power of some wicked witch or demon. Like other myths concerning evil, these need further study. But unlike the hero in such myths, I was not able to rescue Hartley from his slavery. For it was a willing thralldom. He had voluntarily sold his soul into Sarah's keeping. Why?

At one point during the session I had told Hartley that he was "just about the most passive man I've ever met." A passive person means an inactive person—a taker instead of a giver, a follower instead of a leader, a receiver instead of a doer. I could have used a number of other words: "dependent," "infantile," "lazy."* Hartley was monumentally lazy. His relationship with Sarah was that of an infant clinging to its mother. He would not even come into my office alone, much less take the risk or exert the energy to think independently for himself.

Why Hartley was so extremely lazy we do not know for certain. Sarah's comments that his mother was an alcoholic and his father as weak as he suggest that he came from a family in which his parents probably served as lazy role models and he probably failed to receive adequate fulfillment of his infantile needs. We can postulate that by the time he met Sarah he was already a profoundly lazy person, a child in adult's clothing who was unconsciously seeking the strong mother he had never had to take care of him. Sarah filled the bill perfectly, just as he undoubtedly met her requirements for a potential slave. Once the relationship was established, it became a vicious circle, naturally intensifying the sickness of each. Her domination further encouraged his submissiveness, and his weakness further nourished her desire for power over someone.

So Hartley was not simply an unwilling victim of Sarah's evil. This is important, because the case exemplifies a general rule: We do not become partners to evil by accident. As adults we are not forced by fate to become trapped by an evil power; we set the trap ourselves. We shall see this principle in action once again in the next-to-last chapter when we consider the phenomenon of group evil and how vast numbers may so easily participate with each other in the most atrocious behavior.

For the moment, however, we are concerned with the smallest of groups—the single couple—and how two people participate in

* Erich Fromm coined the term "incestuous symbiosis" for one of the three components of the "syndrome of decay," or evil character type. Although lacking the other components, Hartley was a fleshed-out, walking definition of incestuous symbiosis. It suggests that he entered into a submissive relationship with evil precisely because he was partially evil himself. It is true he was not entirely comfortable in his thralldom. Dimly aware that he was caught in a dreadful trap, he obsessed back and forth between the two easiest ways to extricate himself: to kill Sarah or to kill himself. But he was too lazy to even consider the one legitimate escape route open to him: the obvious, more difficult path of psychological independence.

evil. The case of Hartley and Sarah was introduced, in part, by the observation that it seemed impossible to tell which partner of an evil couple was the evil *one*. Both of Bobby's parents seemed evil. Both Mr. and Mrs. R. seemed equally involved in destroying Roger's spirit. But by the very nature of their evil I was unable to get close enough to them to know them well. My purely speculative suspicion is that they were not as equally evil as they seemed. I doubt that it is possible for two utterly evil people to live together in the close quarters of a sustained marriage. They would be too destructive for the necessary cooperation. I suspect, therefore, that one or the other of Bobby's parents was the more dominant in their mutual evil, and I believe the same was true of Mr. and Mrs. R. In every evil couple, if we could examine them closely enough, I imagine we would find one partner at least slightly in thrall to the other, in the same manner as Hartley was in thrall to Sarah, albeit hardly to the same degree.

If the reader feels Hartley and Sarah's relationship was a bizarre one, I agree. I chose it precisely because they were the "sickest" couple of this type I have seen in the years of my practice of psychiatry. Bizarre though it was, the type of relationship it illustrates is quite common. The phenomenon of thralldom in marriage is not rare. Those readers who are psychiatrists will have seen in their everyday practice dozens of such cases. And I suspect that general readers will, on reflection, also be able to recognize this type of marriage among at least some of their acquaintances.

Evil was defined as the use of power to destroy the spiritual growth of others for the purpose of defending and preserving the integrity of our own sick selves. In short, it is scapegoating. We scapegoat not the strong but the weak. For the evil to so misuse their power, they must have the power to use in the first place. They must have some kind of dominion over their victims. The most common relationship of dominion is that of parent over child. Children are weak, defenseless, and trapped in relation to their parents. They are born in thrall to their parents. It is no wonder, then, that the majority of the victims of evil, such as Bobby and Roger, are children. They are simply not free or powerful enough to escape.

For adults to be the victims of evil, they too must be powerless to escape. They may be powerless when a gun is held to their head, as when the Jews were herded into the gas chambers or when the inhabitants of MyLai were lined up to be shot. Or they may be powerless by virtue of their own failure of courage. Unlike the Jews or the inhabitants of MyLai and unlike children, Hartley was physically free to escape. Theoretically he could have just walked away from Sarah. But he had bound himself to her by chains of laziness and dependency, and though titularly an adult, he had settled for the child's impotence. Whenever adults not at gunpoint become victims of evil it is because they have—one way or another—made Hartley's bargain.

## MENTAL ILLNESS AND THE NAMING OF EVIL

The issue of naming is a theme of this work. It has already been touched on in diverse instances: science has failed to name evil as a subject for its scrutiny; the name of evil does not occur in the psychiatric lexicon; we have been reluctant to label specific individuals with the name of evil; in their presence, therefore, we may experience a *nameless* dread or revulsion; yet the naming of evil is not without danger.

To name something correctly gives us a certain amount of power over it. Through its name we identify it. We are powerless over a disease until we can accurately name it as "pneumococcal pneumonia" or "pulmonary embolism." Without such identification we are at a loss as to how to treat it. It makes a great deal of difference from the standpoint of both therapy and prognosis whether we label a person's disorder as "schizophrenia" or "psychoneurosis." Even when we do not have an effective treatment, it is good to have a name. Pityriasis rosea is an ugly and occasionally uncomfortable skin affliction for which there is no adequate therapy. But the patient is happy to pay the dermatologist's fee when told, "All it is is pityriasis rosea. It is *not* leprosy. We don't have any treatment for it, but don't worry, it won't hurt you and it will go away by itself in two to three months."

We cannot even begin to deal with a disease until we identify it by its proper name. The treatment of an illness begins with its diagnosis. But is evil an illness? Many would not consider it so. There are a number of reasons why one might be reluctant to classify evil as a disease. Some are emotional. For instance, we are accustomed to feel pity and sympathy for those who are ill, but the emotions that the evil invoke in us are anger and disgust, if not actual hate. Are we to feel pity and sympathy for parents who give their younger son his older brother's suicide weapon for Christmas? Are we to look kindly on any murderer, except possibly those few so visibly insane as to be obviously "out of their minds"? The people labeled here as evil were not crazy as we ordinarily think of the word. They were not babbling and demented. They were coherent and self-possessed, holding down responsible jobs, making money, apparently functioning smoothly in the social system, and hardly identifiable on superficial inspection as the least bit deranged. But the fact that we are not likely to feel a shred of sympathy for those who are evil speaks only of our own emotional response and not of the reality of whether evil is or is not an illness. Even when we still felt frightened and disgusted by lepers, we recognized leprosy to be a disease.

Beyond our emotional reactions, there are three rational reasons that make us hesitate to regard evil as an illness. Although each of the three reasons is cogent in its own way, I shall nonetheless take the position that evil should indeed be regarded as a mental illness. I will do so in the context of examining the fallacy inherent in each of three arguments.

The first holds that people should not be considered ill unless they are suffering pain or disability—that there is no such thing as an illness without suffering. This is a very old argument, but as bitterly contested today as ever. Even the very word "disease" means suffering. A person is diseased when he or she is experiencing dis-ease—that is, an absence of ease and the presence of discomfort. We most likely define ourselves as ill, of course, precisely because we are suffering in a way that is unwanted and unnecessary.

The "evil" people we have described certainly did not define themselves as ill, nor did they appear to be suffering. They would certainly not have identified themselves as patients. Indeed, as I have said, it is characteristic of the evil that, in their narcissism, they believe that there is nothing wrong with them, that they are psychologically perfect human specimens. If overt suffering and self-definition are the criteria for illness, then the evil are the last ones to be considered mentally ill.

But there are vast problems with this argument. There are a

host of physical diseases that are wholly asymptomatic in their early stages. An executive discovered on a routine physical exam to have a blood pressure of 200/120 may be feeling perfectly fit. Are we not to prescribe medicine to bring his blood pressure down (medicine that is indeed likely to make him feel less fit)? Or are we to wait until he has a fatal or crippling stroke before we consider his hypertension a disease? The Pap test has become a routine part of the regular medical care of women because it detects cancer of the cervix at a time when the cancer is curable but years before it causes the woman any discomfort or disability. Are we to defer our painful surgical treatment until she actually feels bad—which will likely be when her ureters are blocked by tumor and she is irrecoverably dying of kidney failure? If we define diseases only in terms of the suffering they currently produce, then we must state that most cases of high blood pressure and cancer, among others, are not, in fact, diseases. This seems absurd.

Of course, much of the time when physicians tell us that there is something seriously wrong with us, we take them at their word whether we are in actual pain or not. Their definition that we are ill is acceptable to us, and therefore we begin to define ourselves as ill, even when we are not actually feeling ill.

But not always. Consider the case of a farmer who suffers a serious heart attack that results in his losing consciousness and being brought to the hospital. The next day when he is fully alert in the intensive care unit, he struggles to get out of bed and to rip the cardiac monitor off his chest. The nurses tell him to lie back and relax because he has had a heart attack, is seriously ill, and needs to be quiet lest he have another attack. "That's ridiculous," the farmer screams, struggling even harder. "There's nothing wrong with me. My heart's as sound as a dollar. I don't know how you tricked me here, but I've got to get home to milk my cows." When the doctor is called in and several more attempts at reassurance fail, are we to let him get dressed and go home to work his farm? Or are we to restrain him as necessary, rapidly sedate him, and under these conditions continue to give him the true information and the time to come to terms with it?

Or consider an alcoholic in DT's who has not slept for three days, who is shaking like a leaf, whose temperature is 103 degrees and pulse 145, and who is severely dehydrated. He is convinced that the hospital is a Japanese extermination camp and that he must at all costs escape immediately to save his life. Are we to let him dash out of the hospital and run wildly down the streets, hiding behind cars until he drops dead from exhaustion, convulsions, or dehydration? Or are we to restrain him against his will and give him massive doses of Librium until he finally falls into a desperately needed sleep and begins to recover?

Obviously, in each case we would follow the latter alternative because we know that both these men are seriously ill despite the fact that they neither define themselves that way nor accept our definition. For we realize that their inability to define themselves as ill in the face of overwhelming evidence to the contrary is actually a part of the illness itself. Is it not also this way for those who are evil? I am not suggesting that the evil need to be physically restrained or deprived of their civil liberties in the ordinary course of their lives. But I am saying, as I have already said, that the failure of the evil to define themselves as disordered is an essential, integral component of their condition. And I am also saying that disease, whether it be evil or delirium or psychosis or diabetes or hypertension, is an objective reality and is not to be defined by subjective acknowledgment or lack of acknowledgment.

The use of the concept of emotional suffering to define disease is also faulty in several other respects. As I noted in *The Road Less Traveled*,* it is often the most spiritually healthy and advanced among us who are called on to suffer in ways more agonizing than anything experienced by the more ordinary. Great leaders, when wise and well, are likely to endure degrees of anguish unknown to the common man. Conversely, it is the unwillingness to suffer emotional pain that usually lies at the very root of emotional illness. Those who fully experience depression, doubt, confusion, and despair may be infinitely more healthy than those who are generally certain, complacent, and self-satisfied. The denial of suffering is, in fact, a better definition of illness than its acceptance.

The evil deny the suffering of their guilt—the painful awareness of their sin, inadequacy, and imperfection—by casting their pain onto others through projection and scapegoating. They

* Simon and Schuster, 1978.

themselves may not suffer, but those around them do. They cause suffering. The evil create for those under their dominion a miniature sick society.

In reality, we exist not merely as individuals but as social creatures who are integral component parts of a larger organism called society. Even if we were to insist upon suffering in the definition of illness, it is neither necessary nor wise to conceive of illness solely in terms of the individual. It may be that the parents described were not themselves suffering, but their families were. And the symptoms of family disorder—depression, suicide, failing grades, and theft—were attributable to their leadership. In terms of "systems theory," the suffering of the children was symptomatic not of their own sickness but of that of their parents. Are we to consider individuals healthy simply because they are not in pain—no matter how much havoc and harm they bring to their fellow human beings?

Finally, who is to say what the evil suffer? It is consistently true that the evil do not *appear* to suffer deeply. Because they cannot admit to weakness or imperfection in themselves, they must appear this way. They must appear to themselves to be continually on top of things, continually in command. Their narcissism demands it. Yet we know they are not truly on top of things. No matter how competent the parents described thought themselves, we know that in fact they were incompetent in their parental role. Their appearance of competence was just that: an appearance. A pretense. Rather than being in command of themselves, it was their narcissism that was in command, always demanding, whipping them into maintaining their pretense of health and wholeness.

Think of the psychic energy required for the continued maintenance of the pretense so characteristic of the evil! They perhaps direct at least as much energy into their devious rationalizations and destructive compensations as the healthiest do into loving behavior. Why? What possesses them, drives them? Basically, it is fear. They are terrified that the pretense will break down and they will be exposed to the world and to themselves. They are continually frightened that they will come face-to-face with their own evil. Of all emotions, fear is the most painful. Regardless of how well they attempt to appear calm and collected in their daily dealings, the evil live their lives in fear. It is a terror—

and a suffering—so chronic, so interwoven into the fabric of their being, that they may not even feel it as such. And if they could, their omnipresent narcissism will prohibit them from ever acknowledging it. Even if we cannot pity the evil for their inevitably ghastly old age or for the state of their souls after death, we can surely pity them for the lives they live of almost unremitting apprehension.

Whether the evil suffer or not, the experience of suffering is so subjective, and the meaning of suffering so complex, I think it best not to define illness and disease in its terms. Instead, I believe that illness and disease should be defined as *any defect in the structure of our bodies or our personalities that prevents us from fulfilling our potential as human beings.*

Admittedly, we may have some differences of opinion as to what exactly constitutes the human potential. Nonetheless, there are a sufficient number of men and women in all cultures and at all times who have achieved in their full adulthood a kind of gracefulness of existence so that we can generally say of them: "They have become truly human." By which we mean their lives seem almost to touch on the divine. And we can study these people and examine their characteristics.* Briefly, they are wise and aware; they enjoy life with gusto, yet face and accept death; they not only work productively but creatively, and they obviously love their fellow human beings, whom they lead with a benignity of both intent and result.

Most people, however, are so crippled in body and spirit that they cannot possibly ever attain such a lofty condition even through their best efforts without massive therapeutic assistance. Among these crippled legions—the mass of suffering humanity—the evil reside, perhaps the most pitiable of all.

I said there were two other reasons one might hesitate to label evil an illness. They can be countered more briefly. One is the notion that someone who is ill must be a victim. We tend to think of illness as something that befalls us, a circumstance over which we have no control, an unfortunate accident visited on us by meaningless fate, a curse in the creation of which we did not participate.

Certainly many illnesses seem like this. But many others—per-

* See Abraham Maslow's description of "self-actualized" persons in his *Motivation and Personality* (Harper Bros., 1954).

haps the majority—do not conform to such a pattern at all. Is the child who runs out on the street, when he has been told not to, and gets hit by a car, a victim? How about the driver of a car who gets in an "accident" when he is racing well above the speed limit to meet an appointment for which he is late? Or let us examine the enormous variety of psychosomatic illnesses and diseases of stress. Are people who suffer tension headaches because they don't like their jobs victims? Of what? A woman has an asthmatic attack every time she is in a situation in which she feels ignored, isolated, and uncared for. Is she a victim? One way or another, to some extent, all these people and a host of others victimize themselves. Their motives, failures, and choices are deeply and intimately involved in the creation of their injuries and diseases. Although they all have a certain degree of responsibility for their condition, we still consider them ill.

Most recently this issue has been debated in reference to alcoholism—some vigorously insisting that it is a disease and others insisting that because it appears to be self-inflicted, it is not. Not only physicians but courts and legislatures have been involved in this debate, and have reached the conclusion that alcoholism is indeed a disease, despite the fact that the alcoholic may sometimes seem nobody's victim except his or her own.

The issue of evil is similar. An individual's evil can almost always be traced to some extent to his or her childhood circumstances, the sins of the parents and the nature of their heredity. Yet evil is always also a choice one has made—indeed, a whole series of choices. The fact that we are all responsible for the state of health of our souls does not mean that a poor state of health is something other than disease. Once again, I believe we are on safest and soundest ground when we do not define disease in terms of victimization or responsibility but instead hold onto the definition already offered: An illness or disease is any defect in the structure of our bodies or personalities that prevents us from fulfilling our potential as human beings.

The final argument against labeling evil an illness is the belief that evil is a seemingly untreatable condition. Why designate as a disease a condition for which there is neither known treatment nor cure? Had we an elixir of youth in our doctor's black bag, it might make good sense to consider old age a disease, but we do not generally or currently think of it so. We accept old age as an inevitable part of the human condition, a natural process that is our lot and against which we are fools to rage.

This argument, however, ignores the fact that there are a whole host of disorders, from multiple sclerosis to mental deficiency, for which there is no treatment or cure but which we don't hesitate to call diseases. Perhaps we call them diseases because we hope to find the means to combat them. But is this not the case with evil? It is true that we do not currently possess any generally feasible or effective form of treatment to heal the thoroughly evil of their hatred and destructiveness. Indeed, the analysis of evil presented thus far reveals several reasons just why it is an extraordinarily difficult condition to approach, much less cure. But is a cure impossible? Are we to simply throw up our hands in the face of this difficulty and sigh, "It's beyond us"? Even when it is the greatest problem of mankind?

Rather than being an effective argument against it, the fact that we currently do not know how to treat evil in the human individual is the best reason to designate it a disease. For the label of disease implies that the disorder is not inevitable, that healing should be possible, that it should be studied scientifically and methods of treatment should be sought. If evil is an illness, it should then become an object for research like any other mental illness, be it schizophrenia or neurasthenia. It is the central proposition of this book that the phenomenon of evil can and should be subjected to scientific scrutiny. We can and should move from our present state of ignorance and helplessness toward a true psychology of evil.

The designation of evil as a disease also obligates us to approach the evil with compassion. By their nature the evil inspire in us more of a desire to destroy than to heal, to hate than to pity. While these natural reactions serve to protect the uninitiated, they otherwise prevent any possible solution. I do not think we shall come any closer than we are today to understanding and, I hope, curing human evil until the healing professions name evil as an illness within the domain of their professional responsibility.

There is a wise old priest retired to the mountains of North Carolina who has long done battle with the forces of darkness. After he had done me the favor of reviewing a draft of this book he commented: "I am glad that you have labeled evil an illness. It is not only a disease; it is the ultimate disease."

If evil is to be named a psychiatric disorder, is it sufficiently unique to stand in a category all by itself or does it fit into one of the already existing categories? Surprisingly, in view of the degree to which it has been neglected, the present system of classification of psychiatric illness seems quite adequate for the simple addition of evil as a subcategory. The existing broad category of personality disorders currently covers those psychiatric conditions in which the denial of personal responsibility is the predominant feature. By virtue of their unwillingness to tolerate the sense of personal sin and the denial of their imperfection, the evil easily fit into this broad diagnostic category. There is even within this class a subcategory entitled "narcissistic personality disorder." It would, I believe, be quite appropriate to classify evil people as constituting a specific variant of the narcissistic personality disorder.

One related issue, however, must be addressed. It will be recalled that when I confronted Sarah with her responsibility for the nature of her marriage she went off "into left field." In her diatribe about "apples and oranges" and "pseudoscience persecutors" she not only lost her composure, she seemed to lose the thread of her thoughts as well. Her logic disintegrated. Such disorganization in thinking is far more characteristic of schizophrenia than it is of a personality disorder. Could Sarah have been schizophrenic?

Among themselves psychiatrists often refer to something called "ambulatory schizophrenia." By this name we mean people like Sarah, who generally function well in the world, who never develop a full-blown schizophrenic illness or require hospitalization but who demonstrate a disorganization in their thinking—particularly at times of stress—which resembles that of more obvious "classical" schizophrenia. It is not, however, a formal diagnostic category for the very good reason that we do not know enough about the condition to be definite about it. We do not, in fact, know whether it has any real relationship to true schizophrenia.*

* The relationship between evil and schizophrenia is not only a matter for fascinating speculation but also very serious research. Many (but certainly not all) of the parents of schizophrenic children seem to be ambulatory

Despite its lack of clarity, however, the issue must be raised, because many of the evil people seen by psychiatrists are diagnosed as having ambulatory schizophrenia. Conversely, many we call ambulatory schizophrenics are evil people. Although not identical, there seems to be a large overlap of the two categories. It is also realistic to introduce this element of diagnostic confusion. The reality of the matter is that the naming of evil is still in a primitive stage.

Be that as it may, the time is right, I believe, for psychiatry to recognize a distinct new type of personality disorder to encompass those I have named evil. In addition to the abrogation of responsibility that characterizes all personality disorders, this one would specifically be distinguished by:

(a) consistent destructive, scapegoating behavior, which may often be quite subtle.

(b) excessive, albeit usually covert, intolerance to criticism and other forms of narcissistic injury.

(c) pronounced concern with a public image and self-image of respectability, contributing to a stability of life-style but also to pretentiousness and denial of hateful feelings or vengeful motives.

(d) intellectual deviousness, with an increased likelihood of a mild schizophreniclike disturbance of thinking at times of stress.

Thus far I have been speaking of the necessity for the accurate naming of evil from the standpoint of the evil themselves: that we might better appreciate the nature of their affliction, come to know how to contain it, and, I hope, eventually even cure it.

---

schizophrenics or evil or both. Much has been written about the "schizophrenogenic" parent, and usually an ambulatory schizophrenic or evil person is what is described. Does this mean that ambulatory schizophrenia is a variant of true schizophrenia and a simple genetic transmission is involved? Or is schizophrenia in the child the psychological product of its parents' evil destructiveness? Might even evil itself have a genetic basis, as seems the case in most instances of schizophrenia? We do not know, nor will we know until the psychobiology of human evil has become the subject of much scientific research.

But there is another vital reason to correctly name evil: the healing of its victims.

If evil were easy to recognize, identify, and manage, there would be no need for this book. But the fact of the matter is that it is the most difficult of all things with which to cope. If we, as objectively detached, mature adults, have great difficulty coming to terms with evil, think of what it must be like for the child living in its midst. The child can emotionally survive only by virtue of a massive fortification of its psyche. While such fortifications or psychological defenses are essential to its survival through childhood, they inevitably distort or compromise its life as an adult.

It happens, then, that the children of evil parents enter adulthood with very significant psychiatric disturbances. We have been working with such victims, often very successfully, for many years without ever having to employ the word "evil." But it is doubtful that some can be wholly healed of their scars from having had to live in close quarters with evil without correctly naming the source of their problems.

To come to terms with evil in one's parentage is perhaps the most difficult and painful psychological task a human being can be called on to face. Most fail and so remain its victims. Those who fully succeed in developing the necessary searing vision are those who are able to name it. For to "come to terms" means to "arrive at the name." As therapists, it is our duty to do what is in our power to assist evil's victims to arrive at the true name of their affliction. Two case vignettes follow in which it would have been impossible to render such assistance had the therapist not first recognized the face and spoken the name of evil.


## THE CASE OF THE VOODOO DREAM

Angela could not speak.

She entered therapy at the age of thirty because she had grave difficulty relating with anyone intimately. She was a competent teacher who could lecture her students with smooth eloquence. But from the moment she started to relate with me, Angela became tongue-tied. Long periods of silence were occasionally interspersed with brief spasms of almost unintelligible speech. When she attempted to talk she would often break into gasping sobs after only a few words. Initially I felt these sobs reflected overwhelming sadness, but gradually I realized they were a mechanism designed to prevent her from being articulate. They reminded me of a child tearfully trying to protest against unfair treatment by its parents, only to be ordered not to talk back. Angela acknowledged she had similar difficulty speaking in all her intimate relationships, but the problem was clearly at its worst with me. It was also clear I represented an authority figure—a parental figure—for her.

Angela's father had deserted the family when she was five. She could only remember being raised by her mother. Her mother was an odd woman. When Angela, who was Italian, was a dark-haired little girl of eleven, her mother made her dye her hair blond. Angela had not wanted her hair dyed. She liked her black hair. But for some reason her mother wanted to have a blond child, so a blond child she had.

The incident was typical. Her mother seemed to have little capacity or desire to recognize Angela as a separate human being in her own right. Angela had, for instance, no privacy. Although she had her own room, her mother strictly forbade her to close her door. Angela never understood the reason for this prohibition, but it was useless to argue against it. Once at the age of fourteen, she tried; her mother went into a depression that lasted over a month, during which time Angela had to do all the cooking and take care of her baby brother. The first term we developed for Angela's mother was "intrusive." She was unredeemably intrusive. She had no hesitation about intruding on Angela's person or privacy, and would tolerate no interference with her intrusiveness.

In the second year of Angela's therapy we were able to relate her difficulty in talking to her mother's intrusiveness. Angela's silence was a moat that her mother could not cross. No matter how much her mother desired to intrude on Angela's thoughts as well as her person, Angela could preserve the privacy of her mind through silence. Whenever her mother attempted to invade this privacy, Angela became tongue-tied. We also discovered that this moat of silence not only served to keep her mother out but also to keep Angela's anger in. Angela had learned it was folly ever to attempt to contradict her mother; the punishment for this crime was devastating. Consequently she also became tongue-tied whenever she was in danger of expressing her resentment.

Psychotherapy is, of course, a highly intrusive process, and the therapist is invariably an authority figure. Given the facts that I was in a parental role to her and that I desired to penetrate into the innermost recesses of her mind, it is no wonder that Angela dramatically reactivated with me the moat of silence that she had dug during her childhood. Only after she learned there was an essential difference between me and her mother was she able to dispense with this moat. Although I sought to know her thoughts and even to influence them, Angela gradually came to realize that, unlike her mother, I had a consistent and genuine respect for her identity and the unique individuality of her soul. It was two years before she could speak freely with me.

But she was still not free from her mother. Having married a man who, like her father, had then deserted her, Angela—with a child to support—had to rely on her mother for occasional financial assistance. More important, she still clung to the hope that somehow, someday, her mother would change and would appreciate her for who she was. It was at this point, in the beginning of the third year of therapy, that Angela recounted to me the following dream.

"I was in a building. Some kind of occult group of people came in wearing white robes. Somehow I was supposed to be part of an occult, scary ritual. Simultaneously I had occult powers. I could take myself up to the ceiling and float. But I was also part of the ritual. It was not something I was willingly doing. I was captive in the situation. It was very unpleasant."

"What ideas do you have about the dream?" I asked.

"Oh, I know perfectly well where it came from," Angela responded. "Last week at a party there was a couple who had been to Haiti. They were describing their visit to a voodoo place. It was a clearing in the woods. There were stones with bloodstains on them and there were chicken feathers all around. I felt horrified listening to them talk about the scene. I'm sure that's why I had the dream. It was sort of like a voodoo ritual, and it was like I was going to be forced to kill something. Yet, somehow, I was also going to be the victim. Ugh, it was ugly—I don't want to talk about it anymore."

"What else do you think the dream's related to?" I inquired.

Angela seemed annoyed. "Nothing. The only reason I had it was because I heard those people talking of voodoo."

"But that alone doesn't explain the dream," I insisted. "Out of all your experiences the past couple of weeks, you chose that one to dream about. There must be some reason for your choice. There must be some particular reason that voodoo rituals are of concern to you."

"Voodoo rituals don't interest me at all," Angela declared. "I don't even like to think about the dream. It was gory, ugly."

"What is it about the dream that disturbs you the most?" I asked.

"There was something evil there. That's why I don't want to talk about it."

"Perhaps there's something evil going on in your life at the present time," I commented.

"No, no," Angela protested. "It's just that stupid dream—and I wish we could get off the subject."

"Do you think there's anything evil about your mother?" I wondered.

"Sick, not evil," Angela replied.

"What's the difference?"

Angela did not answer this question directly. "Actually, I am angry at my mother," she said instead, "for the ten-millionth time."

"Oh? Tell me about it."

"Well, you know my car died on me last month. I was able to borrow enough from the bank to make a down payment on my new one, but I don't have enough money to make the interest payments. So I called up my mother and asked if she could make me a thousand-dollar interest-free loan. She was really nice about it at the time. 'Of course,' she said. But then the money didn't come. So after a couple of weeks I called her again. She gave me some story about how she couldn't give it to me for another two weeks or she would lose bank interest. I really didn't understand what the problem was, and I began to realize she probably didn't want to lend me the money, although she wasn't going to say so. Then last week I got a phone call from my brother. We've talked about how she always uses him to give me messages she doesn't want to give me herself. Anyway, he just wanted to let me know that my mother maybe had a lump in her breast and maybe would have to have surgery. He said Mother was worried she wouldn't have enough money to take care of her medical needs in her old age. By this time the picture was becoming clear. Finally, three days ago, I received a formal promissory note from my mother for me to sign for the loan. I know she didn't expect me to sign it. A year or so ago I wouldn't have. But fuck her. I need the money and I have no other way to get it. So I signed it. But I still feel guilty."

"You say a year ago you wouldn't have signed it?" I asked.

"I would have felt too guilty. But all the talking I've done about my mother in therapy has made me realize this is just a typical game she plays. She's always about to go into the hospital. She's always about to have surgery. She always offers me something with the right hand and pulls it away with the left."

"How many times would you say your mother's played this sort of game with you?"

"I don't know. Hundreds. Maybe even thousands."

"It's really a kind of ritual, then, isn't it?"

"It sure is."

"So you have been engaged in an evil ritual lately, haven't you?" I commented.

Angela looked at me with dawning recognition. "You think that's what the dream's all about?"

"I think so," I replied. "Even though you've been through this sort of ritual hundreds of times, even though you know she wants you to feel guilty, she still manages to succeed, doesn't she? You still feel guilty."

"Yes. I mean, how do I know she really doesn't have a lump in her breast this time? Maybe I really am being cruel to her."

"So you're never really sure whether you're the victim or the victimizer in this ritual, just as in the dream."

"You're right," Angela agreed. "I always feel guilty."

"The key element in the dream seems to be the evil nature of the ritual," I commented. "What do you think it is about this ritual interaction you have with your mother that makes it evil?"

Angela looked pained. "I don't know. That I'm being cruel to my mother?"

"Angela, how much money does your mother have?" I asked.

"I don't really have any idea."

"I'm not asking you down to the last cent," I said. "But you do know she owns three apartment buildings in Chicago, right?"

"Well, they're not very large," Angela protested.

"No," I said, "they're not skyscrapers. If I remember rightly, they have about ten apartments each. And they're in a good neighborhood. And your mother owns them free and clear. Correct?"

Angela nodded.

"So what do you think these three buildings alone are worth—forget whatever she might have in the bank—do you think they're worth at least half a million dollars?"

"I suppose so," Angela responded grudgingly. "But you know I don't think about money very clearly."

"Yes," I agreed, "I think that's one way you avoid seeing the obvious. Do you think maybe the apartment buildings might be worth even a million dollars?"

"Well, I guess it's possible."

"So you know that your mother has at least between half a million and a million dollars to her name," I continued, with mathematical logic. "Yet your mother acts as if it were a great burden to loan you a thousand dollars so that you and her grandchild can have a car to get around in. She's really quite a wealthy woman, but she talks poverty. And when she talks poverty, she's talking a lie, isn't she?"

"Yes. I guess that's why I get so angry at her," Angela acknowledged.

"Angela, wherever there is evil, there's a lie around," I remarked. "Evil always has something to do with lies. What makes this ritual interaction between you and your mother evil is that it's based on a lie. Not your lie. Your mother's lie."

"But my mother's not evil," Angela exclaimed.

"Why do you say that?"

"Because she just . . . she just isn't, that's why. I mean, she's my mother; I know she's sick, but she can't be evil."

We had returned to the issue. "What's the difference between sick and evil?" I asked.

"I'm not sure," Angela answered, looking not the least bit happy.

"I'm not sure either, Angela," I said. "In fact, I think that evil probably is a kind of sickness. But it's a particular kind of sickness. And calling it a sickness doesn't make it not evil. Whether it's a sickness or not, I think that evil's very real. And I think you have to come to terms with that reality. Your dream suggests that in relating with your mother you are relating with evil. And since you're not able to stop relating with your mother, you had best know as much as you can about what you're doing. I think that, together, you and I must squarely face the issue of whether or not your mother is evil and just what that means—what it has meant for you in the past and what it will mean for you in the future."

To fully appreciate the forces acting on Angela and, even more, on the young woman in the next case vignette, it is necessary that we turn our attention once again to the phenomenon of narcissism. We all of us tend to be more or less self-centered in our dealings with others. We usually view any given situation first and foremost from the standpoint of how it affects us personally, and only as an afterthought do we bother to consider how the same situation might affect someone else involved. Nonetheless, particularly if we care for the other person, we usually can and eventually do think about his or her viewpoint, which may well be different from ours.

Not so those who are evil. Theirs is a brand of narcissism so total that they seem to lack, in whole or in part, this capacity for empathy. Angela's mother apparently did not stop to think that Angela might not want her hair dyed blond. Any more than Bobby's parents stopped to think how he would feel being given his brother's suicide weapon for Christmas. Any more than Hitler, one would suppose, stopped to think about how the Jews felt as they were being pushed into the gas chambers.

We can see, then, that their narcissism makes the evil dangerous not only because it motivates them to scapegoat others but also because it deprives them of the restraint that results from empathy and respect for others. In addition to the fact that the evil need victims to sacrifice to their narcissism, their narcissism permits them to ignore the humanity of their victims as well. As it gives them the motive for murder, so it also renders them insensitive to the act of killing. The blindness of the narcissist to others can extend even beyond a lack of empathy; narcissists may not "see" others at all.

Each of us is unique. Except in the mystical frame of reference, we are all separate entities. Our uniqueness makes of each of us an "I-entity," provides each of us with a separate identity. There are boundaries to the individual soul. And in our dealings with each other we generally respect these boundaries. It is characteristic of—and prerequisite for—mental health both that our own ego boundaries should be clear and that we should clearly recognize the boundaries of others. We must know where we end and others begin.

Angela's mother obviously lacked this knowledge. When she dyed Angela's hair she was behaving as if Angela did not even exist. Angela as a distinct, unique individual with a will and tastes of her own had no reality for her mother. She did not see Angela as Angela. She did not accept the validity of Angela's boundaries. Indeed, the very existence of these boundaries was anathema to her—as was symbolized by her refusal to allow Angela to close her bedroom door. She would have engulfed the entirety of Angela's self into her narcissistic ego had Angela not been able to retreat behind a moat of silence. Growing up, Angela was able to develop and preserve her ego boundaries only through this defense against her mother's narcissistic and assaultive intrusiveness. In a sense she was able to preserve her boundaries only by making them excessive, but then had to pay the price of isolation from others as a result.

Another form of devastation that narcissistic intrusiveness can create is the symbiotic relationship. "Symbiosis"—as we use the term in psychiatry—is not a mutually beneficial state of interdependency. Instead it refers to a mutually parasitic and destructive coupling. In the symbiotic relationship neither partner will separate from the other even though it would obviously be beneficial to each if they could.

Hartley and Sarah clearly had such a relationship. Hartley, the weak one, could not have survived in his infantile state without Sarah to make his every decision for him. But Sarah also could not have survived psychologically without Hartley's weakness to feed her narcissistic need for domination and superiority. They functioned not as two separate individuals but as a single unit. Sarah had engulfed Hartley by mutual consent to the point where he had no will or identity of his own except that small little bit remaining that was reflected in his feeble suicide attempts. He had largely forsaken his ego boundaries, and she had incorporated them into her own.

Since Hartley and Sarah, two middle-aged adults, had "succeeded" in effecting a symbiotic relationship, it is hardly surprising that certain evil and narcissistic parents can succeed in cultivating such a relationship with a child destined to come under their domination. The case vignette that follows describes the lengthy healing, and hence the weaning away, of one such child from a symbiotic relationship with her mother.

## THE CASE OF THE SPIDER PHOBIA

To this day I cannot understand how it was that Billie remained in therapy. The fact that she did remain is an enormous tribute to both the genius of her therapist and the genius of Billie herself. It was a sort of miracle.

Billie was taken to a colleague of mine by her mother because of academic underachievement. Sixteen at the time and very bright, she was doing poorly in school. After six months of therapy Billie's grades had improved slightly. She had also clearly developed a certain attachment to her therapist, a mature and kindly man of infinite patience. At this point her mother stated that the problem was solved. Billie wanted to continue in therapy. Her mother refused to pay for it. Her therapist reduced the already minimum fee to five dollars a session. Billie, whose allowance was five dollars a week and who had two hundred dollars saved, began paying him out of her own money. Soon her mother stopped her allowance. Billie got her first job during her senior year of high school in order to continue to pay for her therapy. That was seven years ago. Billie is still in therapy, but the end is beginning to be in sight.

One of the reasons it is so remarkable that Billie stayed in therapy, paying for it out of her allowance and then out of her meager salary, is that for the first three years Billie did not feel that there was anything the matter with her. On some unconscious level she must have known that something was radically wrong. But consciously she was utterly cool about her "problems." She vaguely wished she could get better grades, yet she was perfectly ready to acknowledge she almost never did her homework. This she blandly attributed to "laziness," and after all, "Aren't many high school kids lazy?" The only thing that could possibly be identified as a symptom was her fear of spiders. Billie hated spiders. Any spider. Whenever she saw a spider she literally ran away in panic. If she noticed a spider in the house—no matter how minuscule or harmless-appearing—she wouldn't stay in the house unless someone killed and removed it. But this phobia was ego-syntonic. While she recognized that almost everybody was much less afraid of spiders than she, Billie concluded that this was because others were insensitive. If they appreciated how really horrible spiders were, then they would be just as afraid as she was.

Since she consciously felt nothing was wrong with her, it is hardly surprising that Billie broke at least as many appointments as she kept. But somehow her therapist "hung in there" over the first three years, and somehow Billie did also. During these years Billie passionately hated her father and adored her mother. A lifelong bank clerk, her father was a shy and taciturn man who seemed to Billie as cold and distant as her mother was warm and close. Billie, the only child, and her mother were companions. They confided in each other their closest secrets. Her mother always had at least several lovers, and throughout her adolescence Billie liked nothing better than to listen to her mother's tales of the ins and outs and ups and downs of her extramarital affairs. There seemed to be nothing wrong in this. Billie's mother blamed her affairs on her husband's isolated, unaffectionate personality. They seemed a natural response to his lack of interest, and Billie and her mother were united in their hatred of him. Against him they felt almost like gleeful coconspirators.

Her mother was as eager to listen to all the sexual and romantic details of Billie's life as Billie was to listen to hers. Billie considered herself very fortunate to have such a loving and interested mother. She was not able to explain why her mother refused to pay for her therapy, but she was hardly able or willing to criticize her mother in this regard. Whenever the issue was raised by her therapist, Billie sidestepped vigorously.

When Billie told her mother about her own boyfriends, there was a lot to tell. Billie was frankly promiscuous. Her mother never criticized this; after all, she had many lovers, too. It was not, however, that Billie wanted to be promiscuous. On the contrary, she yearned painfully for a deep and lasting relationship with a man. But it never seemed to work out. She would fall head over heels in love with a man, almost immediately move into his apartment, but within a few days or a few weeks the relationship invariably soured and Billie was back at home with her parents. Beautiful, intelligent, and charming, Billie never had difficulty finding new lovers. Within a week she would be in love again. But, as always, within a few more weeks, the relationship would be dead. Billie faintly began to wonder if somehow she killed these relationships.

It was this bit of wonder and her pain at being unable to hold onto her lovers that caused Billie to begin working more seriously in therapy. Very gradually the basis of the pattern emerged. Billie couldn't tolerate being alone. Having fallen in love with a man, she would want to go with him wherever he went. She would always sleep with him, whether or not she felt sexual, because that would guarantee that he would stay with her—at least for the night. When they awoke in the morning she would plead with him not to go to work. He would have to tear himself away from her. Inevitably the man would feel suffocated. He would start to break dates. She would redouble her efforts to cling to him. He would feel more suffocated. Finally, on some excuse, he would terminate the relationship. Billie then picked up the first man she could find, even though his intelligence and character were often less than desirable. Unable to tolerate being alone, she was unable to wait long enough for a more deserving lover to appear on the scene. She would fall in love with whoever was closest at hand, cling to him immediately—and the vicious cycle would repeat itself.

Once her fear of being alone was uncovered, it also became clear why Billie had been an underachiever in school. To read a book or write a paper requires solitude. Billie had been unable to do her homework because she had been unwilling to tear herself away from people—particularly from her mother, who was always ready for a chat—long enough to carry out an assignment.

Although it was now identified as a problem, Billie felt helpless to do anything about it. She recognized that her terror of aloneness limited her in certain ways, but what could be done? It was a part of her nature. Self-destructive though the pattern might be, it was just the way she was. She could not even imagine being any other way. So nothing changed except that her phobia of spiders became worse. She would no longer walk with her boyfriends through the woods or even down a shaded street at night, lest she inadvertently brush against a spider.

At this point her therapist took a bold step. He insisted that Billie, who hitherto had always lived either with her lovers or her parents, get an apartment of her own. She refused. It was a ridiculous expense. Oh, of course, it had advantages: she could bring lovers home with her, she could play her stereo whenever she wanted, she could feel more independent. But how could she possibly afford it? Now that she was working steadily, the therapist had raised her fee from five dollars a session to his standard rate of twenty-five. That was more than a hundred dollars a month she was paying him—a quarter of her salary. He offered to reduce his fee again to five dollars an hour. Billie was touched but still couldn't afford it, she claimed. Besides, what would happen if she found a spider in her apartment one night and she was all alone? What would she do then? No, an apartment of her own was out of the question.

My colleague pointed out to her that she was doing absolutely nothing to deal with her fear of being alone. Unless she took some step to actually choose aloneness, he said, he saw no hope for her therapy. There must be some other step, she argued. He asked her to think of one. She could not, but insisted he was being too demanding and would just have to drop the idea. He told her he would refuse to see her anymore unless she got an apartment. She raved at his cruelty. He remained adamant. So finally, in the fourth year of her therapy, Billie rented her own apartment.

Three things immediately happened. One was that Billie became more aware of just what a compelling force her fear of aloneness was. On nights when she was not with a lover she became extremely anxious in her empty apartment. By nine in the evening she could no longer tolerate it and would drive back to her mother's house to chat and then sleep there. On weekends when she had nothing to do she spent the entire time with her parents. During the first six months of renting her apartment she slept there alone on no more than half a dozen occasions. She was paying for an apartment that she was too frightened to use. It was absurd. She became annoyed with herself. She began to think that maybe, just maybe, this fear of aloneness was really sick.

The second thing that happened was that a change seemed to come over her father. When she reluctantly announced she was going to get her own apartment, he suggested that perhaps she would like to have some furniture he had inherited which was sitting unused in a barn. Then, on her moving day, he borrowed a truck from one of his friends and helped her load and unload the furniture. He gave her a bottle of champagne for her house-warming. Once she was settled in, he began a pattern of making her a present of some small object for the apartment every month or so—a new lamp, a print to hang on the wall, a bath mat, a fruit bowl, a set of kitchen knives. These gifts were given unostenta-tiously, wrapped in plain brown paper and quietly dropped off for her at her place of work. But Billie realized they were chosen with care. They were all in good taste. She had not thought of her father before as having good taste. And she knew he had little extra money to spare for such things. Although he remained shy and withdrawn and difficult to talk to, for the first time she could remember Billie was quite touched by his interest in her. She wondered if the interest, subtle though it was, might not have been there all along.

In relation to the apartment, Billie's mother was as unhelpful as her father was generous. Several times she asked her mother for little odds and ends that had been tucked away in corners of the family house, but suddenly her mother seemed to have devel-oped a use for them. Her mother never asked her about the new apartment. In fact, Billie began to notice that whenever she men-tioned the apartment her mother seemed to be annoyed, even cutting. "Don't you think you're being just a bit self-centered talking about your apartment this and your apartment that all the time?" she said on one occasion. Slowly it dawned on Billie that her mother did not want her to move out of the family home. This was the third thing that happened.

It was a thing that snowballed. At first Billie rather enjoyed the fact that her mother was upset about her moving out. Didn't that show how much her mother loved her? And wasn't it nice to always be welcome back at the family home, to have her mother to chat with late into the night, to have her old bedroom always ready for her—not to have to return to her lonely apartment with the possibility of spiders in the dark? But the magic began to go out of this, bit by bit. For one thing, she and her mother no longer had Billie's father to talk against. When her mother railed against him as usual Billie began to say, "Come on, Mom, he's not really that bad. Sometimes I think he's even kind of sweet." This sort of response seemed to inflame her mother. Immediately her mother's remarks about her father would become positively vicious or else she would turn around and start attacking Billie for not being sympathetic. These moments became distinctly unpleasant. Finally Billie had to ask her mother not to talk against her father when they were together, since it invariably ended in a quarrel. Her mother grudgingly complied. But without their mutual enemy, Billie and her mother had much less to talk about. Then there was the matter of Wednesday evenings.

Billie was an office manager for a small publishing company. Every Thursday morning it made a single large weekly shipment to other parts of the country. The nature of Billie's responsibilities required her to be in the office by six o'clock on those mornings. Whenever she spent the night at her parents' house, it somehow seemed impossible, chatting away with her mother, to get to bed before midnight. The result was that on Thursday mornings Billie invariably felt wretched from lack of sleep. With the help of her therapist, she made a vow that on Wednesday night—on just that one night, if on no other night of the week—she would sleep alone in her apartment, and would be back there no later than nine o'clock in the evening.

For the first ten weeks Billie was unable to keep her vow. She was never able to be back in her apartment before midnight. Each week her therapist would ask her how well she had fulfilled her vow, and each week Billie had to confess failure. First she was furious at her therapist. Then she was furious with herself for not being able to stick to her resolution. She began to look seriously at her weakness. For several sessions she talked of her ambivalence about the vow, her fear of the loneliness of her apartment, her desire to remain in the warmth of the family home. At this point her therapist asked Billie if she thought there was any way her mother might be able to help her keep her vow.

Billie was delighted with the idea. She immediately told her mother about the vow and requested her encouragement to leave the house by eight-thirty on Wednesday evenings. Her mother refused. "What you and that therapist of yours do is your business, not mine," she said. Billie felt there was a certain amount of truth in this, but she also began to suspect that her mother might have reasons of her own for not wanting Billie to keep the vow. The suspicion grew. And as it grew, Billie began to observe her mother's behavior on Wednesday nights. She noticed that invariably around eight-thirty her mother would bring up some particularly provocative topic for discussion. Once she recognized this pattern, Billie tried to interrupt it. At eight forty-five, in the middle of one such topic, Billie stood up and announced that she had to leave. "Don't you think you're being rude?" her mother asked. She reminded her mother of her vow and suggested that even if it wasn't her mother's responsibility to help her keep it, perhaps it was her responsibility at least to respect it. They got into a heated argument. Her mother cried. It was after midnight when Billie got back to her apartment.

Thereafter Billie observed that if her mother's genius for bringing up a provocative topic at eight-thirty failed to have an effect, she would then demonstrate an equal genius for starting an argument. By the fourteenth week of her still unkept vow, this pattern too had become clear to Billie. That Wednesday night at eight-thirty her mother started a story. Billie stood up, saying she was sorry she didn't have time to hear it. Her mother began to argue. Billie announced she didn't have time to argue either. She moved to the door. Her mother literally clutched at her sleeve. Billie tore herself away. She was in her apartment at the stroke of nine. Five minutes later the phone rang. It was her mother. Billie had left in such a hurry, she said, she hadn't had time to tell her that the doctor thought maybe she had gallstones.

Billie's fear of spiders became even worse.

At this point Billie still adored her mother. In therapy she had become able to criticize her mother quite freely and accurately, yet she was never actually angry, and she continued to take every possible opportunity to be in her mother's company. It was as if she had developed two brains—a new one that could look at her mother objectively coexisting with the old one that remained utterly unchanged.

Her therapist pressed forward. It was not just on Wednesday evenings, he suggested, that her mother clung to her; perhaps her mother didn't want Billie to leave her or develop a separate existence in any dimension. He reminded her once again that her mother had refused to pay for her therapy as soon as it had become important in Billie's life. Could it be that her mother was jealous of Billie's attachment to therapy because it was an attachment to something other than herself? And why had she so resented Billie's getting her own apartment? Might she not resent Billie's developing independence and separation? Maybe so, Billie countered, but her mother had never objected to her having boyfriends and lovers. Didn't this indicate that her mother had no desire to hold onto her? Perhaps, her therapist acknowledged, but then it might also indicate simply that her mother wanted Billie to be a carbon copy of herself. Perhaps her mother used Billie's promiscuity to justify her own. Besides, the more alike the two of them were, the less the chance they would ever separate. And so the struggle went on, week after week, month after month, endlessly back and forth over the same issues, with no sign of resolution in sight.

But a subtly enormous change did occur in the sixth year of her therapy. Billie began to write poetry. At first she showed her poems to her mother. Her mother was not particularly interested. But Billie was proud of her poetry. It was a new, surprising dimension of herself. It was uniquely her, something her own. She bought an elegant leatherbound volume in which to record her poems. The urge to write did not come often, but when it did, it was compelling. For the first time in her life, when she was working on a poem, Billie found herself enjoying being alone. Indeed, she had to be alone. She couldn't concentrate in her parents' house, with her mother's constant interruptions. So when the urge hit her she would suddenly stand up and announce that she had to return to her apartment. "But it's not Wednesday night," her mother would shriek. And Billie would have to tear herself away from her mother once again. It was after one such episode, when she was describing to her therapist how her mother had clutched at her as she was leaving to write, that Billie commented, "She was like a goddamn spider."

"I've been waiting a long time for you to say that," her therapist exclaimed.

"Say what?"

"That your mother's like a spider."

"So?"

"But you hate and fear spiders."

"I don't hate my mother," Billie said. "And I don't fear her either."

"Maybe you should."

"But I don't want to."

"So you hate and fear spiders instead?"

Billie missed her next appointment. When she returned, her therapist suggested she had skipped the appointment because she was angry at him for making a connection between her mother and her spider phobia. Billie missed the next two appointments. But when she finally came back, she was ready to face it. "All right," she said, "so I've got a phobia. What is a phobia, anyway? How does it work?"

Phobias are the result of displacement, her therapist explained. They occur when a normal fear or revulsion toward something is displaced onto something else. People employ this defensive displacement because they do not want to acknowledge the original fear or revulsion. In Billie's case, she didn't want to acknowledge her mother's evil. Naturally. What child would want to think of her mother as malicious or destructive? Like any child, Billie wanted to believe that her mother loved her, that her mother was safe and kind and good. But to believe this she somehow had to get rid of the fear and revulsion she instinctively felt toward her mother's evil. She did this by directing the fear and revulsion toward the spiders. Spiders were the evil ones—not her mother.

"But my mother is not evil," Billie proclaimed. It was true that her mother was not keen on her becoming independent, and that she used all manner of wiles and tricks to try to keep Billie from developing a fully separate existence. But this was not a matter of evil. It was just because her mother was lonely. And she, Billie, understood about loneliness. It was terrible to feel lonely. It was also human. Humans are social creatures; they need each other. The fact that her mother clung to her from loneliness was hardly evil; it was only human.

"While loneliness is human," her therapist responded, "the inability to tolerate it is hardly a necessary part of the human condition." He went on to explain that it was the task of parents to assist their children to achieve their own independence and separateness. In order to succeed in this task it was essential for parents to tolerate their own loneliness so as to allow and even encourage their children to eventually leave them. Instead, to discourage such separation not only represented a failure in the parental task but a sacrificing of the child's growth to the parent's own immature self-centered desires. It was destructive. Yes, he thought, it was evil. And Billie was right to be afraid of it.

Slowly Billie came to see it. And the more she saw the more her eyes were opened. She began to notice hundreds of infinitely subtle little ways in which her mother continually attempted to retain her spirit in her clutches. In her leatherbound book Billie wrote one evening:

> Ambiguity and guilt
> Can really drive one crazy—
>
> You send me my clean laundry,
> Which you did.
> In it you include the first turned
> Leaf of fall.
>
> Manipulation? Guilt?
> . . . your method really works.

Yet little changed. Billie, now twenty-three, still spent most nights sleeping in her parents' house and most of her free time with her mother. Although falling behind on her payments for therapy, she would pay a substantial portion of her week's salary to take her mother out to lunch at the most expensive restaurant in the area. And the pattern of her relationships with men continued unaltered—the falling in love, the clinging, the suffocating, the breaking up, the frantic searching, the falling in love again— man after man, time after time. And she was just as terrified of spiders as ever. The hard part was yet to come.

"Nothing's happening," Billie complained in therapy one day.

"That's the way it feels to me too," her therapist responded.

"Well, why not?" Billie demanded. "It's been seven years I've been seeing you now. What the hell more do I have to do?"

"Figure out why you still have your spider phobia."

"I've recognized that my mother is a spider," Billie replied.

"Then why do you keep dropping into her lair and web?"

"You know. Like her, I'm lonely."

Her therapist looked at Billie. He hoped she was ready. "So maybe, in part, you too are a spider," he said.

Billie sobbed for the remainder of the session. But the next session she was there, right on time, even eager for the painful work ahead. It was true; she felt like a spider sometimes. When men started to leave her she clutched at them—just as her mother clutched at her. She hated them for going. She didn't care about their feelings. She didn't care about them. She wanted them for herself. Yes, it was like something evil in her, an evil urge, an evil part of her taking over. The spider phobia had not only helped her to deny her mother's evil, she had used it to deny the evil in herself.

It was all so connected and intertwined. She had identified with her mother. They were so much the same. How could she genuinely fight against her mother's evil unless at the same time she fought against herself? How could she condemn her mother for holding onto her without condemning herself for refusing to tolerate her own loneliness? How could she stop trying to trap men in her own web—men who ought to stand free and tall and strong, just as she ought to stand free and tall and strong? The problem was not how to extricate herself from her mother's web anymore, since her mother's identity was so much hers; the problem was to extricate herself from herself. And how in God's name do you do that?

But Billie is doing it. In the name of God or her true self she is somehow beginning to separate from her mother, to definitively break free from their symbiotic relationship. In her leatherbound book she recently wrote:

> Amazing to me, how your disease
> Pops up in me all the time,
> Part of my very being, without me
> Even knowing.
> So hard to fight an enemy
> One can't see;
>
> So scary to think you're in me,
> So incorporated into my thinking and feeling

That it is indistinguishable
From *me*.

It is me.

I feel like a mulatto who is
Part of the Ku Klux Klan,
Hating the very essence of part of me,
Working on eradicating part of myself.

This is probably the hardest thing
That I ever will do.
Sometimes it feels so unnatural.

I often wonder how it is that I
Became different from you;
To have the will to want to be
Different than you.

It looks as if Billie is beginning to break the chain.

# 4

# CHARLENE:
# A TEACHING CASE

Ξ  I HAVE NOTED how difficult it is to examine evil people in depth, because it is their nature to avoid the light. Denying their imperfection, the evil flee both self-examination and any situation in which they might be closely examined by others. Yet in this chapter a woman will be described who—seemingly evil to some degree—nonetheless submitted herself to extensive psychoanalytic psychotherapy.

Although rare, this case is not one of a kind. I myself attempted to treat one other such patient and have supervised therapists working with several remarkably similar cases. In every instance, although lengthy, the treatment was a failure.

It is not fun to fail. But it can be highly educational—in the psychotherapy business as well as in the rest of life. We probably have even more to learn from our failures than from our successes. Certainly no patient ever taught me more than the one to be described. It is my hope that she will also serve others. Examining such questions as why she entered treatment in the first place, why she persisted in it for some four hundred sessions, and why she totally failed to be affected by it, perhaps we can ultimately arrive at a depth of understanding out of which we will be able to help to heal the Charlenes of this world.

## IN THE BEGINNING, CONFUSION

In the beginning there was nothing to mark Charlene as particularly unusual. She came to me at age thirty-five with a complaint of depression following a breakup with her boyfriend. Her depression did not seem severe.

She was petite and rather attractive but not a remarkable beauty. She had a capacity for humor and obvious high intelligence. Clearly, however, she was an underachiever in the game of life. For reasons that were initially vague she had repeatedly failed in an undemanding college. Nonetheless, after a year of proving her worth as a volunteer, she was hired by her Episcopal church as its director of religious education. Six months later she was fired by the rector. She attributed this to his capriciousness. But the pattern continued. She lost seven more jobs before obtaining the one as a telephone operator that she held when she came to see me. Similarly, her recent breakup with her boyfriend was only the last in a long, unbroken string of failed romantic relationships. In fact, Charlene had no real friends at all.

Still, people usually enter therapy for one kind of underachievement or another and, although marked, Charlene's lack of success was hardly unique. Little did I know she would turn out to be the "damndest" patient with whom I had ever worked.

Exploring her background, I found that Charlene seemed to have few illusions about her parents. Except for considerable money, there was apparently little they had given her. Preoccupied with his inherited wealth, her father had been utterly uninvolved with the care of her or her younger sister, Edith. Their mother, a fanatic Episcopalian, who mouthed the words of Jesus continually, was unabashed in her hatred of her husband. "If it weren't for you girls, I would have left him long ago," she told them at least once a week. "Of course," Charlene noted wryly, "even though Edie and I have been out of the house for over a decade, she still hasn't left."

Edie had become a lesbian. Charlene considered herself bisexual. Edie was doing well in the banking business but was not happy. Whenever she considered herself to have a problem, Charlene had no compunction about blaming her parents. "They really fucked us up—my father in love only with his stocks and bonds and my mother with her gas bubbles and her prayer book." Certainly her parents did sound uncaring, even nasty and wicked.

But lots of patients have wicked parents. Even Charlene's unusual religious faith did not distinguish her. After being fired from her job at the church Charlene had gradually drifted into a cult of sorts that proclaimed a hodgepodge of Hindu, Buddhist, Christian, and esoteric theology, along with a belief in "the love vibrations of meditation." But such cults are a dime a dozen, and this one seemed to encourage neither fanaticism nor dependency. Her membership in it seemed natural enough in view of her mother's misuse of Christianity and her own fury at the rector who had fired her.

What did distinguish Charlene, however, was my confusion in relation to her.

Generally, by the time they have spent five or six hours in therapy with a patient, psychiatrists will have at least a superficial understanding of the patient's problem. There will be at least a tentative diagnosis. After four dozen sessions with Charlene I still did not have the foggiest idea of what was wrong with her. Underachievement, yes. But why, no.

Frustrated, I went through a check list of diagnostic categories in my mind, asking her very specific questions. I wondered, for instance, whether she might have an obsessive-compulsive neurosis, and I questioned her about all the possible symptoms of this neurosis, such as ritualistic behavior. Charlene understood perfectly. With considerable enthusiasm she described several minor rituals she had performed during her early adolescence—a common, almost normal time for such behavior. She would arrange the objects in her room in a certain way and in certain sequences before she felt comfortable going to sleep at night. As a child she had been told that in the army soldiers were required to make their beds so tightly that the drill sergeant could bounce a quarter off them. So each morning when she was thirteen and fourteen, Charlene would bounce a quarter off her bed, always before she brushed her teeth. "But by the time I was fifteen," she said, "I realized these things were a silly waste of time, and I just stopped doing them. I haven't had any rituals since." So I was stumped once again. And I remained stumped. Another three dozen sessions were to go by before I got the first inkling of Charlene's character.

One day after nine months of therapy, when she handed me a check for the preceding month, I noticed that it was issued from a different bank. "You've changed banks?" I questioned casually.

Charlene nodded. "Yes, I had to."

"You had to?" I picked up my ears.

"Yes, I ran out of checks."

"You ran out of checks?" I repeated dumbly.

"Yes, haven't you noticed?" Charlene sounded a bit piqued. "Each check I've given you has had a different design on it."

"No, I haven't noticed," I acknowledged. "But what has that got to do with changing banks?"

"You're not very swift, are you?" Charlene countered. "I ran out of new designs at my old bank, so I had to get a new checking account in order to have new designs."

More confused than ever, I asked, "Why do you have to use a different design each time?"

"Because it's a love offering."

"A love offering?" I repeated once again, bewildered.

"Yes. Whenever I write a check to anyone, I ask myself what his or her particular design is at that point in time. It's a matter of vibrations, you see. Through love I tune in on their vibrations and then I make the selection. But I never like to give a person the same design more than once, and my old bank only had eight different designs. Actually, it's because of you I had to change banks, since this is the ninth check I've given you. Still, I had to change because of the electric company anyway. But they're more impersonal. It's hard to get vibrations off of them."

I was dumbfounded. Perhaps I should have picked up on the issue of "love" right there and then. But I was overwhelmed by the bizarreness of this minor but repetitive interaction. "It sounds like a bit of a ritual," was the best comment I could make.

"Yes, I suppose you could call it a ritual."

"But I thought you didn't have any rituals."

"Oh, I've got lots of rituals," Charlene answered gaily.

And she did. Over the next few sessions she told me of dozens of rituals. Almost every single thing she did was connected, one way or another, with a ritual. It became abundantly clear that Charlene did indeed have a form of an obsessive-compulsive disorder. "Since you've got dozens of rituals," I queried, "how come when I asked you about rituals four months ago you told me you didn't have any?"

"I just didn't feel like telling you. Maybe I didn't trust you enough."

"But you were lying."

"Of course."

"Why should you pay me fifty dollars an hour to help you and then lie to me so I didn't know how to help?" I asked.

Charlene looked at me archly. "I'm certainly not going to tell you anything until I think you're ready to know it," she replied.

Now that she had "confessed" her rituals, it was my hope that Charlene would become increasingly open in our work together and I, consequently, less confused. It was not to be, however. Only gradually did it begin to dawn on me that she was a "person of the lie." Although during the months and years ahead she would, willy-nilly, reveal one aspect or another of herself, Charlene remained largely enigmatic. And I remained confused. Which was the way she wanted it. She continued until the end to withhold information from me, if for no other reason than to keep control of the show. And while my understanding of her was to deepen, so was my awe of her basic incomprehensibility.

## ONE WAY OR THE OTHER: INFANT OR ADULT

Shortly after revealing her rituals Charlene began revealing something else: her intense desire for me.

This was not surprising, at first. I cared for Charlene. She kept her appointments and paid for them faithfully, presumably from an earnest desire for growth. I was eager to meet her efforts with dedication of my own. Anything she said, everything that happened to her, was of deep interest and import to me. It is natural for a patient in response to consistent attentiveness to romantically desire the therapist when he or she is of the opposite sex. This is especially the case when the patient never succeeded, during childhood, in overcoming the Oedipal dilemma.

All healthy children experience sexual desire for the parent of the opposite sex. This desire usually reaches its peak around the age of four or five and is referred to as the Oedipal dilemma. It places the child in a dreadful predicament. The romantic love of the child for the parent is a hopeless love. The child will say to its parent, "I know you tell me that I can't have sex with you because I'm a child, but just look at how grown-up I am acting and you will change your mind." This grown-up act requires enormous energy, however, and ultimately cannot be sustained by the child. It becomes exhausted. Resolution of the dilemma finally occurs when the exhausted child accepts the reality that it is a child and cannot—and no longer desires to—pull off the appearance of adulthood. In so doing, the child also realizes it cannot have its cake and eat it too; it cannot both sexually possess its parent and at the same time be a child. It therefore opts for the advantages of being a child and renounces its premature sexuality.* The Oedipal dilemma has been resolved. Everyone breathes a sigh of relief—particularly the child, who becomes visibly happier and more relaxed.

In psychotherapy the patient who failed to resolve the Oedipal dilemma during childhood must essentially undergo the same process in relation to the therapist during adulthood. He or she must learn to give up the therapist as a romantic, sexual love object and settle for being the therapist's child on a symbolic level. Once this occurs, things go very smoothly. The patient can relax and enjoy the therapist's parental ministrations. Unimpeded, he or she will then absorb the therapist's wisdom and love.

Only it did not go that way between Charlene and me.

The first inkling I had that this stage of her treatment was not progressing well was a growing sense of revulsion I began to experience toward her. This was highly unusual in my experience. When an attractive woman patient desires me, my usual problem is how not to respond in kind. I will have my own sexual feelings and fantasies for her and must make sure these in no way interfere with my judgment and my commitment to the therapeutic role. Certainly I usually have no difficulty feeling warmly toward patients who entrust their love to me.

---

* Among the reasons that the Oedipus complex is so important in psychiatry is that adults who have failed to resolve it usually have great difficulty in accomplishing many of the renunciations required for successful adult adjustments. They still have not learned that they cannot have their cake and eat it too.

Yet with Charlene it was another matter. I had no positive sexual fantasies about her. To the contrary, the thought of a sexual relationship with her made me actually nauseated. Even the notion of nonsexually just touching her gave me a faintly queasy feeling. And it didn't get better. The more time passed, the more my gut desire was to keep a distance from her.

Possibly my growing sense of revulsion was not primarily a sexual response. It was also not unique to me. Another patient, a quite perceptive and intelligent woman, began one session by asking, "You know that lady who always comes to see you before me?"

I nodded. She was referring to Charlene.

"Well, she gives me the willies. I don't know why—I've never even talked to her. She just comes into the waiting room, gets her coat, and leaves. She's never said a word to me, but she gives me the willies."

"Maybe it's because she isn't friendly," I suggested.

"No—I'd just as soon not talk to your other patients. It's something else. It's like—well, I don't know how to put it—it's like there's something evil in her."

"She doesn't look strange, does she?" I asked, fascinated.

"No, she looks just like an ordinary person. She dresses well. She might even be a professional woman. But something about her gives me the creeps. I can't put my finger on it. But if I've ever seen someone who's evil, she's the one."

Whether or not my sense of revulsion was primarily sexual, Charlene's sexual behavior during our sessions was quite extraordinary. Ordinarily when a woman patient experiences affection for me, she is shy, even secretive about it at first. Not so Charlene. She who routinely withheld information from me was blatant about her seductive intent.

"You're cold," she said accusingly. "I don't see why you won't hold me."

"Perhaps I could hold you if you needed comforting," I replied, "but your desire to be held feels sexual to me."

"You and your nit-picking distinctions," Charlene exclaimed. "What difference does it make whether I want to be comforted sexually or in some other way? Either way I need comforting."

"You do not need a sexual relationship with me," I tried to explain again and again. "You can have that with anyone. What you are paying me for is a more special kind of care."

"Well, I don't think you care for me at all. You're stiff and distant. You're not warm. I don't see how you're going to be able to help me when you don't even feel warm toward me."

I was beginning to wonder about this myself. Always Charlene caused me to wonder if I was the right therapist for her.

There was also an illicit, sneaky, invasive quality to Charlene's desire for me. In the summer she used to come early to our sessions and would sit in our garden. Had she asked my permission to do this, I do not think I would have begrudged it. I like people to enjoy the flowers that are my wife's and my hobby. But she never asked. Several nights when we did not have appointments I looked outside to see Charlene parked in front of our house, just sitting in her car listening to the radio playing softly in the darkness. It was eerie. When I asked her about it she simply said, "You know you're the man I love. It's natural to want to be near someone you love."

One day when we did not have an appointment I came into our library to find Charlene sitting reading one of my books. I asked her what she was doing there. "It's a waiting room, isn't it?" she replied.

"It's a waiting room when you have an appointment," I responded. "When I'm not seeing patients, it's a private room in my house."

"Well, for me it's a waiting room," Charlene said with utter comfort. "When you have your office in your home, you have to expect to lose some of your privacy."

After ascertaining that she had no valid reason for seeing me, I practically had to order her out. More than any other time in my life, I personally felt something of what it must be like for a woman to receive unsolicited advances and even to be in fear of rape. Indeed, twice at the end of a session Charlene actually grabbed me and attempted to embrace me before I pushed her away.

A major reason children often fail to resolve the Oedipus complex is that they have failed to receive adequate parental love and attention in the years before the age of four—the so-called pre-Oedipal years. Solving the Oedipal dilemma is like building the first story of a house. It simply cannot be done unless there is a foundation to build upon. Many signs pointed to the probability that Charlene had been emotionally deprived from the beginning. Her mother was clearly an ungiving woman. Charlene had no memory whatsoever of either parent ever holding her. She dreamed frequently of breasts. She ritualistically followed the strange dietary laws of her cult, with the result that she was always searching for odd organic foods and, when dining with others, always eating something different from them—something special. In psychoanalytic terms Charlene's most basic problem was not an unresolved Oedipus complex but a condition of pre-Oedipal oral fixation.

Charlene's yearning to touch and be touched by me was, in fact, a yearning for mothering—the warm, no-strings-attached cuddling of which she had been deprived. I experienced her desire for touching as repulsive and threatening. Yet was not touching exactly what she desperately needed? In order to heal her, should I not have done the very thing I found so distasteful? Should I not have taken Charlene on my lap, held her and fondled her and kissed her and caressed her until she was finally at peace?

Perhaps so, perhaps not. I seriously considered it. But in so doing I realized something. I realized that although I was willing to nurture Charlene as a sick and hungry infant, she was unwilling to receive that kind of attention. She was unwilling to assume the role of child, much less infant, in relation to me. The essence of my distaste for touching her lay in her insistence that the touching be sexual. She saw herself not as a hungry child but an adult on the make. I repeatedly attempted, through a variety of means, including the use of the couch, to help her take a more passive, trusting, childlike posture with me. All my attempts failed. Throughout all the four years she worked with me Charlene insisted on controlling the show. To have been like a young child she would have had to give me the reins, to have let me care for her parentally instead of demanding that I care for her sexually. But this she would not do. She wanted the reins in her hands every moment.

The process of deep healing, at least within the psychoanalytic framework, requires the patient to regress on some level to some degree. It is a difficult and frightening requirement. It is no easy thing for adults, accustomed to independence and the psychologic trappings of maturity, to allow themselves to become like young children again, dependent and so very vulnerable. And the deeper the disturbance—the more hungry and painful and wounding the patient's childhood—the more difficult it is to return to the childhood condition within the therapeutic relationship. It is like a death. Yet it can be accomplished. When it is, healing will result. When it does not, the foundation cannot be reconstructed. No regression, no healing; it is as simple as that.

If I had to put my finger on a single cause for Charlene's failure to be healed in the long years she spent with me, it would be her failure to regress. When patients succeed in regressing, there is an entirely different quality to their demeanor in therapy. They develop a peacefulness they did not have before. They have a kind of trusting innocence, which can be suspended at any moment, given the need, but which can also be easily recaptured. The interaction between patient and therapist becomes not only smooth but even playful and joyful. It is an ideal partnership of loving mother and child. Had this state of affairs been achieved with Charlene, and had it seemed necessary to do so, I have no doubt that I could and would have taken her on my lap and given her all she needed. But this state of affairs did not come to pass. Although in her core she was obviously an infant, there was never anything innocent or truly trusting about her. She continued until the end to act the adult on the make. "I still don't see why," Charlene said three years into therapy.

"Still don't see what?" I asked.

"I don't see why a child shouldn't have sex with its parents."

I patiently explained once again that it is the parents' job to assist their child toward independence—and independence from one's parents is always retarded by incestuous ties.

"But this wouldn't be incest," Charlene said. "You're not my father."

"I may not be your actual father," I responded, "but my role as your therapist is a parental one. My job is to help you grow, not to sexually satisfy you. You can get sex elsewhere, with your peers."

"But I am your peer," she exclaimed.

"Charlene, you're my patient. You've got all kinds of big problems you need help with. I want to help you with those problems. I do not want to sleep with you."

"But even though I'm your patient, I can still be your peer."

"Charlene, the plain fact of the matter is that you are not my peer. You can't even hold a menial job for more than a few months. You haven't even learned to find your way around in broad daylight. Psychologically you're practically an infant. And that's okay. You had lousy parents, and you've got all kinds of reasons to still be an infant. But stop trying to pretend you're my peer. Why don't you just relax and enjoy my attention as a parent? I really want to love you that way. But please stop trying to possess me sexually. Give it up, Charlene."

"I won't give it up. I want you and I intend to have you."

Although she could not have been more blatant about what she wanted from me, I still sensed Charlene's advances as inherently dishonest. She was trying to obtain breast-feeding under the guise of sex. She sought infantile nurturance in the disguise of adult sexuality—which is not in itself such an uncommon phenomenon, except that Charlene steadfastly refused to let the disguise be penetrated. Time and time again I said to her, one way or another: "You really want me to mother you. That's okay. That's nice. I'd like to do that. It's something you need. In fact, you deserve it. You were cheated of it in the past, and you deserve to have it made up to you. Forget about this sex stuff. You're not ready for it. You're too young. Relax. Lie back and enjoy the warmth I can give you. Let me nurture you."

But she did not. To a certain extent this was because she regarded my offer as a trap—as well she might, since the kind of mothering she had received as a young child had been a trap. Had this fear alone been the source of her resistance, however, it could probably have been worked through and overcome. But the issue of pure power was more important. It was not simply that she was afraid to give me a maternal power over her. Rather it was that she did not want to relinquish any power for any reason. She wanted healing, but she was not willing to lose anything, give up anything, in the process. It was as if she demanded of me, "Heal me, but don't change me." She wanted not only to be nurtured but to be the boss of the nurturer.*

When Charlene berated me for my lack of warmth and desire

* The desire for regression to a state of union with the mother was one of the three characteristics Erich Fromm found in his analysis of the evil personality pattern, or "syndrome of decay" (*The Heart of Man: Its Genius for Good and Evil* [Harper & Row, 1964]). He labeled this desire "incestuous symbiosis." Certainly I found this desire in Charlene. But I have also found it in many others. A crucial factor in evil, I suspect, is not simply a regressive yearning for Mother (which can be used for healing) but rather the attempt to obtain Mother without regression—an insistence on receiving mothering without relinquishing either the adult role or any of the power associated with it.

to hug her, she kept saying, "I just want you to affirm me. How can I be cured by a therapist who won't even affirm me?" This was an important word. The essence of maternal love for the infant is affirmation. The ordinary, healthy mother loves her infant for no reason other than simply the fact that it is here. The infant does not have to *do* anything to earn her love. There are no strings attached to it. The love is unconditional. She loves the infant for itself, as it is. This love is a statement of affirmation; it says, "You are of great value simply because you exist."

During the second and third year of its life the mother begins to increasingly expect certain things, such as toilet training, from her child. And when this happens her love inevitably becomes, to at least some degree, conditional. She now says, "I love you, but . . ." "But I wish you would stop tearing up the books." "But I wish you would stop pulling the lamp off the table." "But I wish you would help me by going to the potty so I don't have to wash these diapers anymore." The child learns the words "good" and "bad." And it learns it can continue to be fully affirmed only by being a good child. Now it has to earn its affirmation. And so it is forever after. The period of unconditional affirmation lasts only as long as infancy. As psychological adults we have all learned, to a greater or lesser degree, that in order to be loved it is our responsibility to make ourselves lovable.

A key element in Charlene's behavior was her request—no, her demand—that I love her regardless of how she behaved—that I affirm her not just for who she might become but for who she was, sickness and all. In so doing I would give her what she desired from me—the love of a mother for her infant, the consistently unconditional love that can be experienced only in infancy. It is no wonder that this was so, because we had evidence that she had failed to receive from her mother the unconditionally affirming love during her infancy which ought to be the heritage of every child. Of this heritage she had been cheated. But it was impossible for me to make it up to her. For she demanded that I love her unconditionally as a sick adult. She insisted that I love her as a mother would an infant, but she insisted also that I treat her as an adult peer. If for no other reason, her demand was impossible to fulfill because it was a demand to affirm her sickness.* Charlene did not want to be healed. She wanted to be loved, not

---

* In Martin Buber's words, the evil insist upon "affirmation independent of all findings" (*Good and Evil* [Charles Scribner's Sons, 1953], p. 136).

changed. She wanted to be loved for herself, neurosis and all. Although she would never say so, it gradually became clear that Charlene remained in therapy with the intent to obtain my love *without* therapy—that is, to have both my love and her neurosis: to have her cake and eat it too.


## A LAW UNTO HERSELF

By now Charlene's willfulness had become evident. Yet the depths of that willfulness still did not become clear until the third year of her therapy, when I realized that Charlene was actually autistic.

Mental health requires that the human will submit itself to something higher than itself. To function decently in this world we must submit ourselves to some principle that takes precedence over what we might want at any given moment. For the religious this principle is God, and so they will say, "Thy will, not mine, be done." But if they are sane, even the nonreligious submit themselves, whether they know it or not, to some "higher power"—be it truth or love, the needs of others, or the demands of reality. As I defined it in *The Road Less Traveled*,* "Mental health is an ongoing process of dedication to reality at all costs."

The utter failure to submit oneself to reality is called autism. The word comes from the Greek root *auto*, meaning "self." The person who is autistic is oblivious to certain essential dimensions of reality. Such people literally live "in a world of their own" in which the self reigns supreme.

When I asked Charlene why she wanted sex with me, her answer was always perfectly simple: "Because I love you." Although I repeatedly raised the issue of its genuineness, to Charlene the reality of her "love" was unquestionable. To me, however, it was autistic. When she gave me a different check each month, she thought she was doing so *for* me. In her mind there was some connection between me and the particular pattern of that month's check. But the connection was all in her mind. The reality was not only that I couldn't have cared less which pattern she used but also that her selection had nothing to do with the reality of me.

* Simon and Schuster, 1978.

As far as she was concerned, Charlene loved everyone. The cult to which she belonged espoused as its principal doctrine the love of mankind. Charlene saw herself proceeding through the world spreading gifts and gentle kindness wherever she walked. My own experience of her love, however, was that it invariably excluded the reality of me. One winter evening, for instance, a few minutes after we had completed a session, I made myself a martini and went into the living room, ready to settle down by the fire for a rather rare time of relaxation in which I could get caught up with my mail. I heard the grinding noise of someone repeatedly attempting to start a car. I went outside. It was Charlene.

"I don't know what's wrong," she said. "I can't get it started."

"You're not out of gas, are you?" I asked.

"Oh, I don't think that could be it," she replied.

"You don't think? What does the gas gauge read?"

"Oh, that reads empty," Charlene answered gaily.

I might have laughed if I'd not been annoyed. "Since your gauge reads empty, what makes you think you're not out of gas?"

"Oh, it always reads empty."

"What do you mean," I asked, "it always reads empty? Is it broken?"

"No. At least I don't think so. You see, I never buy more than a couple of gallons at a time. That way I'll be sure not to waste any. Besides, it's fun to guess when I need some more. I'm pretty good at it."

"How often do you guess wrong and run out?" I asked in amazement at the discovery of this new, extraordinary ritual.

"Oh, not often. Maybe three or four times a year."

"And I don't suppose it's possible this could be one of those times?" I said with an edge of sarcasm. "What are you going to do now?"

"If I can come in and use your phone, I'll call AAA."

"Charlene, it's nine o'clock at night and we're way out in the country. What do you think they're going to do about it?"

"Well, sometimes they come out at night. The only other thing I could do is borrow some gas from you."

"I'm afraid I don't have any extra gas lying around," I replied.

"We could siphon some out of your car, couldn't we?" Charlene asked.

"I suppose so," I acknowledged, "except I don't think we have anything to siphon with."

"Oh, I have a siphon tube," Charlene answered brightly. "I keep it in the trunk. I always like to be prepared."

So I searched for a pail and a funnel. Then I used her siphon tube, getting a mouthful of gasoline in order to initiate the suction. I gave her a gallon. Her car started right up and she drove off. I was very cold when I came in. My martini was warm and diluted. I couldn't taste it for the gasoline. I couldn't taste anything for the rest of the evening except gasoline—the bad taste she had literally left in my mouth.

Two days later Charlene came in for her next session. She mentioned nothing of the debacle following her previous one. Finally I asked her how she'd felt about what had happened.

"Oh, I thought it was neat," she replied. "I really enjoyed it."

"You enjoyed it?" I queried.

"Sure. It was exciting. It was kind of like an adventure, figuring out how to siphon the gasoline and get the car started. And we shared it together. Do you know, that's the first time we've ever actually done anything together? It was fun working with you out there in the dark."

"How do you think I felt about it?" I asked.

"I don't know. I assume you enjoyed it too."

"Why do you assume that?"

"I don't know why. Didn't you enjoy it?"

"Charlene," I asked, "did the thought ever cross your mind that I might have had something else to do the other evening rather than help you start your car, something I might have wanted to do more?"

"No. I thought people liked to help other people. At least I do. Don't you?"

"Charlene," I asked again, "were you at any time during the incident uncomfortable or embarrassed? Did you feel bad at all about having to use my help to get out of a mess that you were responsible for?"

"Oh, it wasn't my fault."

"It wasn't?"

"No," Charlene stated flatly. "The car had less gas in it than I thought. That's not my fault. I suppose you might say that I should have estimated better, but on the whole I do pretty well.

As I told you, I only run out three or four times a year. That's a pretty good average."

"Charlene," I said, "I've been driving three times as long as you and I've never run out of gas."

"Well, apparently not running out of gas is a big deal to you. I mean, you're really uptight about it. It's not my fault you're so uptight about it."

I gave up. For the moment I was just too tired of batting my head against the impregnable walls of Charlene's obliviousness. As far as she was concerned, my feelings did not really exist.

Autism is narcissism in its ultimate form. For the complete narcissist, others have no more psychologic reality than a piece of furniture. Narcissists have only what Martin Buber calls "I-I relationships."* While I have no doubt Charlene truly believed that she loved me, her "love" was all in her head. It did not exist as any objective reality. To herself she was a "light unto the people," emanating joy and happiness wherever she went. All that I and others experienced of her, however, was the irritating chaos and confusion she invariably left in her wake.

Charlene didn't stumble into chairs, but it was more than just me or other people to which she was oblivious. She was, for instance, continually getting lost when she drove any significant distance. This symptom puzzled me for the longest time—perhaps because the answer was so obvious. But as soon as I became aware of her autism, the puzzle was simple. Complaining that on the previous day she had ended up in Newburgh, New York, when she had intended to go to New York City, I commented, "It sounds as if you missed the turnoff from Interstate Eighty-four onto Interstate Six eighty-four."

"That's it," Charlene exclaimed happily. "It was Six eighty-four I wanted."

"But you've been that way to New York City a number of times, and the turn is clearly marked. How could you have missed it?"

"Well, I was humming a tune and I was trying to figure it out in my head."

"So you weren't concentrating."

---

* See Buber's *I and Thou,* trans. Walter Kaufmann (Charles Scribner's Sons, 1970).

"That's what I just told you, isn't it?" Charlene responded, annoyed.

"Since you're always getting lost," I persisted, "maybe the problem is always the same. Maybe you just don't pay attention to road signs."

"Well, I can't do two things at once. I can't work out a tune and be expected to concentrate on road signs at the same time."

"Correct," I said. "You can't play your own tune, so to speak, and expect the Highway Department to dance to it. If you don't want to get lost, you have to pay attention to signs. If you want to lose yourself in fantasy, then you're going to get lost in relation to the external world. I'm sorry, Charlene, but that's the way it is."

Charlene jumped off the couch. "This session is not going the way I intended it," she said coldly. "I do not intend to lie here and be harangued like a child. I will see you next week."

It was not the first time Charlene had walked out of a session. Still, I pleaded with her. "Charlene, you've got more than half your time left. Please stay and let's try to work it out. It's a very important issue."

But my office door slammed irrevocably shut.

I began at this point also to understand another one of Charlene's symptoms: her inability to hold a job for more than a few months. During our two and a half years together, until this point, Charlene had held four different positions, which were interspersed with long periods of unemployment. On the eve of starting a fifth job I asked her, "Are you nervous?"

She looked genuinely surprised. "No, why should I be?"

"If I were starting a new job, I'd be nervous," I said. "Particularly if I'd been fired so many times before. I'd be scared I wouldn't be able to succeed. Actually, I'm a bit scared whenever I go into any new situation in which I don't know the rules."

"But I do know the rules," Charlene countered.

I looked at her, dumbfounded. "How can you know the rules of a job you haven't even begun?"

"My job's to be an aide at the state school for the retarded. The woman who hired me said the patients are like children. I know all about how to take care of children. After all, I had a younger sister, and I was a Sunday school teacher, wasn't I?"

Exploring the issue further, I gradually realized that Charlene was never nervous when entering any new situation because she always knew the rules beforehand. Because she herself always made them up. The fact that they were her rules and not her employer's never seemed to matter to her. Nor the fact that confusion inevitably resulted. Playing by her predetermined rules, with utter disregard for the way her employers wanted things done, she could never understand why people on the job soon became annoyed with her and, in relatively short order, totally fed up, if not frankly furious. "People are so unkind," she would explain. She repeatedly complained that I too was unkind. Charlene placed great stock in kindness.

The reason she had been unable to graduate from college similarly became clear. Charlene seldom produced her papers when they were due, and when she did, they were seldom on the subject assigned. A psychologist to whom I had referred Charlene for consultation described her as having "an IQ that would sink a battleship." Yet she had flunked out of a mediocre college. Repeatedly I attempted to explain to her—sometimes gently, sometimes forcefully—how her disregard of others was at the core of her failures, and how self-destructive was her extreme narcissism. But "The world is too inflexible" was the closest she ever came to acknowledging the problem. "And unkind."

Toward the end of therapy the problem was elucidated theologically as well as psychologically.

"Everything seems meaningless," Charlene complained to me one day.

"What is the meaning of life?" I asked her with seeming innocence.

"How should I know?" she replied with obvious irritation.

"You're a dedicated religious person," I responded. "Surely your religion must have something to say about the meaning of life."

"You're trying to trap me," Charlene countered.

"That's right," I acknowledged. "I am trying to trap you into seeing your problem clearly. What does your religion hold to be the meaning of life?"

"I am not a Christian," Charlene proclaimed. "My religion speaks of love, not of meaning."

"Well, what do Christians say as to the meaning of life? Even if it isn't what you believe, at least it's a model."

"I'm not interested in models."

"You were raised in the Christian Church. You spent almost two years as a professional teacher of Christian doctrine," I went on, goading her. "Surely you're not so dumb as to be unaware of what Christians say is the meaning of life, the purpose of human existence."

"We exist for the glory of God," Charlene said in a flat, low monotone, as if she were sullenly repeating an alien catechism, learned by rote and extracted from her at gunpoint. "The purpose of our life is to glorify God."

"Well?" I asked.

There was a short silence. For a brief moment I thought she might cry—the one time in our work together. "I cannot do it. There's no room for *me* in that. That would be my death," she said in a quavering voice. Then, with a suddenness that frightened me, what seemed to be her choked-back sobs turned into a roar. "I don't want to live for God. I will not. I want to live for me. My own sake!"

It was another session in the middle of which Charlene walked out. I felt a terrible pity for her. I wanted to cry, but my own tears would not come. "Oh, God, she's so alone," was all I could whisper.

## THE DREAM OF THE MARVELOUS MACHINE

Throughout our work together Charlene steadfastly maintained her insistence not only that she loved me but also that she wanted to be "well." I had long ago come to suspect that both were pretenses—although, most likely, pretenses she herself believed.* The unconscious, however, has a beautiful and tenacious tendency to speak the truth. So it was, near the end, that Charlene's unconscious did seem to reveal to me, with quite striking clarity, the reality of our relationship.

"I had a dream last night," Charlene recounted at the begin-

* It is perhaps not without significance that Malachi Martin, in *Hostage to the Devil*, has labeled the first, longest, and most difficult stage of an exorcism the "pretense." Whether or not she was conceivably possessed, Charlene's pretense was penetrated only by her own unconscious. It was never acknowledged by her consciously.

ning of her fourth year in therapy. "It took place on another planet. My people were at war with an alien race. For a long time it had been unclear who would win the war. But I had constructed a marvelous machine that was both offensive and defensive. It was enormous and very complicated, with many different weapons systems. It could shoot torpedoes under water, fire rockets for great distances, spray chemicals, and do many other things. With it we knew we could win the war. I was in the process of putting the finishing touches on this machine in my laboratory when a man came in. He was an alien, one of our enemy. I knew that he had come to try and destroy my machine before we could put it to use. But I was not alarmed. I felt supremely confident. There seemed to be plenty of time. I thought I would have sex with him and then could get rid of him before he got to the machine. There was a couch on one side of my laboratory. We lay down on it and began to make love. But then, just as we were getting into it, he suddenly jumped up from the couch and ran to the machine to attack it. I dashed over and began to push the buttons that would activate the defensive weapons systems, which would kill him and blast him away. But they didn't work. I hadn't quite finished checking them and hadn't test-fired them before. I pushed buttons and pulled levers frantically. In the midst of doing this I awoke in great agitation. It was unclear when I awoke whether I would succeed in repelling his sneak attack or whether he would succeed in destroying my beautiful machine."

One of the many remarkable things about this dream was Charlene's violent reaction to its interpretation.

"What is your predominant feeling about the dream?" I asked. "The one you had after you awoke?"

"Fury. I was furious."

"What were you most furious about?"

"The trickster," Charlene replied. "The man cheated me. He seemed willing to go to bed with me. I thought he cared for me. But then, just as my senses were lulled, he left off and started attacking my machine. He pretended that he cared for me, but all he was after all along was the machine. He tricked me. He used me."

"But weren't you using him and deceiving him just as much?" I asked.

"How do you mean?"

"Well, you knew he was after your machine in the first place," I explained. "I'm not sure why you should be so upset with him when he was simply doing what you knew he'd come there to do. And it seems to me that you were attempting to deceive him by taking him to bed. While you apparently wanted him sexually, I don't hear in the dream that you cared for him. Indeed, it was your intent to get rid of him, perhaps even kill him, once the sex was over. You described it as something you thought you could get away with."

"No, he tricked me," Charlene insisted. "He pretended that he loved me, and he really didn't."

"Whom do you suppose he represented?" I asked.

"Oh, it could be you. He looked something like you, blond and tall," Charlene answered. "I figured it was probably you as soon as I was fully awake."

"So, do you think you're angry at me for deceiving you?"

Charlene looked at me as if I were an idiot stating the obvious. "Of course I'm angry at you. You know that. I tell you all the time that you don't care for me enough. You almost never sympathize with me. You make very little effort to understand what I feel."

"And I won't make our relationship a sexual one."

"Yes, and you won't do that either."

"But I'm not trying to deceive you about that," I commented. "I've made it very clear that I have no intention of relating with you sexually."

"But you're deceptive when you say you care for me," Charlene maintained. "I daresay you honestly do *think* you care for me. But that's just you deceiving yourself. You're always so self-satisfied, anyway. You'd be much different if you really cared for me."

"If the man in the dream represents me," I asked, "what do you think the machine represents?"

"The machine?"

"Yes, the machine."

"Well, I hadn't thought about that," Charlene responded with some confusion. "I suppose it might represent my intelligence."

"You certainly do have a formidable intelligence," I commented.

"And I do think that you and your therapy are trying to undermine my intelligence." Charlene was obviously warming up to this interpretation. "I've told you that. You've sometimes even made me begin to believe things I don't believe. You do try to rob me of my intelligence and my will."

"But in the dream your intelligence seems to be devoted entirely to combat," I remarked. "It's filled with these offensive and defensive systems. It serves you only as a weapon."

"Well, I do need to have my wits about me in dealing with you," Charlene responded happily. "You're pretty intelligent too. A rather formidable opponent."

"Why do I have to be your opponent?" I asked.

Charlene looked stunned. "Well, in the dream you're my opponent, aren't you?" she finally said. "You're trying to destroy my machine."

"Suppose, instead of representing your intelligence," I suggested, "the machine represents your neurosis. It's true that I'm trying to destroy your neurosis."

Charlene bellowed, "NO!"

It was a No of such force and power that I shrank back into my chair. "No?" I asked weakly.

"NO. It's not my neurosis."

Again I felt blasted back into my chair. To this day I do not know how loudly Charlene said this, but I felt as if she had screamed it at me with all the intensity of which the human voice could possibly be capable.

"Why do you say it's not your neurosis?" I finally inquired, fearful of her wrath.

"Because it was beautiful," Charlene wailed. She went on, almost crooning to the image of the machine. "My machine was a thing of beauty. It was intricate. It was intricate beyond belief. It could do so many things. It had been constructed with such care and ingenuity. It had so many levels and operations. It was a masterpiece of engineering. He should never have attempted to destroy it. It was the most beautiful thing ever made."

"But it didn't work," I added quietly.

Charlene screamed again. "It did. It did work. It would have worked. I just hadn't had enough time. All I needed was a little more time to test it. It would have worked beautifully. I only needed to put the finishing touches to it."

"I really do think the machine represents your neurosis, Charlene," I said. "Your neurosis is large and complicated. You have constructed it over many, many years. It does serve many functions for you, but it's cumbersome and constantly tripping you up and not working when you need it. And it keeps you from being close to people, for it was built for warfare—to protect you from people, as you probably needed to be protected from your parents. But you don't need such protection now. You need to be open to people, not to be at war with them. You don't need that machine. It's getting in your way. It's only a weapons system, designed solely for warfare—to keep people away."

"It was not designed just for warfare," Charlene howled like a beast wounded. "It did other things too. It had many peaceful uses as well."

"Like what?" I asked.

Charlene again looked confused. For a moment she seemed to be searching her memory, and then, with utter seriousness and apparent genuineness, she proclaimed, "Well, for instance, down near the bottom there was a part that could repair damaged cuticles—you know, like on your toenails. It was very helpful that way."

Almost involuntarily I did something that I probably should not have done. I laughed.

Charlene jumped off the couch. "The machine is not a neurosis," she declared in cold, regal fury. "You are not to refer to it as such again. And this session is now terminated." Within a second, before I could even remonstrate, she was out of the office and gone once again.

Charlene returned on schedule for her next appointment. And she continued in therapy for six months. But we never got any further than the attempt to interpret this dream. We worked on this or that without success, and whenever I attempted to return to the dream, she refused. She was quite serious when she said that I was not to refer to it again.

## NO-WIN

Charlene had cast me in her dream as an enemy alien. In reality I was no stranger to her. She had been seeing me two to four times each week for over three years. I believe I had done my best to be loving and to fully earn the substantial sums she paid

me. She herself said and believed that she loved me. Yet her unconscious—that reservoir of truth in us all—labeled me an enemy
and alien.

In a way I perceived her similarly. When I recoiled from her
embraces it was, I think, partly out of a fear for my own safety.
Must I not, therefore, have perceived her on some level as an
enemy? Moreover, there existed in Charlene something that—try
as I might—I never came to understand and with which I was
never able to empathize. She was, I suppose, as alien to me as I
to her. She perpetually accused me of being unkind and unsym-
pathetic, and I often wondered if she might not be right—that
perhaps I should have referred her to a different, somehow more
empathic therapist. But I didn't know anyone who seemed better
suited. And, in fact, she had failed with a previous therapist and
was to fail with my successors.

Be that as it may, there were many times when Charlene
seemed to be moved by desires beyond my comprehension—
motives so obscure as to be out of the range of my human experience. More than anything else, it is this "inhuman" something,
out of reach of ordinary psychodynamic understanding, that I
have labeled—rightly or wrongly—evil. But I cannot be absolutely certain whether it was alien to me because it was evil or
whether I called it evil because it was so alien.

I can think of no better way to sum up this incomprehensible—
this alien—something than to describe Charlene's response to the
weather. She had no enthusiasm whatsoever for spring or autumn
days of sunshine or for the loveliest of sunsets. Only one type of
weather pleased her: gray days. Then she came in whistling.
Charlene liked gray days. Not the soft, misty days of autumn
when the leaves fall quietly. Not days of summer along the
coast when the fog swirls around in great blowing sheets. But the
ordinary, dullest gray days. The kind of days you are likely to
get in New England in the middle of March, when winter has
left its detritus on the ground: broken, rotted tree limbs, mud-
slurped earth, and filthy patches of decaying snow. The days of
unrelieved gray. The dismal days. Why? Why did Charlene
love these ugliest days that everyone else hates? Did she love
them because they made the rest of us miserable? Or did she love
them for their own ugliness and vibrate to something in them
so utterly alien that we have no name for it? I do not know.

Fearfully—because I had never done so with any patient before—I did confront Charlene that last year with what seemed to me to be her evil. The first time was several months before her dream of the "magnificent machine." "Charlene," I told her, "you go around creating chaos and confusion in the world and in here in your therapy. You used to claim it was accidental. Now we've learned it is often your intention to do so. But I still don't understand why it's your intention."

"Because it's fun."

"Fun?"

"Yes, it's fun to confuse you. I've told you. It gives me a sense of power."

"But wouldn't it be more fun," I asked, "to get a sense of power out of being genuinely competent?"

"*I* don't think so."

"Does it bother you that you're having this fun at the expense of other people?"

"No. Maybe it would if I seriously hurt somebody. But I don't, do I?"

Charlene was right. She never did seriously hurt anyone else as far as I knew. She just annoyed the hell out of everyone. And it did hurt herself. Why should she enjoy it? It seemed to me I ought to press on. "Charlene," I said, "even though your destructiveness may be minor, it still seems to me that there's something—well, something evil about your delight in it."

"I suppose you could say that," Charlene responded blandly.

"Charlene, I can't believe you," I retorted. "Here I've virtually called you evil, and you don't seem the least bit upset by it."

"So what do you want me to do about it?"

"Well, you could begin by feeling bad about the possibility that you're evil."

"Do you happen to know of a good exorcist in the neighborhood?" Charlene suddenly asked.

I was totally unprepared for the question. "No," I acknowledged lamely.

"What's the point of getting all upset about it, then?" Charlene asked cheerfully.

I felt dizzy, almost punch-drunk, as if I'd just badly lost a round in a boxing match to a vastly superior fighter. I retreated. But I began—for the first time in my life—to study the phenomena of possession and exorcism. It all seemed bizarre. I really did not know what to make of my reading on the subject. I did, however, learn that at least a few of the writers I read seemed not only sane but responsible and caring. I decided to try again four months later.

"Charlene, do you remember a few months ago when you asked me if I knew of a good exorcist?" I asked.

"Sure, I remember everything we talk about."

"Well, I still don't know of one. But I've been reading up on the subject. I believe I could help you find one if you wanted."

"Thanks, but I'm more into bioenergetics at the moment."

"Damn it, Charlene," I almost exploded, "we're talking about the issue of evil, not some little tension or anxiety. The issue isn't a little blemish. The issue is something very ugly."

"And I told you," Charlene said archly, "I'm interested in bioenergetics. I'm not interested in exorcism. Period. I do wonder, however, how you can possibly work with me if you think I'm evil. How can you affirm me? How can you give me the sympathy I need? It's what I've been saying all along: you don't really care for me."

I retreated again. And returned over and over again to confront her willfulness, self-centeredness, self-destructiveness, and failures. Over and over again to urge her to regress, to let me love her as a child, to let me care for her in the only way I could, on the only terms that seemed healthy. It was all I knew how to do. But—as I now expected—nothing changed. I didn't know how else to proceed except to wait, with less and less hope, for a miracle.

Sick though she was in psychiatric terms, Charlene could hardly be called "unstable." To the contrary, she was frighteningly stable. Impervious to her autism. Immutable. Among all the things about her that did not change was her refusal to submit to the "rules" of therapy and the requirements for honesty. Although she had chosen from time to time to reveal this or that, she continued throughout to withhold most of the crucial information that would have made genuine therapy possible. She remained in control of almost every session until the end.

It was to my absolute amazement, therefore, when one afternoon she came in for the four hundred and twenty-first session, lay down on the couch, and for the next fifty minutes proceeded to tell me smoothly and honestly exactly what she was thinking and feeling. No one had ever done better. For those fifty minutes she was the perfect patient. Except, unknown to me, she was still withholding what was most crucial. With five minutes to go in the session, I expressed my amazement and appreciation at how well she had done.

"I thought you'd be pleased," she said.

"But what happened," I asked, "to suddenly cause you to behave so differently in here, to freely tell me things instead of turning the session into a fight and struggle?"

"I wanted to show you that I could do it," she replied, "that I can free-associate and follow the rules just like you want me to."

"Well, you've certainly done that," I answered. "It was beautiful. I hope you'll be able to continue."

"No, I won't."

"Won't what?" I asked dumbly.

"Won't do it again. This is our last session. I've decided not to return. You're not the right therapist for me."

There were thirty seconds left in the session. I attempted to remonstrate. No, she would not return to discuss the matter. My next patient was waiting. I kept him waiting for fifteen minutes. But she would not budge. She had decided she needed a less "rigid" therapist, and that was all there was to it. Finally I had to let her leave. I wrote her several letters, but I never saw her again. It was a remarkable tour de force.


## EVIL AND POWER

It was also remarkably petty.

Charlene's desire to make a conquest of me, to toy with me, to utterly control our relationship, knew no bounds. It seemed to be a desire for power purely for its own sake. She did not want power in order to improve society, to care for a family, to make herself a more effective person, or in any way accomplish anything creative. Her thirst for power was unsubordinated to anything higher than itself.

Consequently it was totally tasteless. There was a kind of artistry with which she could operate—such as her talent for timing when she brought down the curtain on our relationship. But the artistry had no grand design. Unsubmitted even to the requirements of plot, it lacked coherence. The performance was ultimately meaningless.

Because of this silly, petty quality to her life, Charlene may not seem an important character. The only consequence of her role in the drama of life was the string of merely minor annoyances she caused one employer after another. But suppose she had been the employer rather than the employee. Suppose she had inherited not a small trust fund but a whole corporation to manage with her devious destructiveness. Or, more feasibly, simply suppose that Charlene became a mother. Then the rather ridiculous bumbling comedy of her life would be suddenly transformed into an ugly tragedy.

At one point I defined evil as "The exercise of political power—that is, the imposition of one's will upon others by overt or covert coercion—in order to avoid . . . spiritual growth." What made Charlene's existence more of a slapstick comedy than a gruesome tragedy was the mere fact that she possessed virtually no political power to exercise. Give her a husband and she would likely have become a Sarah. Give her a child and she would likely have been a Mrs. R. Give her a nation and she would likely have been a Hitler or an Idi Amin.

Because their willfulness is so extraordinary—and always accompanied by a lust for power—I suspect that the evil are more likely than most to politically aggrandize themselves. Yet at the same time, being unsubmitted, their extreme willfulness is likely to lead them into political debacles. It is conceivable to me that there may have been, deep inside, some hidden instinct for goodness in Charlene that led her to avoid successful mating or the quest for authority over others. Certainly I have known many people who have medically or socially sterilized themselves precisely because of an awareness that they would make incompetent parents. So I do not know for sure whether Charlene was such a politically impotent person because she was the less or because she was the more evil. All evidence pointed to utter willfulness as the sole cause of her failure to be effectively wicked. But I would like to give her the benefit of the doubt.

Be that as it may, Charlene was a failure. Whatever the reason that she was no major villain, she was utterly unable to be creative. Whether or not it was a blessing in disguise, her impotence was still impotence. And impotence is no laughing matter. I have used the metaphor of comedy to describe her ineffectiveness. Now that its usefulness is at an end, I want to retract the metaphor. I do not think Charlene was funny in her impotence. I do not think it is funny when any human being is less of a human being than he or she can be. Intellectually brilliant, Charlene was infinitely less. Although apparently quite happy as she plowed through life leaving a wake of minor chaos behind her, and remarkably content with her impotence, I think she was one of the saddest people I have ever met.

And I am sad that I couldn't help her. Whether or not her coming "for help" was a lie, she still came to me. She needed—and hence deserved—more than I could give her at the time. Her impotence and failure were my own.

## IF I HAD IT TO DO OVER AGAIN

When I worked with Charlene I knew practically nothing about radical human evil. I did not believe in the existence of either the devil or the phenomenon of possession. I had never attended an exorcism. I had never heard of the word "deliverance." The very name of evil was absent from my professional vocabulary. I had received no training on the subject. It was not a recognized field of study for a psychiatrist or for that matter, any supposedly scientific person. I had been taught that all psychopathology could be explained in terms of known diseases or psychodynamics, and was properly labeled and encompassed in the standard *Diagnostic and Statistical Manual*. The fact that American psychiatry almost totally ignored even the basic reality of the human will had not yet struck me as ridiculous. No one had ever told me of a case like Charlene. Nothing had prepared me for her. I was like an infant.

I cut my eyeteeth on Charlene. She was, without question, one of the major beginnings of this book.

What I learned through Charlene and during the years since is insignificant in relation to what needs to be known about human evil. But it is enough that, had I to do it over again, I would work with Charlene very differently. And, conceivably, our work might succeed.

First of all, I would make the diagnosis of evil in Charlene's case with both far greater rapidity and far greater confidence. I would not be misled by her obsessive-compulsive features into thinking that I was dealing with an ordinary neurosis, or by her autism into considering for months whether or not I had uncovered a strange variant of schizophrenia. I would not spend nine months in confusion, or over a year making useless Oedipal interpretations. When I did finally come to the conclusion that Charlene's most basic and real problem was evil, I did so very tentatively, and when I confronted her with it, I did so without any sense of authority. I do not believe that the diagnosis of evil is one that should be made lightly. Nonetheless, all that I have learned since has confirmed my then tentative conclusions. Had I to do it over again, I believe I could put my finger on Charlene's problem in three months instead of three years, and with a firmness that might possibly be healing.

I would begin with my confusion. I know now that one of the characteristics of evil is its desire to confuse. I had been aware of my confusion within a month of beginning work with Charlene but assumed it to be my stupidity. I never entertained the notion in the first year that possibly I was confused because she wanted to confuse me. Today I would make that as a possible hypothesis and begin to test it quite quickly. Had I done that kind of testing with Charlene, it is more than likely that the diagnosis would have evolved in short order.

Might not such a cool competence in dealing with her case have driven Charlene right out of treatment? Yes, it is a distinct possibility.

We must ask why Charlene came into treatment in the first place. Her avowed reason that she wanted help was never manifested. What was evident was a desire to toy with me and seduce me. Then we must ask why she stayed in treatment as long as she did. Here again the answer would seem to be that, in my naïveté and willingness to take her at face value, I offered her the ongoing pleasure of playing with me and the ongoing hope that she could succeed in seducing me, possessing me, or conquering me. Last, we must ask why Charlene finally left treatment when she did. The most obvious conjecture would be that as I increasingly "got her number," the possibility of my seduction became more and more hopeless and her capacity to toy with me more and more limited.

Had it become clear early in the course of our work that I not only recognized her evil but had the power to combat it, it is indeed quite possible that Charlene would have beat a hasty retreat from an engagement she so obviously could not "win." But if she had, would such an outcome not be preferable to what did transpire? Certainly it would have saved her thousands of dollars. I cannot see that there is any virtue in a four-year treatment failure over a four-month treatment failure. I believe, however, that there is an even chance that Charlene would have stayed in therapy. I believe this for three reasons.

One reason is that I suspect Charlene was not irredeemably evil. We must bear in mind that it is highly uncharacteristic for the evil to ever subject themselves to the searing light of psychotherapy. It is possible Charlene took the risk out of the strength of her desire to "beat" me. It is also possible that she took the risk because a part of her—a small part, to be sure—did indeed want help; it is possible that her evil was not of the thoroughbred variety. Actually, the two possibilities are not at all mutually exclusive. People are often "of two minds," and at least some who are evil may be ambivalently so. My leading hypothesis is that Charlene entered treatment out of both a desire to conquer me and a desire to be healed.

Still, the part of her that desired conquest seemed the larger. How, then, can I suppose that had I responded to her more knowledgeably she would ever have allowed *herself* to be conquered—that she could ever have lost the battle in order to win her soul? One reason is the issue of authority. I have learned these past years that evil—whether it be demonic or human—is surprisingly obedient to authority. Why this is so I do not know. But I know that it is so.

Let me stress that authority over the power of evil does not come easily. It is gained by enormous exertion in addition to knowledge. Such exertion can be born only of love. I believe that when I worked with Charlene I had the love, but it was useless without the knowledge. Now that I have the knowledge, I would take her on again—gladly, if I had the chance—but I would shudder at the energy that would be required of me. Genuine love is always ultimately sacrificial. There are no words strong enough to describe the matter. I never had the confidence to do true battle with Charlene's evil. I know now that he or she who would do true battle with evil must expect to be depleted beyond imagination—perhaps even beyond recovery. So I would today take quick (but not easy) authority over Charlene's evil. And out of my newfound knowledge I would do something else I did not do before: I would address her fear.

I have earlier pointed out that the evil are to be pitied—not hated—because they live their lives in sheer terror. On the surface Charlene appeared fearless. She was not afraid of the things that usually make us humans anxious: running out of gas, missing the exit on the throughway, entering on a new job. But now I know her superficial, almost silly equanimity masked depths of terror known to few. Her insistence on controlling every aspect of our relationship was rooted in panic: the dread that she might lose control of it. God knows what might happen to her if she allowed herself to be in the care of an "alien"! Her demand that I affirm her stemmed from the fear she was unaffirmable, the demand that I love her, from the terror that I would not freely do so.

So I would go for her fear. I would expose it to her. I would sympathize with her. "God, Charlene," I would say, "I don't know how you can live with all that terror. I surely wouldn't want to be in your shoes. I don't envy you your constant dread." At the time, I wasn't able to give Charlene the sympathy she often demanded. Today I would be. Of course she might utterly reject the terms on which it was given. On the other hand, it would be a very genuine compassion that I would offer, and through it she might come to realize that she did indeed desperately need healing.

Finally, I would offer her that healing. When I was working with her I felt almost overwhelmed by Charlene's sickness. I wasn't sure I had the power to cure her. Now, in fact, I know that I, alone, did not and still do not have the power and that the psychoanalytic method I used was not wholly the right approach to her. Then I knew no other way to go. Today is different. I do know another approach, far more appropriate and possibly effective in such a case. Today, if I could see evidence that a healthy part of her wanted the whole to be healed, I would with conviction and authority offer Charlene the possible means of her salvation: deliverance and exorcism.

# OF POSSESSION
# AND EXORCISM

## Ξ DOES THE DEVIL EXIST?

Five years ago when I began work on this book I could no longer avoid the issue of the demonic. The cases of George and Charlene had tentatively raised the issue, but neither required its resolution. Writing directly on the subject of evil was another matter, however. Having come over the years to a belief in the reality of benign spirit, or God, and a belief in the reality of human evil, I was left facing an obvious intellectual question: Is there such a thing as evil spirit? Namely, the devil?

I thought not. In common with 99 percent of psychiatrists and the majority of clergy, I did not think the devil existed. Still, priding myself on being an open-minded scientist, I felt I had to examine the evidence that might challenge my inclination in the matter. It occurred to me that if I could see one good old-fashioned case of possession I might change my mind.

Of course I did not believe that possession existed. In fifteen years of busy psychiatric practice I had never seen anything faintly resembling a case. Admittedly, for the first ten of those years I might, with my prejudice, have walked right over one and not known it. But in the five years since George and Charlene

I had been vaguely open to the possibility and still had not seen a case. I doubted that I ever would.

But the fact that I had never seen a case did not mean such cases, past or present, were out of the question. I had discovered a large volume of literature on the subject—none of it "scientific." Much of it seemed naïve, simplistic, shoddy, or sensational. A few authors, however, seemed thoughtful and sophisticated, and they invariably stated that genuine possession was a very rare phenomenon. I therefore could not assume it to be unreal on the basis of limited experience.

So I decided to go out and look for a case. I wrote around and let it be known that I was interested in observing cases of purported possession for evaluation. Referrals trickled in. The first two cases turned out to be suffering from standard psychiatric disorders, as I had suspected, and I began making marks on my scientific pistol.

The third case turned out to be the real thing.

Since then I have also been deeply involved with another case of genuine possession. In both cases I was privileged to be present at their successful exorcisms. The vast majority of cases described in the literature are those of possession by minor demons. These two were highly unusual in that both were cases of Satanic possession. I now know Satan is real. I have met it.

The reader will be naturally disappointed—even skeptical—that I am not going to describe either of these cases in depth. But there are a number of compelling reasons for my withholding such descriptions. The most compelling is that to describe just one of these cases would completely unbalance this book. Each case was extraordinarily complex—far more so than usual psychiatric patients. To begin to do justice to one of them would require a small book in itself. Genuine possession, as far as we know, is very rare. Human evil, on the other hand, is common. Since the relationship between possession and ordinary evil is obscure at best, it would be highly unrealistic to devote half these pages to the subject. Nonetheless, I might be tempted to do so were it not for the fact that there is a book that describes quite well five cases of possession—Malachi Martin's *Hostage to the Devil.** All of my experience confirms the accuracy and depth of understanding of

* Bantam Books, 1977.

Martin's work, and a case description of my own would contribute practically nothing beyond his writings.

The skeptical reader is likely to ask, "How can you hope to prove to me the reality of the devil when you don't even present your evidence?" The answer is that I don't hope to convince the reader of Satan's reality. Conversion to a belief in God generally requires some kind of actual encounter—a personal experience—with the living God. Conversion to a belief in Satan is no different. I had read Martin's book before witnessing my first exorcism, and while I was intrigued, I was hardly convinced of the devil's reality. It was another matter after I had personally met Satan face-to-face. There is no way I can translate my experience into your experience. It is my intent, however, that, as a result of my experience, closed-minded readers will become more open-minded in relation to the reality of evil spirit.

Finally, on the basis of two cases alone, I am simply not able to offer a broad, in-depth, scientific presentation on the subjects of evil spirit, possession, and exorcism. It is an old maxim of science that once you answer a question, others immediately take its place. Previously I had a single question: Does the devil exist? Now that this has been answered in the affirmative to my personal satisfaction, I have several dozen new questions I did not have before. The mystery is enormous.

Nonetheless, I am equally compelled to recount some of what I think I have learned from my rather extraordinary experience in these matters. Being convinced of the reality of demonic possession, however rare, I am equally certain that clergy and psychotherapists and human-service institutions are seeing such cases, whether they know it or not. To help the victims of possession, they will need all the assistance they can get. Martin's book is certainly the place to start. But while he describes cases at least as well as I could, he is not a psychiatrist, and I think I do have some important insights to offer in addition to his. These insights center around the psychiatric aspects of possession and the psychotherapeutic aspects of exorcism. Moreover, obscure though it might be, I do believe there is some relationship between Satanic activity and human evil. This book would not be complete without offering the little we do seem to know about "The Father of Lies."

# CAUTION: HIGH VOLTAGE

One might think of exorcism and psychotherapy as utterly different, mutually exclusive approaches. The two exorcisms I witnessed, however, both seemed to me to be psychotherapeutic processes—in method as well as outcome. Indeed, a week after one exorcism, the patient, who had been seeing psychiatrists for many years, exclaimed, "All psychotherapy is a kind of exorcism!" And in my experience, all good psychotherapy does in fact combat lies.

The differences between psychoanalytic psychotherapy and exorcism fall into two categories: conceptual frames of reference and the use of power.

Almost innumerable volumes have been written about the conceptual frames of reference of Christianity and psychoanalysis, and it is not now appropriate to delve more deeply into the subject. What is appropriate is to point out that these frames of reference need not be mutually exclusive. I have been combining them in various mixtures in ordinary psychotherapy for some years with many patients and apparently with considerable success.* Increasing numbers of other therapists have been doing likewise.

As to the use of power, psychoanalytic psychotherapy and exorcism are *radically* different. Traditional psychotherapy—whether it be psychoanalytically oriented or not—deliberately makes little or no use whatsoever of power. It is conducted in an atmosphere of total freedom. The patient is free to quit therapy at any time. Indeed, he or she is free to leave even in the middle of a session—as Charlene, in fact, not infrequently did. Except for the threat of refusing to see the patient anymore (which is virtually never a constructive maneuver) the therapist has no weapons with which to push for change beyond the persuasive power of his or her own wits, understanding, and love.

Exorcism is another matter. Here the healer calls upon every power that is legitimately, lovingly available in the battle against the patient's sickness. First of all, exorcism, as far as I know, is

---

* The speech I give to professional therapists which is most frequently in demand is entitled, "The Use of Religious Concepts in Psychotherapy."

always conducted by a team of at least three or more. In a sense the team "gangs up" on the patient. Unlike traditional therapy, in which it is one "against" one, in exorcism the patient is outnumbered.

The length of an exorcism session is not preset but is at the discretion of the team leader. In ordinary psychotherapy the session is no more than an hour, and the patient knows this. If they want to, patients can evade almost any issue for an hour. But exorcism sessions may last three, five, even ten or twelve hours—as long as the team feels is required to confront the issue. Also, the patient may be forcefully restrained during an exorcism session—and, indeed, frequently is—which is one of the reasons for the team approach. He or she cannot, like Charlene, walk out whenever things get unpleasant.

Finally—and most important—the exorcism team, through prayer and ritual, invokes the power of God in the healing process. For the nonbeliever this may seem like an ineffective measure, or else its effectiveness would be explained in terms of the mere power of suggestion. Speaking as a believer, I can only offer my personal experience of the presence of God in the room during the exorcisms I witnessed.* Indeed, as far as the Christian exorcist is concerned, it is not he or she who successfully completes the process; it is God who does the healing. The whole purpose of the prayer and ritual is to bring the power of God into the fray.

So it is that exorcism is seen by its practitioners in terms of spiritual warfare. The strategy is not, one hopes, that "all is fair in war." But the exorcist does believe it is legitimate to use any and every loving means—to ask for any loving help and use any loving resource—that can be summoned or otherwise made available in the battle.

The key word is "loving."

Because it not only condones but insists on the use of power, I consider exorcism to be a dangerous procedure. Power is always subject to misuse. But the simple fact of its potential danger is hardly reason to outlaw it. The four-hour neurosurgical procedure that I underwent three years ago to relieve the pressure of

---

* A confirmed atheist who witnessed the same exorcisms did not have that same experience, although there is much about them he cannot explain. For me, however, the power of God on these occasions was palpable.

disc and bone on the spinal cord in my neck was dangerous; it also made it possible for me to be writing these very words this very moment instead of being a bedridden quadriplegic or insane with chronic pain. From my vantage point, exorcism stands in relation to ordinary psychotherapy as radical surgery does to lancing a boil. Radical surgery can be not only healing but life-saving, and, in fact, may be the only way to heal in certain cases unresponsive to more conservative therapy.

One issue to be considered in relation to the use of power in exorcism is that of brainwashing. I have struggled with this issue and have concluded that exorcism is indeed a form of brainwashing. One individual whose exorcism I witnessed was highly ambivalent after the procedure—simultaneously feeling relieved, profoundly grateful, and raped. In the years since then the feelings of gratitude and relief have, if anything, increased, and the sense of rape has faded—as does the trauma of surgery.

What prevents exorcism from being true rape is that, as with surgery, the individual consents to the procedure. One safeguard against the misuse of power in exorcism is to bear in mind the extreme importance of this issue of consent. I suspect some exorcists consider it too lightly. And perhaps one thing we practitioners of traditional medicine and surgery can contribute to exorcism is an insistence on "informed consent." So it is that before surgery we will formally and legally read patients their rights—or rather a list of rights they are consenting to forfeit. During the procedure of exorcism patients forfeit a great deal of their freedom. I firmly believe this forfeiture should be under legal conditions and conducted in a legal manner. Before the procedure patients should sign not simple but elaborate authorization forms. They should know exactly what they are letting themselves in for. And if a patient is clearly incapable of such awareness, a guardian should be legally appointed to make a reasoned decision for him or her.*

Other safeguards should be employed as well. An objective

---

* This last position may currently verge on the idealistic and impractical. In specific, desperate instances I would probably forgo it. Conservative lawyers would argue that no patient who is possessed or in need of exorcism is mentally competent to give such authorization. And the courts would likely not authorize the procedure of exorcism, except on the testimony of traditional psychiatrists, who do not believe in it to begin with.

record should be kept of the proceedings which can be made public if the patient or guardian desires. At the very least, this record should be an audiotape. Preferably it should be a video-tape.* A relative should be present if one suitably detached can be found.

But the greatest safeguard is love. Only with love can exorcists discern between interventions that are "fair" and necessary and those that are manipulative or truly violating. Only with love can practitioners be sure to keep the patients' best interests in mind at all times and be certain of resisting the omnipresent human tendency to become unscrupulous and enamored with power. Indeed, in all serious cases more is required than knowledge and skill; it is only love that can heal.

Exorcism is not a magical procedure—unless one considers love to be magical. As in psychotherapy, it makes use of analysis, of careful discernment, of interpretation, of encouragement, and of loving confrontation. It differs from traditional psychotherapy only as open-heart surgery differs from a tonsillectomy. Exorcism is psychotherapy by massive assault.

Like any massive assault, it is potentially quite dangerous and should be used only in cases so severe that lesser varieties of psy-chotherapy are doomed to failure. Moreover, it should be re-garded an experimental procedure until it has been scientifically investigated. In exorcism one is dealing with very high voltages.

The whole purpose of an exorcism is to uncover and isolate the demonic within the patient so that it can then be expelled. The demonic can have a tremendous energy of its own. Perhaps there are cases in which this energy is too powerful for either the patient or the team to cope with. Or the patient may not truly desire to be rid of it. Then the outcome of an exorcism would probably leave the patient worse off than before. The result could conceivably even be fatal. In such cases it would

---

* This safeguard does not simply have moral-legal utility; it is a potentially invaluable aid in the healing process. The exorcism team may need the record to check their remembrance of events in the heat of battle with the emotionless validity of tapes. Review of the tapes may also be extremely helpful to the patient, who often has difficulty believing that "it really all happened," and can be a very effective tool in the more ordinary psycho-therapy that should invariably follow an exorcism. Finally, given the pa-tient's permission, such tapes will be invaluable for both research and teaching purposes.

be better if the "high voltage" demonic energy had never been tapped into or uncovered in the first place. Before both exorcisms in which I participated, the patients signed consent forms acknowledging their awareness that the exorcism might fail and that they might even die as a result of the procedure. (This should give the reader some notion of their courage and desperation.)

Then there is the danger to the exorcist and the other team members. From my limited experience, I suspect Martin may have overemphasized the physical dangers. But the psychological dangers are real and enormous. Both the exorcisms I witnessed were successful. I shudder to think what the effect would have been on the exorcist or other team members—on me—if they had failed. Even though all team members had been carefully chosen for their psychological strength as well as their love, the procedures were stressful for everyone. And even though the outcome was successful, most had emotional reactions to contend with in the weeks afterward.

I might add that exorcism is not what one would ordinarily think of as a "cost effective" procedure. The first (and easier) required a team of seven highly trained professionals to work (without payment) four days, twelve to sixteen hours a day. The second involved a similar team, of nine men and women, who worked twelve to twenty hours a day for three days. Not that it is necessarily always such a massive undertaking. I remind the reader that both cases were apparently unusual in being Satanic possession.

Difficult and dangerous though they were, the exorcisms I witnessed were successful. I cannot imagine how otherwise the two patients could have been healed. They are both alive and very well today. I have every reason to believe that had they not had their exorcisms they would each be dead by now.


## ASPECTS OF DIAGNOSIS AND TREATMENT

The two persons whose exorcism I witnessed were dramatically different people. One was hypomanic and intermittently psychotic before the procedure; the other was neurotically depressed but eminently sane. One was of very average intelligence, the other of very superior intelligence. One was a loving parent, one an abusive parent. The one who looked sicker had the easier exorcism; the one who looked more sane had the deeper possession and the more ghastly struggle for healing. There was a unique flavor to each of their personalities.

But some aspects of their possession and exorcism were strikingly similar. I am going to speak now throughout this subsection about these similarities because they may serve as guidelines in the understanding of the nature of possession and exorcism. I can do so, however, only with the caveat that two cases do not a science make, and one should not expect a case to conform to such guidelines.

From both these cases I would conclude that possession is no accident. I very much doubt that somebody can go walking down the street one day and have a demon jump out from behind a bush and penetrate him. Possession appears to be a gradual process in which the possessed person repeatedly sells out for one reason or another. The primary reason both these patients sold out seemed to be loneliness. Each was terribly lonely, and each, early in the process, adopted the demonic as a kind of imaginary companion. But there were also secondary reasons involved—reasons that I suspect might be primary in other cases.

In one patient the process seemed to begin with involvement in the occult at the age of twelve.* In the other the process ap-

* It seems clear from the literature on possession that the majority of cases have had involvement with the occult—a frequency far greater than might be expected in the general population. It is difficult to discern which comes first: the occult involvement or the possession. I do not mean to imply that most people who involve themselves with the occult will become possessed. But they do seem to increase their chances. The traditional Church has spoken of the danger of the occult as far back as its literature goes.

From the beginning the traditional Church has recognized the reality that certain human beings could have "supernatural" powers, such as ESP or prophetic ability. It labeled such powers "charisms," or gifts. By this word, "gift," the Church implies that such powers should be given to humans by God at a time and for a purpose of God's own choosing. When one involves oneself in the occult, wittingly or unwittingly, one is attempting to obtain, maintain, or enhance such power for one's own purposes. This the Church calls magic. Practitioners of the occult often also refer to it as magic, but they distinguish between white magic and black magic. White magicians decry black magicians for practicing their art for malevolent motives but feel comfortable with their own practice because they are convinced of their loving motives. But it is very easy to be self-deceptive about one's motives. So, as far as the Church is concerned, magic is magic, and all of it is black or potentially so.

parently began at the age of five with something more ghastly than what one would ordinarily consider occult.

Possession in both cases seemed to create what psychiatrists call fixation at the age of its onset. During the exorcism one patient, when the healthy self was free to speak, gave the most poignant expression of fixation I have ever heard: "I haven't learned anything these past twenty years. I'm really just twelve years old. How can I possibly function after the exorcism? I'm way too young to be married and have children. How can I have sex and be a parent when I'm only twelve?" After the exorcism the other patient, whose possession began at age five, had to deal in intensive psychotherapy with all manner of five-year-old fears, misconceptions, issues, and transferences.

Both patients were highly predisposed to their possession by multiple stresses before and after the onset of their possession. Both were victims of human evil as well as demonic evil. In particular, while both had been supported by the traditional Church in some minor ways, each had been deeply hurt in major ways by evil people under the guise or auspices of the Church.

Just as possession is a process, exorcism is also a process. In fact, exorcism begins not only long before the "exorcism proper" but even before the patient is first seen by the exorcist. Psychotherapists should understand this. Usually the biggest step in the healing process in ordinary cases occurs when the client first decides to see a psychotherapist. In such situations people have already identified themselves as ill and have made the decision to work against their illness and to enlist professional help in that work. At some point both these patients decided to fight back against their possession. Friendly though it had seemed at first, they had eventually concluded that the demonic within them did not have their best interests in mind. And so the struggle began. Indeed, it is probably only because of that struggle that the possession ever comes to light. It is because there is a struggle going on between an intact human soul and the infesting demonic energy that Martin correctly states that all cases of what we call possession ought more properly be referred to as "partial possession" or "imperfect possession."*

The diagnosis of possession is not an easy one to make. Neither of these two cases had "bulging eyes" or demonstrated any clearly

* *Hostage to the Devil.*

supernatural phenomena before the exorcism proper. Both showed multiple manifestations of routine mental illness such as depression or hysteria or loosening of associations. Authorities who encounter cases often like to ask, "Is the patient possessed or is he or she mentally ill?" It is not a valid question. As far as I can currently understand these matters, there has to be a significant emotional problem for the possession to occur in the first place. Then the possession itself will both enhance that problem and create new ones. The proper question is: "Is the patient just mentally ill or is he or she mentally ill and possessed?"

My first case was a patient who had originally gone to another psychiatrist to be treated for an actual complaint of possession. The psychiatrist—unusually skilled, open-minded and caring—did not believe this self-diagnosis and repeatedly attempted to treat the case with drugs or psychotherapy, without any success. (It should be noted that this very wise man was most helpful to the patient later, both before and after the exorcism.) Even after I had been called into the case a year later, I spent four hours with the patient before I had the first subtle inkling that something might be going on beyond standard psychopathology.

My second case had been in fairly intense analytically oriented psychotherapy with an unusually experienced spiritually oriented woman for over a year and a half before the therapist even began to suspect that possession might be involved. It was the therapist in this case who first raised the issue. Indeed, the therapist believes it is precisely because of the gains that the patient made in psychotherapy that the possession began to be revealed.

The time from the beginning of the specific evaluation of the issue of possession until the exorcism proper was six months in one case and nine months in the other. In each case the diagnosis was made not on the basis of a single finding but on a whole conglomeration and pattern of many findings over time.

In both cases the major distinction in differential diagnosis was between possession and multiple personality disorder. In these cases there were two distinguishing features. In multiple personality disorder the "core personality" is virtually always unaware of the existence of the secondary personalities—at least until close to the very end of prolonged, successful treatment. In other words, a true dissociation exists. In these two cases, however, both patients were either aware from the beginning or were readily made aware not only of the self-destructive part of them but also that this part had a distinct and *alien* personality. Not that they were not confused by this secondary personality. To the contrary, it quickly became clear that the secondary personality *desired* to confuse them. In many ways the secondary personality seemed like a personified resistance. The second differentiation is that while in multiple personality disorders the secondary personality may play the role of the "whore" or "the aggressive one" or "the independent one" or someone with other unacknowledged traits, it has never been reported to my knowledge as being frankly evil. In both these cases before exorcism the secondary personality was revealed to be blatantly evil.

A crucial part in this diagnostic uncovering process was an attempted deliverance. Deliverance is a sort of "mini-exorcism" frequently conducted over the past two decades by charismatic Christians to treat people suffering from "oppression" (defined as a sort of halfway state between demonic temptation—which the charismatics would say we all undergo—and frank possession).* In one case the deliverance itself was a failure, but when the patient was vigorously confronted afterward by part of the deliverance team (which had originally numbered four), an utterly evil persona temporarily emerged. The deliverance team of three in the second case was successful after six hours in identifying a lesser demonic spirit and in apparently casting it out. The patient (not a hysterical type of person in the least) experienced dramatic, extraordinary improvement for six weeks. But then the bottom fell out. Overnight the patient regressed to severe life-

---

* There is a good deal of controversy over these matters of "oppression" and deliverance. Many charismatics practice deliverance in cases in which I would find no evidence of demonic involvement. Indeed, they will attempt to cast out such things as "spirit of alcoholism," "spirit of depression," or "spirit of revenge." They report many instances of dramatic success. Yet some of us wonder how long-lasting such "cures" are, how many failed cases go unreported, and whether these almost casual and generally untrained interventions may not frequently be actually harmful. There is no way of knowing until the work of deliverance practitioners can be scientifically evaluated. For the present I still must pay some heed to one of my mentors who believes that "oppression" is a false category—that there is either possession or not and that there is either an exorcism or not. In his words, "The charismatics generally are not dealing with true demons, but occasionally they catch a real fish."

threatening illness, and shortly began to hear "the voice of Lucifer." I can only speculate as to the reasons for the very temporary success of this deliverance. Ultimately it is mysterious. But it did serve to strengthen our suspicion that the demonic was playing a major role in this person's illness.

Something now must be said of the utmost importance. While both these patients demonstrated blatantly evil secondary personalities, they were *not* evil people. I never experienced either of them as evil. Unlike Charlene, they did not *feel* evil to me. Although I said that Charlene might have been a candidate for exorcism, it is likely she would not have been. I suspect that even if I had been able to tease apart her healthy from her sick self, I might have found her secondary personality to be the healthy one and her core personality to be evil. I am not sure that exorcism can be conducted with such a configuration.

But in these cases it was very different. Not only did the core personality of each seem healthy, it seemed unusually good and potentially saintly. In fact, I admired both of these people very much even before the exorcisms. As I have indicated, they came to exorcism precisely because they had struggled against their possession for some years. A mature psychiatrist team member said, following one of the exorcisms, "I have never seen a person of such courage." Indeed, I have reason to suspect that the potential holiness of these two people was one of the reasons for their possession. More will be said about this later.

Martin has labeled the first and usually longest stage of an exorcism the "Pretense." My experience confirms this. What he meant by the Pretense is that the demonic hides within and behind the person. For the exorcism to occur, the Pretense must be broken; the demonic must be uncovered and brought into the open. Martin did not, however, comment upon the process nature of exorcism. The overriding question during the lengthy evaluation of both these patients was, "Is this person truly possessed?" To answer this question and proceed to the exorcism proper, the Pretense must be at least partially penetrated. The crucial aspect of the evaluation period is this partial penetration.

It is not the only aspect. During the evaluation the core personality needs to be both educated and encouraged. The encouragement is particularly necessary toward the end, because it is my impression from these two cases that as the exorcism proper approaches, the demonic activity "heats up" and the patients experience considerable torment.

One of the many risks of exorcism is that one cannot go into the exorcism proper with absolute, total certainty about the diagnosis of possession. In fact, one should not go into it with total certainty. For the exorcism proper is the final stripping away of the Pretense so as to come face-to-face with the demonic. I would never want to see that done by someone without the support of a loving, well-prepared team, as well as a large amount of scheduled time and careful planning. One of these patients had to be restrained for two hours during the exorcism proper; the other required almost continuous restraint for more than a day! The situation is analogous to performing major brain surgery for a suspected tumor. The surgery should not be attempted unless one is pretty sure that the tumor is there. But one cannot often be absolutely certain of what will be found until the skull flap is lifted away and the surgery has begun. So my advice would be to proceed as people proceeded in these two cases: evaluate slowly and painstakingly up to the point at which the diagnosis of possession is 95 percent certain, but do not attempt to go beyond that point before the commencement of the exorcism proper.

Once the exorcism proper was begun, with appropriate prayer and ritual, in both these cases silence seemed the most effective of the many means used for the final penetration of the Pretense. The team would speak either with the patient's healthy core personality or the demon(s) but would refuse to speak with some unclear mixture of the two. It took some time before the team in each case became adept at doing this. For the demon itself seemed to have a marked ability to draw the exorcist or team into confusing conversation that went nowhere. But as the team became more perceptive and steadfastly refused to be sucked in, both these patients began to alternate between a progressively more healthy-appearing core personality and a progressively more ugly secondary personality, until suddenly the secondary personality took on inhuman features and the Pretense was broken.

As a hardheaded scientist—which I assume myself to be—I can explain 95 percent of what went on in these two cases by traditional psychiatric dynamics. For instance, the effectiveness of the aforementioned "silent treatment" requires no demons for explanation. Perhaps particularly because they were lonely people, thirsting for relationships, the technique encouraged the appearance of separate selves (which could be related with) and hence the necessity to choose between those selves. In regard to the possession, I could talk in terms of "splitting" and "psychic introjects." And in regard to the exorcisms, I could talk in terms of brainwashing, deprogramming, reprogramming, catharsis, marathon group therapy and identification. But I am left with a critical 5 percent I cannot explain in such ways. I am left with the supernatural—or better yet, subnatural. I am left with what Martin called the Presence.

When the demonic finally spoke clearly in one case, an expression appeared on the patient's face that could be described only as Satanic. It was an incredibly contemptuous grin of utter hostile malevolence. I have spent many hours before a mirror trying to imitate it without the slightest success. I have seen that expression only one other time in my life—for a few fleeting seconds on the face of the other patient, late in the evaluation period. Yet when the demonic finally revealed itself in the exorcism of this other patient, it was with a still more ghastly expression. The patient suddenly resembled a writhing snake of great strength, viciously attempting to bite the team members. More frightening than the writhing body, however, was the face. The eyes were hooded with lazy reptilian torpor—except when the reptile darted out in attack, at which moment the eyes would open wide with blazing hatred. Despite these frequent darting moments, what upset me the most was the extraordinary sense of a fifty-million-year-old heaviness I received from this serpentine being. It caused me to despair of the success of the exorcism. Almost all the team members at both exorcisms were convinced they were at these times in the presence of something absolutely alien and inhuman. The end of each exorcism proper was signaled by the departure of this Presence from the patient and the room.

The critical moment of the exorcism is what Martin calls the "expulsion." It cannot be rushed. In both the exorcisms I witnessed, it was initially attempted prematurely. I cannot fully explain what happens at this moment, but I can state that the role of the exorcist in this moment is the least important. The desperate prayers of the team are more important. These prayers are for God or Christ to come to the rescue, and each time I had a sense that God did just that. As I said earlier, it is God that does the exorcising.

But let me amend that. Human free will is basic. It takes precedence over healing. Even God cannot heal a person who does not want to be healed. At the moment of expulsion both these patients voluntarily took the crucifix, held it to their chests and prayed for deliverance. Both chose that moment to cast their lots with God. Ultimately it is the patient herself or himself who is the exorcist.

I do not want to denigrate the man (I have never heard of a female exorcist, but I have no reason to believe that there shouldn't be one, and quickly) who is the designated exorcist—I want only to put his power in perspective. In truth, the role of exorcist is a heroic one. But the essence of the role is not any magical power at the time of expulsion. It is the gentleness and caring and patience and discernment and willingness to suffer with which he shepherds the whole exorcism process from beginning to end. It is upon his shoulders alone that the final decision rests as to whether or not the patient is truly possessed, and whether to proceed with the massive undertaking of the exorcism proper. It is he who must gather the team together, discerning who would fit and who would not. It is he who prepares both patient and team as best he can, nurturing their trust and understanding. It is he who makes crucial decisions about timing and direction during the course of the exorcism proper. It is he who must bear the fullest pain of the clash with the demonic, just as it is he who must bear the responsibility if the exorcism fails. And last, it is he who must pick up the pieces after the exorcism proper, dealing not only with the emotional reactions of all the team members but supervising the patient during the extremely critical period when he or she is utterly vulnerable and requires intense care before being finally led to safety.

Both patients of whom I have been speaking required at least two hours a day of psychotherapy for some weeks following the exorcism proper. It is a draining time.

Satan does not easily let go. After its expulsion it seems to hang around, desperately trying to get back in. In fact, in both cases it very much looked for a short while as if the exorcism proper had failed. The patients had returned largely to their pre-exorcism condition. Nonetheless, within a few hours it was possible to discern a subtle but extraordinary change. All the old complexes were back in place, but it was as if the energy had gone out of them. The change was that now these patients could listen and what they heard could now have an effect. In one case, psychotherapy became possible for the first time. In the other, more was accomplished in fifty hours of intense psychotherapy following the exorcism proper than in five hundred hours preceding it. These patients moved extraordinarily fast. It was as if they were catching up for all those lost years. But, perhaps because it moved so fast, it was tumultuous therapy, making great demands on the therapist.

I feel it important to warn others that my experience of Satan demonstrates that it does not easily let go. Satan will not only tell the patient it is still around but in one case repeatedly misled the patient into believing that it was still inside. In these cases perhaps the greatest and most diabolic of all temptations for both patient and exorcist was to believe that the exorcism proper had been a failure when in fact it had been a success.

It seemed as if the exorcism proper moved the patients from a position of demonic possession to what has been called demonic attack. The tempting, threatening, and frightening voices that each heard were at least as active afterward as before. But, as one patient said, "Before, it was like I was a little embryo, totally surrounded and hidden by them so that I could not be me. Now I am me, and while I still hear the voices, they're coming from outside of me." Or, as the other said, "Before, the voices were in control of me; now I'm in control of them."

The voices only very gradually faded away for these patients. But what was not gradual was their improvement. Given the severity of their psychopathology before their exorcisms, the rapidity of their progress to health is not explainable in terms of what we know about the ordinary psychotherapeutic process.

The teams deserve some additional mention. Each member of both came not nearly so much out of curiosity as out of love. Each, as well as the exorcist, was there at considerable personal risk and sacrifice. Consider, for instance, those two team members who offered their houses for the exorcisms. If one begins to hunt for a place to hold an exorcism—other than the patient's house which was unfeasible in each of these cases—one begins to realize the full meaning of the expression "There was no room . . . in the inn." Psychiatric hospitals don't currently want exorcisms going on in their midst. Nor do convents or monasteries. So it was up to two brave people in these cases to step forth not only with their bodies but with their homes. I have said that the presence of God was virtually palpable in the room. I do not think this was an accident. I suspect that whenever seven to ten people gather together at personal risk, motivated by love and healing, God will be there (as His Son assured us He would) and that healing will occur.

I mentioned that the primary reason each of these patients had originally sold out to the demonic was from loneliness. They were not only lonely people, but were accustomed to being lonely, and when they came to exorcism each was still basically a loner. Their courage in doing so may be all the more apparent when it is realized that neither was basically a trusting person. A major reason that the team was crucial in each exorcism was that the team gave the patients their very first experience of a true community.* There is no doubt in my mind that this experience was an essential factor in the success of both exorcisms.

Many skills were required in each of these battles with the demonic: analytic detachment, compassionate involvement, intellectual formulation, intuitive insight, spiritual discernment, deep understanding of theology, thorough knowledge of psychiatry, great experience with prayer, and others. No one person can possess all these skills. I suppose in easier exorcisms the team may be needed only to restrain the patient. But in those of which I'm speaking, while the exorcist was the coordinator in charge, a true team approach was absolutely necessary. The talents of all team members were used.

I also had a sense in both exorcisms that our weaknesses and mistakes were being used as well. It is said that Christ can use even our sins. I have spoken of the presence of God in those rooms. It may sound mystical, but when I reflected on each event, it seemed as if God or Christ had been choreographing the whole show.

The most common reaction of team members following the completion of these exorcisms was expressed by one woman

---

* Within Christian circles a great deal is spoken these days of "Christian community." But a group of nominal Christians does not a Christian community make. On the other hand, despite the fact that some team members were self-defined atheists or admittedly lukewarm Christians, there is no doubt in my mind that at each exorcism the team assembled was a true "Christian community."

when she said, "I never want to go through anything like that again, but I wouldn't have missed it for the world." Strangely, the exorcisms were healing not only for the patients but for a number of the team members as well. Another team member, a man, two weeks afterward reported: "You don't know this, but I've always had a small, cold, hard place in my heart. It's gone now. And I find I have become a better therapist." In fact, even some of the people who were not at the exorcisms but were praying for their success seemed to experience a certain healing. Mystically again, I have an inchoate sense that these exorcisms were not just isolated events but somehow almost cosmic happenings.

Still, it is the patients who served as the very center and focal point of these happenings. I salute them. Through the torment and courage of their struggle with Satan they won a great victory not only for themselves but for many.

## RESEARCH AND TEACHING

While I have endeavored to my utmost to be objective, the fact remains that the preceding account of two cases of possession and exorcism is a subjective one of my personal experience. I am certain that each team member would write a different tale. I believe that the phenomena of possession and exorcism need to be studied scientifically. It is more than a matter of idle scientific curiosity. While genuine possession may be a rare phenomenon, the subject represents a veritable untapped gold mine for scientific unearthing. Hemophilia is a rare disease, but its study did much to illumine the whole physiology of blood-clotting. In the same way, the study of possession and exorcism will further illumine not only the physiology of evil but our very understanding of human meaning.

There is a resistance to such scientific study—a part of the more general resistance of science toward the spiritual and "supernatural." It is interesting that while possession and exorcism have never been scientifically studied, to my knowledge, in America or Europe, Western anthropologists have written extensively about exorcismlike healing rituals in distant foreign or "primitive" cultures. It is as if it is somehow "OK" to study such things "over there" at a considerable distance from us as long as we don't look at what's going on closer to home among ourselves.

I do not mean to decry such anthropological research. To the contrary, I think we need more of it. The two cases I witnessed were ones of possession by a spirit that has been well described in Christian literature under the name of Satan. Would that same spirit be identifiable—under a different name—in the exorcisms of Hindus or Hottentots? Is Satan merely a demon that attacks Judeo-Christians or is it a cross-cultural, universal enemy? It is an important question.

The resistance to the scientific study of such matters close to home comes from many of the religious as well as the scientific-minded. I once proposed the establishment of an "Institute for the Study of Deliverance" to an organization of scientifically and religiously oriented professionals who were rather at odds with each other. For the first time in years they were able to unite in opposition to my proposal for the scientific study of religious healing, ranging from prayer through deliverance to exorcism. "There are too many variables; your operational definitions are fuzzy; it's inherently unresearchable," said the scientific. "Everyone knows prayer works, and you shouldn't tamper with faith," said the religious.

Actually, there are more real or worrisome problems with such an institute. For I have grave doubts that the process of exorcism should ever be institutionalized. I have said that in both cases described the team members assembled at great personal risk and sacrifice, and I profoundly suspect that this is one of the reasons the exorcisms succeeded. I am not at all sure that an exorcism could be successfully conducted by rotating shifts of nine-to-five salaried "human service" employees.

Beyond that, it is questionable just how scientifically exorcisms can be "researched." Were I to conduct an exorcism, I would not exclude from the team any mature Hindu, Buddhist, Muslim, Jew, atheist, or agnostic who was a genuinely loving presence. But I would without hesitation exclude a nominal Christian or anyone else who was not such a presence. For the presence of one unloving person in the room is likely not only to cause the exorcism to fail but to subject the team members as well as the patient to the possibility of grave harm. If lovingness is incompatible with scientific objectivity, then there can or should be no such thing as a scientific, on-the-spot observation of an exorcism. At an exorcism the only observers are the participants.

Still, it would be nice indeed to have at least some institutional support for such healing endeavors. Both patients whose cases I recounted were gravely ill from a psychiatric standpoint before their exorcisms. It would have been much easier if there had been a psychiatric hospital available to care for acknowledged cases of possession. And it would have been much easier for all concerned if the institutional Church had been more open to offering its sponsorship, blessing, and service. While there was cooperation from some Church authorities in both cases, the more general response of the Church was to try to avoid any involvement. The Church's fear of repercussions in such cases is both natural and realistic but not necessarily humane.

At the very least, a centralized data bank and study center is required. To this center could be sent reports of cases and video tapes of exorcisms. With thorough safeguards for confidentiality, authorized behavioral scientists could come to the center to examine the data. Although much of the true flavor and spiritual energy of the experience would be missing from such data, it would still be sufficient basis for many valuable scientific studies.

The center could also serve for teaching. It could develop standards for diagnosis and treatment which would diminish the number of irresponsible exorcisms and deliverances that are likely to occur. It could also conduct training seminars for appropriately selected people. While genuine possession may be rare, we do know that there are more cases than can be treated by currently available competent exorcists.

## THE FATHER OF LIES

Toward the end of one exorcism, in response to a comment that the spirit must really hate Jesus, the patient, with a full-blown Satanic facial expression, said in a silky, oily voice, "We don't hate Jesus; we just test him." In the middle of the other exorcism, when asked whether the possession was by multiple spirits, the patient with hooded, serpentine eyes answered quietly, almost in a hiss, "They all belong to me."

As the title of a recent article asks, "Who in the hell is Satan?"*

* *U.S. Catholic*, Feb. 1983, pp. 7–11.

I don't know.

The experience of two exorcisms is hardly sufficient for one to unravel all the mystery of the spiritual realm. Nor would the experience of a hundred be sufficient. But I think I now know a few things about Satan and also have the basis to make a few speculations.

While my experience is insufficient to prove Judeo-Christian myth and doctrine about Satan, I have learned nothing that fails to support it. According to this myth and doctrine, in the beginning Satan was God's second-in-command, chief among all His angels, the beautiful and beloved Lucifer. The service it performed in God's behalf was to enhance the spiritual growth of human beings through the use of testing and temptation—just as we test our own children in school so as to enhance their growth. Satan, therefore, was primarily a teacher of mankind, which is why it was called Lucifer, "the light bearer."* As time went by, however, Satan became so enamored with its adversarial functions that it began to employ them more for its own delight than on God's behalf. This we see in the Book of Job. Coincidentally, God decided that something more was required than simple testing for the uplifting of mankind; what was required was both an example of His love and an example to live by. So He sent His only son to live and die as one of us. Satan was superseded by Christ both in function and in God's heart. It was so enamored of itself that Satan perceived this as an intolerable personal insult. Puffed up with pride, it refused to submit to God's judgment of the precedence of Christ. It rebelled against God. Satan itself created the situation in which heaven became literally not big enough for the both of them. So Satan was inevitably, by its own doing, immediately cast out into hell, where, once the light bearer, it now dwells in darkness as the Father of Lies, nursing continual dreams of revenge against God. And through the angels at its command, who joined it in its rebellion and fall, it

---

* The original meaning of the words "satan" and "devil" were not pejorative, as they are today. "Devil" and "diabolic" come from the Greek verb *diabalein*, meaning simply "to oppose." The word "satan" commonly meant "adversary." In the Book of Numbers, God Himself stated that He was proceeding against Balaam as a satan. Seeing the necessity for mankind to be tested and tempted by something in *opposition* to His own will, God delegated this oppositional (diabolic) and adversarial (satanic) function to the chief of His archangels.

now wages continual war against God's design. Where once it existed to spiritually uplift mankind, it now exists to spiritually destroy us. In the battle for our souls it attempts to oppose Christ at every turn. Satan perceives Christ as its personal enemy. As Christ in spirit lives, so is Satan the living Antichrist.

The spirit I witnessed at each exorcism was clearly, utterly, and totally dedicated to opposing human life and growth. It told both patients to kill themselves. When asked in one exorcism why it was the Antichrist, it answered, "Because Christ taught people to love each other." When further questioned as to why human love was so distasteful, it replied, "I want people to work in business so that there will be war." Queried more, it simply said to the exorcist, "I want to kill you." There was absolutely nothing creative or constructive about it; it was purely destructive.

Perhaps the greatest problem of theodicy is the question why God, having created Satan in the first place, simply didn't wipe it out after its rebellion. The question presupposes that God would wipe anything out. It assumes that God can punish and kill. Perhaps the answer is that God gave Satan free will and that God cannot destroy; He can only create.

The point is that God does not punish. To create us in His image, God gave us free will. To have done otherwise would have been to make us puppets or hollow mannequins. Yet to give us free will God had to forswear the use of force against us. We do not have free will when there is a gun pointed at our back. It is not necessarily that God lacks the power to destroy us, to punish us, but that in His love for us He has painfully and terribly chosen never to use it. In agony He must stand by and let us be. He intervenes only to help, never to hurt. The Christian God is a God of restraint. Having forsworn the use of power *against* us, if we refuse His help, He has no recourse but, weeping, to watch us punish ourselves.

This point is unclear in the Old Testament. There God is depicted as punitive. But it begins to become clear with Christ. In Christ, God Himself impotently suffered death at the hands of human evil. He did not raise a finger against His persecutors. Thereafter in the New Testament we hear echoes of the punitive Old Testament God, one way or another, saying that "the wicked will get what's coming to them." But these are only echoes; a punishing God does not enter the picture ever again.

While many nominal Christians still today envision their God as a giant cop in the sky, the reality of Christian doctrine is that God has forever eschewed police power.

Of the Holocaust as well as of lesser evils it is often asked, "How could a loving God allow such a thing to happen?" It is a bleeding, brutal question. The Christian answer may not suit our tastes, but it is hardly ambiguous. Having forsaken force, God is impotent to prevent the atrocities that we commit upon one another. He can only continue to grieve with us. He will offer us Himself in all His wisdom, but He cannot make us choose to abide with Him.

For the moment, then, God, tormented, waits upon us through one holocaust after another. And it may seem to us that we are doomed by this strange God who reigns in weakness. But there is a dénouement to Christian doctrine: God in His weakness will win the battle against evil. In fact, the battle is already won. The resurrection symbolizes not only that Christ overcame the evil of His day two millennia ago but that He overcame it for all time. Christ impotently nailed upon the cross is God's ultimate weapon. Through it the defeat of evil is utterly assured. It is vitally necessary that we struggle against evil with all the power at our command. But the crucial victory occurred almost two thousand years ago. Necessary and even dangerous and devastating though our own personal battles may be, unknown to us they are but mopping-up operations against a retreating enemy who has long since lost the war.

This idea that Satan (and its works), despite all appearances, is actually on the run offers a possible answer to a major question of mine. I have spoken of the factors that predisposed both of the two patients to their possession. But what about the far greater number of children who are also lonely victims of human evil and have even more serious character defects as a result yet who do not apparently become possessed? Why not? I also mentioned a quality of potential holiness in the personalities of both patients. I wonder if they did not become possessed precisely because of this potential holiness. I wonder if Satan did not specifically invest its energy in attacking them because they represented a particular threat to its designs. Perhaps Satan does not have the energy left to go wherever there is human weakness. Perhaps it is frantically engaged in attempting to put out the fires.

Be that as it may, as Martin points out, it is terribly important to understand that Satan is a spirit. I have said I have met Satan, and this is true. But it is not tangible in the way that matter is tangible. It no more has horns, hooves, and a forked tail than God has a long white beard.* Even the name, Satan, is just a name we have given to something basically nameless. Like God, Satan can manifest itself in and through material beings, but it itself is not material, nor is it even its manifestations. In one case described it manifested itself through the patient's writhing serpentine body, biting teeth, scratching nails, and hooded reptilian eyes. But there were no fangs, no scales. It was, through the use of the patient's body, extraordinarily and dramatically and even supernaturally snakelike. But it is not itself a snake. It is spirit.

Herein lies an answer, I suspect, to a question that has been asked through the ages: Why do demonic spirits have such an attachment to bodies? During one of the exorcisms I witnessed the exorcist attempted to so enrage Satan that it would leave the possessed's restrained body to attack him, the exorcist. The maneuver did not work. Despite its obvious homicidal fury at the exorcist, nothing happened. And slowly it dawned on us that the spirit either could not or would not leave the patient's body under such conditions. This led us to two conclusions. One, already mentioned, is that ultimately the patient had to be the exorcist. The other is that *Satan has no power except in a human body*.

Satan cannot do evil except through a human body. Although "a murderer from the beginning," it cannot murder except with human hands. It does not have the power to kill or even harm by itself. It must use human beings to do its deviltry. Although it repeatedly threatened to kill the possessed and the exorcists, its threats were empty. Satan's threats are always empty. They are all lies.

In fact, *the only power that Satan has is through human belief in its lies*. Both patients became possessed because they bought its false seductive promise of "friendship." Possession was maintained because they believed its threats that they would die without it. And the possession was ended when both chose to believe its lies

* John A. Sanford suggests that the horned image of Satan was derived from the pre-Christian horned male God of the British: "the gods of the old religion always become the devils of the new" (*Evil: The Shadow Side of Reality* [Crossroad, 1981], p. 118).

no longer but to transcend their fear by trust in the resurrected Christ and to pray to the God of Truth for deliverance. During each exorcism Satan's lies were confronted. And each exorcism was concluded successfully by a conversion of sorts—a change of faith or value system. I now know what Jesus meant when he so frequently said, "By your faith you have been healed."

So we are back to lies. Whatever relationship it might have to the "people of the lie," I know no more accurate epithet for Satan than the Father of Lies. Throughout both exorcisms it lied continually. Even when it revealed itself, it did so with half-truths. It was revealed to be the Antichrist when it said, "We don't hate Jesus, we just test him." But the reality is that it does hate Jesus.

The list of lies it spoke was endless—sometimes almost a boring litany. The major ones I remember were: humans must defend themselves in order to survive and cannot rely on anything other than themselves in their defense; everything is explainable in terms of negative and positive energy (which balance out to be zero), and there is no mystery in the world; love is a thought and has no objective reality; science is whatever one chooses to call science; death is the absolute end to life—there is no more; all humans are motivated primarily by money, and if this appears not to be the case, it is only because they are hypocrites; to compete for money, therefore, is the only intelligent way to live.

Satan can use any human sin or weakness—greed and pride, for instance. It will use any available tactic: seduction, cajolery, flattery, intellectual argument. But its principal weapon is fear. And in the postexorcism period, after its lies had been exposed, it was reduced to haunting both patients with dully repetitive threats: "We will kill you. We will get you. We will torture you. We will kill you."

As well as being the Father of Lies, Satan may be said to be a spirit of mental illness. In *The Road Less Traveled* I defined mental health as "an ongoing process of dedication to reality at all costs."* Satan is utterly dedicated to opposing that process. In fact, the best definition I have for Satan is that it is *a real spirit of unreality*. The paradoxical reality of this spirit must be recognized. Although intangible and immaterial, it has a personality, a

* Simon & Schuster, 1978, p. 51.

true being. We must not fall back into Saint Augustine's now discarded doctrine of the "privatio boni," whereby evil was defined as the absence of good. Satan's personality cannot be characterized simply by an absence, a nothingness. It is true that there is an absence of love in its personality. It is also true, however, that pervading this personality is an active presence of hate. Satan wants to destroy us. It is important that we understand this. There are quite popular systems of thought these days, such as Christian Science or the Course in Miracles, which define evil as unreality. It is a half-truth. The spirit of evil is one of unreality, but it itself is real. It really exists. To think otherwise is to be misled. Indeed, as several have commented, perhaps Satan's best deception is its general success in concealing its own reality from the human mind.

Although it has a real power, Satan also has glaring weaknesses—the same weaknesses that caused its banishment from heaven. Martin noted that exorcisms can reveal not only extraordinary demonic brilliance but also extraordinary demonic stupidity. My observations confirm this. Were it not for its extraordinary pride and narcissism, Satan would probably not reveal itself at all. Its pride overcomes its intelligence, so that the demon of deceit is also a showoff. If it had been thoroughly clever, it would have left the two patients long before their exorcisms. But it could not allow itself to lose. It wanted only to win, so in both cases it hung in there until the bitter end—with the result that I and others today now know its reality.

In the same way, Satan's intelligence is afflicted with two other blind spots I have observed. One is that by virtue of its extreme self-centeredness, it has no real understanding of the phenomenon of love. It recognizes love as a reality to be fought and even to be imitated, but utterly lacking it itself, it does not understand love in the least. Its reality appears to Satan only like the reality of a bad joke. The notion of sacrifice is totally foreign to it. When human beings at an exorcism are speaking in the language of love, it does not comprehend what they are saying. And when they are behaving with love, Satan is completely ignorant of the ground rules.

Interestingly, particularly in view of the purpose of this book, Satan also does not understand science. Science is an antinarcissistic phenomenon. It assumes a profound human tendency to self-deception, employs the scientific method to counteract it, and holds truth higher than any personal desire. Deceiver of itself as of others, Satan cannot understand why any beings would not want to deceive themselves. Enamored with its own will and hater of the light of truth, it basically finds human science incomprehensible.

Satan's weaknesses should not encourage us to overlook its strength. It propounds its lies with extraordinary power. It may not be so remarkable that it possessed the two people I have described when they were lonely children. But in each exorcism I witnessed the exorcist—strong, mature, and faithful—temporarily incapacitated by confusion in one case and by despair in the other as a result of the power of its lies.

I think it is necessary that we should hate Satan as well as fear it. Yet, as with evil people, I think it is ultimately more to be pitied. In Christian eschatology (the study of the last days) there are two scenarios for Satan. In one all human souls, having been converted to light and love, reach out to the spirit of hate and falsehood in friendship. Finally realizing itself to be totally defeated, with no human body left to possess, with all immune to its power, out of utter loneliness it breaks down and accepts the offer of friendship, and thereby in the end even Satan is converted. That is the scenario I pray for. But, as I have said, free will takes precedence over healing. In the other scenario, refusing ever to lose, Satan forever rejects the "humiliating" hands of friendship and suffers its icy solitariness until the end of time. A friend who participated in one of the exorcisms with me said afterward, "You know, Scotty, you had told me about the dreariness of evil, and how it is to be more pitied than hated, but I did not believe you. Yet one of my most profound impressions of the exorcism was of how boring it was—that endless string of silly lies. And when I saw that beast writhing in stupid agony for all eternity, I knew what you had meant."

For the sake of clarity I have possibly talked about Satan with too much definitiveness. I described the greater part of both exorcisms as a process of separation. Yet even at their clearest moments it was often impossible to fully distinguish whether the voice talking was that of the patient's unconscious or one of a true demon. Perhaps it will forever be impossible to totally discern exactly where the human Shadow leaves off and the Prince of Darkness begins. It is appropriate to conclude by focusing on the supernatural mystery of Satan. The evidence of the exorcisms was sufficient for me to become a believer in its existence, and I cannot deny the reality of the healing that occurred, but I am left with many more questions than before—too many even to detail.

One of the more important questions concerns the existence of lesser demons. Both cases I witnessed were of Satanic possession, while those in the literature are almost always ones of more minor possession. Is my experience just accidental or somehow by mysterious design? Actually, lesser demons were seemingly encountered in both cases. In one the team went through four successive named spirits (each representing a particular lie) before the Antichrist was reached. In the other the patient was delivered of a lesser spirit with apparent dramatic but temporary healing before "Lucifer" mysteriously took its place. What was going on? Were these lesser spirits individual entities in their own right or were they simply reflections of the underlying Satan? I do not know. There is, however, some evidence to suggest that there is less freedom in the world of demons than in the world of human beings—that, by virtue of their cowardice and terror and belief in their own lies, lesser demons act in such strict obedience to their superiors that they tend to lack individuality as we ordinarily think of it.

The most important question, however, is the role that Satan plays in human evil. What is the influence of Satan on thoroughly evil people such as Bobby's and Roger's parents and Sarah and Charlene? As I have said, both the possessed people I saw did not, like them, seem to me evil; and Martin correctly states that the rare cases we call possession should more properly be termed "partial," "incomplete," or "imperfect" possession. Martin suggests the hypothesis that "perfectly possessed" human beings may exist, even abound, but he offers this hypothesis only as a highly tentative one. Could the thoroughly evil people I have described be cases of perfect possession? I do not know. Perhaps it is even a moot question. Since they are the least likely to submit themselves to psychotherapy, the truly evil are even less likely to undergo an exorcism through which the demonic would be fully discovered. If there is such a thing as perfect possession, it is highly likely to preclude its own revelation.

So I have no idea whether Satan actively recruits the commonly evil to its work. I suspect not. Given the dynamics of sin and narcissism, I suspect they recruit themselves. But until such time as we have greater knowledge of Satan, my understanding remains faint.

# MYLAI:
# AN EXAMINATION
# OF GROUP EVIL

Ξ  BEFORE EXORCISM (in part, deservedly) fell into ill repute during an Age of Science and Rationalism, exorcists were openly recognized in the Church hierarchy. Referred to as a "minor order," they were near the bottom of the status structure. It was, and still is, I think, an appropriate positioning. Demanding and sacrificial though it might be, I have come to perceive the role of exorcist as a relatively easy one. It is an unusual and rewarding privilege to encounter evil in a form in which it can be isolated and cast out.

The ordinary parish priest or minister is not in so fortunate a position. The evil she or he commonly encounters in parishioners, in vestry meetings, and in society is not so discrete or curable. It is more subtle and penetrating and devastating. And no matter how loving and intelligent, such a clergy-person must battle blindly with the forces of darkness. There will seem to be few, if any, clear successes. It is to an example of these diffuse cancerous forces at work in our society that we now turn our attention.

## THE CRIMES

On the morning of March 16, 1968, elements of Task Force Barker moved into a small group of hamlets known collectively as MyLai in the Quang Ngai province of South Vietnam. It was intended to be a typical "search-and-destroy mission"—that is, the American troops were searching for Vietcong soldiers so as to destroy them.

Relative to other units operating in Vietnam, the troops of Task Force Barker had been somewhat hastily trained and thrown together. In the previous month they had achieved no military success. Unable to engage the enemy, they had themselves sustained a number of casualties from mines and booby traps. The province was considered to be a Vietcong stronghold, one in which the civilian population was largely controlled and influenced by the Communist guerrillas. It was generally felt that the civilians aided and abetted the guerrillas to such a degree that it was often difficult to distinguish the combatants from the noncombatants. Hence the Americans tended to hate and distrust all Vietnamese in the area.

Army intelligence had indicated that the Vietcong were currently being harbored by the villagers of MyLai. The task force expected to find combatants there. On the eve of the operation there seemed to be a mood of anticipation; finally they would engage the enemy and succeed in doing what they were there for.

The nature of the instructions given to the enlisted men and junior officers that evening by the senior officers was at best ambiguous in regard to the distinction betwen combatant and noncombatants. All troops were supposed to be familiar with the Geneva Convention, which makes it a crime to harm any noncombatant or, for that matter, even a combatant who has laid down his arms because of wounds or sickness. Whether they were, in fact, familiar with the convention is another matter. It is probable, however, that at least some of the troops were not familiar with the Law of Land Warfare from the U.S. Army Field Manual, which specifies that orders in violation of the Geneva Convention are illegal and not to be obeyed.

Although essentially all elements of Task Force Barker were involved one way or another in the operation, the primary element of ground troops directly involved was C Company, 1st Battalion, 20th Infantry of the 11th Light Infantry Brigade. When "Charlie" Company moved into the hamlets of MyLai they discovered not a single combatant. None of the Vietnamese was armed. No one fired on them. They found only unarmed women, children, and old men.

Some of the things that then happened are unclear. What is clear, however, is that the troops of C Company killed at least somewhere between five and six hundred of those unarmed villagers. These people were killed in a variety of ways. In some instances troops would simply stand at the door of a village hut and spray into it with rifle fire, blindly killing those inside. In other instances villagers, including children, were shot down as they attempted to run away. The most large-scale killings occurred in the particular hamlet of MyLai 4. There the first platoon of Charlie Company, under the command of Lieutenant William L. Calley, Jr., herded villagers into groups of twenty to forty or more, who were then slaughtered by rifle fire, machine gun fire, or grenades. It is important to remember, however, that substantial numbers of unarmed civilians also were murdered in the other hamlets of MyLai that day by the troops of other platoons under the command of other officers.

The killing took a long time. It went on throughout the morning. Only one person tried to stop it. He was a helicopter pilot, a warrant officer, flying in support of the search-and-destroy mission. Even from the air he could see what was happening. He landed on the ground and attempted to talk to the troops, to no avail. Back in the air again, he radioed to headquarters and superior officers, who seemed unconcerned. So he gave up and went about his business.

The number of soldiers involved can only be estimated. Perhaps only about fifty actually pulled triggers. Approximately two hundred directly witnessed the killings.* We might suppose that within the week at least five hundred men in Task Force Barker knew that war crimes had been committed.

The failure to report a crime is itself a crime. In the year that followed, no one in Task Force Barker attempted to report the atrocities that had occurred at MyLai. This crime is referred to as the "cover-up."

The fact that the American public learned about MyLai at all was due solely to a letter that Ron Ridenhour wrote at the end of March 1969 to several congressmen about the atrocities—more than a year after they had occurred. Ridenhour had not himself

---

* Eventually charges were to be considered against *twenty-five*, of whom only *six* were brought to trial. One, Lieutenant Calley, was convicted.

been a part of Task Force Barker but had later heard of the
atrocities in idle conversation from friends who had been at
MyLai, and he wrote his letter three months after his return to
civilian life.

In the spring of 1972 I was chairman of a committee of three
psychiatrists appointed by the Army Surgeon General, at the request of the Chief of Staff of the Army, to make recommendations for research that might shed light on the psychological
causes of MyLai, so as to help prevent such atrocities in the future. The research we proposed was rejected by the General
Staff of the Army, reportedly on the grounds that it could not
be kept secret and might prove embarrassing to the administration and that "further embarrassment was not desirable at that
time."

The rejection of the recommendations of the committee for
research is symbolic of several issues. One is that any research
into the nature of evil is likely to prove embarrassing, not only
to those who are the designated subjects of the research but also
to the researchers themselves. If we are to study the nature of
human evil, it is doubtful how clearly we will be able to separate
*them* from *us;* it will most likely be our own natures we are examining. Undoubtedly, this potential for embarrassment is one of
the reasons we have thus far failed to develop a psychology of
evil.

The rejection by the General Staff of our recommendations
for research also highlights the fact that in considering the evil
at MyLai—as in all our other considerations of evil—we suffer
from a simple lack of scientific knowledge. In tune with what
has preceded, much of what follows is only speculative. We will
inevitably be limited to speculation until such time as we have
been able to develop, through scientific research, a body of
knowledge that constitutes a genuine psychology of evil.


## PREFACE TO GROUP EVIL

Triggers are pulled by individuals. Orders are given and executed
by individuals. In the last analysis, every single human act is ultimately the result of an individual choice. No one of the individuals who participated in the atrocities at MyLai or in their

cover-up is blameless. Even the helicopter pilot—the only one brave enough and good enough to attempt to stop the massacre—can be blamed for not reporting what he saw beyond the first echelon of authority over him.

Until now our focus has been on specific individuals whom I have labeled "evil" and distinguished from the vast majority of other individuals I have designated "not evil." Even if we allow that this sharp distinction is somewhat arbitrary—that there is a whole continuum between those who are thoroughly evil and those who are not at all evil—we are left facing a problem: How is it that approximately five hundred men, the majority of whom were undoubtedly not evil as individuals, could all have participated in an act as monstrously evil as that at MyLai? Clearly, to understand MyLai, our focus must not be limited solely to individual evil and individual choice. This chapter, therefore, concentrates on the phenomenon of group evil as being somewhat distinct from, although in many respects similar to, the phenomenon of individual evil. The relationship between individual and group evil is not a new subject for study. There is even a book on the subject specifically examining the same events: *Individual and Collective Responsibility: The Massacre at MyLai.** It is, however, the work of philosophers and not written from a psychological standpoint.

For many years it has seemed to me that human groups tend to behave in much the same ways as human individuals—except at a level that is more primitive and immature than one might expect. Why this is so—why the behavior of groups is strikingly immature—why they are, from a psychological standpoint, less than the sum of their parts—is a question beyond my capacity to answer.† Of one thing I am certain, however: that there is more than one right answer. The phenomenon of group immaturity is—to use a psychiatric term—"overdetermined." This is to say that it is the result of multiple causes. One of those causes is the problem of specialization.

Specialization is one of the greatest advantages of groups.

* Ed. Peter A. French (Cambridge, Mass.: Schenkman Pub. Co., 1972).
† It is an extremely important question, however, deserving great thought and research. It is an issue not only specific to group evil in general—as if that were not enough—but crucial to the understanding of all human group phenomena, from international relations to the nature of the family.

There are ways groups can function with far greater efficiency than individuals. Because its employees are specialized into executives and designers and tool- and diemakers and assembly-line workers (who are in turn specialized), General Motors can produce an enormous number of cars. Our extraordinarily high standard of living is entirely based on the specialization of our society. The fact that I have the knowledge and the time to write this book is a direct result of the fact that I am a specialist within our community, utterly dependent on farmers, mechanics, publishers, and booksellers for my welfare. I can hardly consider specialization in itself evil. On the other hand, I am thoroughly convinced that much of the evil of our times is related to specialization and that we desperately need to develop an attitude of suspicious caution toward it. I think we need to treat specialization with the same degree of distrust and safeguards that we bring to nuclear reactors.

Specialization contributes to the immaturity of groups and their potential for evil through several different mechanisms. For the moment I will restrict myself to the consideration of only one such mechanism: the fragmentation of conscience. If at the time of MyLai, wandering through the halls of the Pentagon, I stopped to talk with the men responsible for directing the manufacture of napalm and its transportation to Vietnam in the form of bombs, and if I questioned these men about the morality of the war and hence the morality of what they were engaged in, this is the kind of reply I invariably received: "Oh, we appreciate your concerns, yes, we do, but I'm afraid you've come to the wrong people. We're not the department you want. This is the ordnance branch. We just supply the weapons—we don't determine how and where they're used. That's policy. What you want to do is talk to the policy people down the hall." And if I followed this suggestion and expressed the same concerns in the policy branch, this was the response: "Oh, we understand that there are broad issues involved, but I'm afraid they're beyond our purview. We simply determine how the war will be conducted—not whether it will be conducted. You see, the military is only an agency of the executive branch. The military does only what it's told to do. These broad issues are decided at the White House level, not here. That's where you need to take your concerns." So it went.

Whenever the roles of individuals within a group become specialized, it becomes both possible and easy for the individual to pass the moral buck to some other part of the group. In this way, not only does the individual forsake his conscience but the conscience of the group as a whole can become so fragmented and diluted as to be nonexistent. We will see this fragmentation again and again, one way or another, in the discussion that follows. The plain fact of the matter is that any group will remain inevitably potentially conscienceless and evil until such time as each and every individual holds himself or herself directly responsible for the behavior of the whole group—the organism—of which he or she is a part. We have not yet begun to arrive at that point.

Bearing in mind the psychological immaturity of groups, we shall be examining aspects of both the MyLai crimes: the atrocities themselves and their cover-up. The two crimes are quite interwoven. Although the cover-up may seem less atrocious than the atrocities, they are part of the same ball of wax. How is it that so many individuals could have participated in such a monstrous evil without any of them being so conscience-stricken as to be compelled to confess?

The cover-up was a gigantic group lie. Lying is simultaneously one of the symptoms and one of the causes of evil, one of the blossoms and one of the roots. It is why this book is entitled *People of the Lie*. Until now we have been considering individual people of the lie. Now we will also be considering a whole people. Certainly, by virtue of their extraordinarily common—that is, communal—participation in the cover-up, the men of Task Force Barker were a "people of the lie." By the time we are finished we may even conclude that the American people, at least during those war years, were also a people of the lie.

As with any lie, the primary motive of the cover-up was fear. The individuals who had committed the crimes—who had pulled the triggers or given the orders—obviously had reason to fear reporting what they had done. Court-martial awaited them. But what of the much larger number who only witnessed the atrocities yet also said nothing of that "something rather dark and bloody"?* What did they have to fear?

---

* Phrase from the Ron Ridenhour letter.

Anyone who thinks for a while about the nature of group pressure will realize that for a member of Task Force Barker to report the crime outside of that group would require great courage. Whoever did so would be labeled a "squealer" or "stool pigeon." There is no more dreadful label that can be applied to a person than that. Stool pigeons often get murdered. At the very least they are ostracized. To the ordinary American civilian, ostracism may not seem such a horrible fate. "So, if you get kicked out of one group, you can just join another," may be the reaction. But remember that a member of the military is not free to just join another group. He can't leave the military at all until his enlistment is up. Desertion itself is an enormous crime. So he is stuck in the military and, indeed, in his particular military group, except at the discretion of the authorities. Beyond this the military does other things quite deliberately to intensify the power of group pressure within its ranks. From the standpoint of group dynamics and from military group dynamics in particular, it is not bizarre that the members of Task Force Barker failed to report the group's crimes. Nor is it surprising that the man who finally did report the crimes was neither a member of the Task Force group nor even a member of the military at the time he did the reporting.

Yet I suspect there is another extremely significant reason that the crimes of MyLai went unreported for so long. Not having spoken with the individuals involved, I offer it purely as conjecture. But I did speak with many, many soldiers who were in Vietnam during those years, and I am deeply familiar with the attitudes prevailing in the military at that time. My profound suspicion, therefore, is that to a considerable extent the members of Task Force Barker did not confess their crimes simply because they were not *aware* that they had committed them. They knew, of course, what they had done, but whether they appreciated the meaning and nature of what they had done is another matter entirely. I suspect that many of them did not even consider what they had done a crime. They did not confess because they did not realize they had anything to confess. Some undoubtedly hid their guilt. But others, I suspect, had no guilt to hide.

How can this be? How can a sane man commit murder and not know he has murdered? How is it that a person who is not basically evil may participate in monstrous evil without the awareness of what he has done? It is this question that will serve as a focal point for the discussion that follows on the relationship between individual and group evil. In attempting to answer this question, I will proceed in the consideration of evil up the ladder from the level of the individual to the level of the small group (Task Force Barker) to the levels of ever larger groups.

## UP THE LADDER OF COLLECTIVE RESPONSIBILITY

### THE INDIVIDUAL UNDER STRESS

When I was sixteen I had all four wisdom teeth removed during my spring vacation. For the next five days not only did my jaw hurt but it was swollen shut. I could eat no solid food—only liquids or spiceless baby food. The fetid taste of blood was constantly in my mouth. By the end of those five days my level of psychic functioning had been reduced to that of a three-year-old. I had become utterly self-centered. I was whiny and irritable with others. I expected them to be in constant attendance upon me. When some little thing did not go exactly the way I wanted it precisely when I wanted it, tears came to my eyes and my displeasure was mighty.

I believe that anyone who has been in significant chronic pain or discomfort—say, for a week or so—will recognize the experience I have just described. In a situation of prolonged discomfort we humans naturally, almost inevitably, tend to regress. Our psychological growth reverses itself; our maturity is forsaken. Quite rapidly we become more childish, more primitive. Discomfort is stress. What I am describing is a natural tendency of the human organism to regress in response to chronic stress.

The life of a soldier in a combat zone is one of chronic stress. Although the Army did as much as possible to minimize the stress on its troops in Vietnam (providing entertainment whenever possible, rest and recreation periods, and other forms of relaxation) the fact of the matter is that the troops of Task Force Barker were in a chronically stressful situation. They were at the other end of the world from their homes. The food was poor, the insects thick, the heat enervating, the sleeping quarters uncomfortable. Then there was the danger, usually not as severe as in other wars, yet probably even more stressful in Vietnam because it was so unpredictable. It came in the form of mortar rounds in the night when the soldiers thought they were safe, booby traps tripped on the way to the latrine, mines that blew a soldier's legs off as he strolled down a pretty lane. The fact that Task Force Barker did not find the expected enemy in MyLai that memorable day was symbolic of the nature of the combat in Vietnam; the enemy appeared when and where it was unexpected.

Besides regression, there is another mechanism whereby human beings respond to stress. It is a mechanism of defense. Robert Jay Lifton, who studied the survivors of Hiroshima and other disasters, has called it "psychic numbing." In a situation in which our emotional feelings are overwhelmingly painful or unpleasant, we have the capacity to anesthetize ourselves. It is a simple sort of thing. The sight of a single bloody, mangled body horrifies us. But if we see such bodies all around us every day, day after day, the horrible becomes normal and we lose our sense of horror. We simply tune it out. Our capacity for horror becomes blunted. We no longer truly *see* the blood or *smell* the stench or *feel* its agony. Unconsciously we have become anesthetized.

This capacity for emotional self-anesthesia obviously has its advantages. Undoubtedly it has been built into us through evolution and enhances our ability to survive. It allows us to continue to function in situations so ghastly we would fall apart if we preserved our normal sensitivity. The problem, however, is that this self-anesthetizing mechanism seems not to be very specific. If because we live in the midst of garbage our sensitivity to ugliness becomes diminished, it is likely that we will become litterers and garbage-strewers ourselves. Insensitive to our own suffering, we tend to become insensitive to the suffering of others. Treated with indignity, we lose not only the sense of our own dignity but also the sense of the dignity of others. When it no longer bothers us to see mangled bodies, it will no longer bother us to mangle them ourselves. It is difficult indeed to selectively close our eyes to a certain type of brutality without closing them to all brutality. How can we render ourselves insensitive to brutality except by becoming brutes?

I think we can assume, therefore, that after a month in the field with Task Force Barker—a month of poor food, of poor sleep, of seeing comrades killed or maimed—the average soldier was more psychologically immature, primitive, and brutish than he might otherwise have been in a time and place of less stress.

I have spoken of the relationship between narcissism and evil, and I have said that narcissism is a condition out of which human beings normally mature. We may think of evil, then, as a kind of immaturity. Immature humans are more prone to evil than mature ones. We are impressed not only by the innocence but also by the cruelty of children. An adult who delights in picking the wings off flies is correctly deemed sadistic and suspected to be evil. A child of four who does this may be admonished but is considered merely curious; the same action from a child of twelve is cause for worry.

If we grow out of evil and narcissism, and since we normally regress in the face of stress, can we not say that human beings are more likely to be evil in times of stress than in times of comfort? I believe so. We asked how it happened that a group of fifty or five hundred individuals—of whom only a very small minority could be expected to be evil—could have committed such a monstrous evil as MyLai. One answer is that because of the chronic stress they were under, the individuals of Task Force Barker were more immature and hence more evil than would be expected in a normal situation. As a result of stress the normal distribution of goodness and evil had shifted in the direction of evil. As we shall see, however, this is but one of many factors that accounted for the evil at MyLai.

Having considered the relationship between evil and stress, it is appropriate to comment on the relationship between goodness and stress. He who behaves nobly in easy times—a fair-weather friend, so to speak—may not be so noble when the chips are down. Stress is the test for goodness. The truly good are they who in time of stress do not desert their integrity, their maturity, their sensitivity. Nobility might be defined as the capacity not to regress in response to degradation, not to become blunted in the face of pain, to tolerate the agonizing and remain intact. As I have said elsewhere, "one measure—and perhaps the best measure —of a person's greatness is the capacity for suffering."*

* *The Road Less Traveled* (Simon & Schuster, 1978), p. 76.

GROUP DYNAMICS: DEPENDENCY AND NARCISSISM

Individuals not only routinely regress in times of stress, they also regress in group settings. If you do not believe this, watch a Lions Club meeting or a college reunion. One aspect of this regression is the phenomenon of dependency on the leader. It is quite remarkable. Assemble any small group of strangers—say a dozen or so—and almost the very first thing that happens is that one or two of them rapidly assume the role of group leader. It does not happen by a rational process of conscious election; it just happens naturally—spontaneously and unconsciously. Why does it happen so quickly and easily? One reason, of course, is that some individuals are either more fit to lead than others or else desire to lead more than the rest. But the more basic reason is the converse: most people would rather be followers. More than anything else, it is probably a matter of laziness. It is simply easy to follow, and much easier to be a follower than a leader. There is no need to agonize over complex decisions, plan ahead, exercise initiative, risk unpopularity, or exert much courage.

The problem is that the role of follower is the role of child. The individual adult as individual is master of his own ship, director of his destiny. But when he assumes the role of follower he hands over to the leader his power: his authority over himself and his maturity as decision-maker. He becomes psychologically dependent on the leader as a child is dependent on its parents. In this way there is a profound tendency for the average individual to emotionally regress as soon as he becomes a group member.

From the standpoint of a therapist who leads a therapy group, this regression is not welcomed. It is, after all, the therapist's task to encourage, foster, and develop the maturity of his or her patients. Hence much of the work of a group therapist will be to confront and challenge the patients' dependency within the group, then to step aside so that the patient may risk assuming a leadership position and thereby learn how to exercise mature power in a group setting. A therapy group that has been successfully led will be one in which all the members have come to share equally in the leadership of the group according to their unique individual capacities. The ideal mature therapy group is a group composed entirely of leaders.

Most groups, however, do not exist for the purpose of psychotherapy or personal growth. The purpose of the First Platoon,

Charlie Company of Task Force Barker was not to train leaders but to kill Viet Cong. Indeed, for its purpose the military has developed and fostered a style of group leadership that is essentially the opposite of a therapy group. It is an old maxim that soldiers are not supposed to think. Leaders are not elected from within the group but are designated from above and deliberately cloaked in the symbols of authority. Obedience is the number-one military discipline. The dependency of the soldier on his leader is not simply encouraged, it is mandated.* By nature of its mission the military designedly and probably realistically fosters the naturally occurring regressive dependency of individuals within its groups.

In situations such as MyLai the individual soldier is in an almost impossible situation. On one hand, he may vaguely remember being told in some classroom that he is not required to forsake his conscience and should have the mature independence of judgment—even the duty—to refuse to obey an illegal order. On the other hand, the military organization and its group dynamics do everything to make it just about as painful and difficult and unnatural as possible for the soldier to exercise independence of judgment or practice disobedience. It is unclear whether Charlie Company's orders were to "kill anything that moved," or to "waste the village." But if they were, is it surprising that the troops followed those orders of their leaders? Would we have expected them to mutiny en masse instead?

If mutiny en masse seems farfetched, could we not at least have anticipated that a few individuals would have been brave enough to rebel against their leadership? Not necessarily. I have already made note of the fact that patterns of group behavior are remarkably similar to the behavior of an individual. This is because a group is an organism. It tends to function as a single

---

* Even civilians will commit evil with remarkable ease under obedience. As David Myers described in his excellent article "A Psychology of Evil" (*The Other Side* [April 1982], p. 29): "The clearest example is Stanley Milgram's obedience experiments. Faced with an imposing, close-at-hand commander, sixty-five percent of his adult subjects fully obeyed instructions. On command, they would deliver what appeared to be traumatizing electric shocks to a screaming innocent victim in an adjacent room. These were regular people—a mix of blue-collar, white-collar and professional men. They despised their task. Yet obedience took precedence over their own moral sense."

entity. A group of individuals behave as a unit because of what is called group cohesiveness. There are profound forces at work within a group to keep its individual members together and in line. When these forces to cohesiveness fail, the group begins to disintegrate and ceases to be a group.

Probably the most powerful of these group cohesive forces is narcissism. In its simplest and most benign form, this is manifested in group pride. As the members feel proud of their group, so the group feels proud of itself. Once again, the military deliberately does more than most organizations to foster pride within its groups. It does so through a variety of means, such as developing group insignia—unit standard flags, shoulder patches, even special uniform deviations such as the green berets—and encouraging group competition, ranging from intramural sports to the comparison of unit body counts. It is no accident that the common term for group pride is a military one: esprit de corps.

A less benign but practically universal form of group narcissism is what might be called "enemy creation," or hatred of the "out-group." We can see this naturally occurring in children as they first learn to develop groups.* The groups become cliques. Those who do not belong to the group (the club or clique) are despised as being inferior or evil or both. If a group does not already have an enemy, it will most likely create one in short order. Task Force Barker, of course, had a predesignated enemy: the Viet Cong. But the Viet Cong were largely indigenous to the South Vietnamese people, from whom they were often impossible to distinguish. Almost inevitably the specified enemy was generalized to include all Vietnamese, so that the average American soldier did not just hate the Viet Cong, he hated "Gooks" in general.

It is almost common knowledge that the best way to cement group cohesiveness is to ferment the group's hatred of an external enemy. Deficiencies within the group can be easily and painlessly overlooked by focusing attention on the deficiencies or "sins" of the out-group. Thus the Germans under Hitler could

---

* Psychologists have observed that when similar groups of twelve-year-old male campers without restraining adult leadership were encouraged to compete with each other, the benign competition soon changed into violent "warfare on a twelve-year-old scale" (Myers, "A Psychology of Evil," p. 29).

ignore their domestic problems by scapegoating the Jews. And when American troops were failing to fight effectively in New Guinea in World War II, the command improved their esprit de corps by showing them movies of Japanese committing atrocious acts. But this use of narcissism—whether unconscious or deliberate—is potentially evil. We have extensively examined the ways in which evil individuals will flee self-examination and guilt by blaming and attempting to destroy whatever or whoever highlights their deficiencies. Now we see that the same malignant narcissistic behavior comes naturally to groups.

From this it should be obvious that the failing group is the one likely to behave most evilly. Failure wounds our pride, and it is the wounded animal who is vicious. In the healthy organism failure will be a stimulus to self-examination and criticism. But since the evil individual cannot tolerate self-criticism, it is in time of failure that he or she will inevitably lash out one way or another. And so it is with groups. Group failure and the stimulation of group self-criticism act to damage group pride and cohesiveness. Group leaders in all places and ages have therefore routinely bolstered group cohesiveness in times of failure by whipping the group's hatred for foreigners or the "enemy."

Returning to the specific subject of our examination, we will remember that at the time of MyLai the operation of Task Force Barker had been a failure. After more than a month in the field the enemy had still not been engaged. Yet the Americans had slowly and regularly sustained casualties. The enemy body count, however, was zero. Failing in its mission—which was to kill in the first place—the group leadership was all the more hungry for blood. Given the circumstances, the hunger had become indiscriminate, and the troops would mindlessly satisfy it.

### THE SPECIALIZED GROUP: TASK FORCE BARKER

I have already mentioned the potential for evil in specialization. In so doing I spoke of how the specialized individual is in a position to pass the moral buck to some other specialized cog in the machine or onto the machine itself. Even when I was speaking of the regression that individuals undergo when they take the role of followers in a group, I was talking of specialization. The follower is not a whole person. He whose accepted role it is neither to think nor lead has defaulted his capacity to think and lead.

And because thinking and leading are no longer his specialty or duty, he usually defaults his conscience in the bargain.

Turning from consideration of the specialized individual to the specialized group, we will see the same sorts of dangerous forces at work. Task Force Barker was a specialized group. It did not exist for many purposes—to play football or build dams or even to feed itself. It existed for only one highly specialized purpose: to search for and destroy the Viet Cong in Quang Ngai Province in 1968.

An important fact to bear in mind about specialization is that it is seldom either accidental or random. It is usually highly selective. It is not by accident that I am a psychiatrist. I chose to be one and selectively performed those tasks necessary to prepare myself for this specialized role. Moreover, I not only selected the role but was also selected for it by society. By many different stages I was examined to see if I met the qualifications for membership in the "club." Any specialty group is a particular breed as a result of both self-selection and group selection. Were you, for instance, to attend a convention of psychiatrists and observe their dress, diction, carriage, and particular brand of argumentativeness, you would conclude we are a peculiar breed indeed.

Let us look at another, even more typical example: a police force. One does not become a policeman by accident. It is only because particular kinds of people want to become policemen that they apply for the job in the first place. A young man of lower-middle-class origins who is both aggressive and conventional, for instance, would be quite likely to seek a position on the force. A shy, intellectual youth would not. The nature of police work allows for the expression of a certain amount of aggression in the service of the law, and at the same time encourages the containment of aggression through a highly structured organization dedicated to respect for the law. It fits the psychological needs of the first young man. He quite naturally gravitates toward it. Should he find during the period of his training and early duty that the work is not satisfying or that he is somehow not compatible with the rank and file of other policemen, he will either resign or be weeded out. The result is that a police force is usually a quite homogeneous group of people who have much in common with each other and who are distinctly different from other types of groups, such as antiwar demonstrators or college English majors.

From these examples we can discern three general principles regarding specialized groups. First, the specialized group inevitably develops a group character that is self-reinforcing. Second, specialized groups are therefore particularly prone to narcissism—that is, to experiencing themselves as uniquely right and superior in relation to other homogeneous groups. Finally, the society at large—partly through the self-selection process described—employs specific types of people to perform its specialized roles—as, for instance, it employs aggressive, conventional men to perform its police functions.

We have already mentioned that Task Force Barker was a specialized group, existing solely for the purpose of conducting search-and-destroy missions in Quang Ngai Province. What the reader may not realize, however, is the large amount of selection and self-selection involved in the creation of that group. Although citizens were drafted into the military at that time, Task Force Barker was hardly a random sample of the American population. The most pacifistic members of society exempted themselves by going to Canada or declaring themselves conscientious objectors. Those less pacifistic members who desired to avoid combat duty usually chose to enlist in the military rather than be drafted. Through enlistment they could choose duty in the Air Force or Navy or some noncombat specialty within the Army, highly unlikely to land them in Vietnam. Task Force Barker consisted either of career military personnel who had deliberately chosen the combat arms or young "grunts" who had done likewise (or for some reason had failed to avoid the quite easily escapable role of foot soldier).

Until the end of 1968, well after MyLai, the Vietnam war was almost entirely fought, on the American side, by volunteers. For many career personnel a tour of duty in Vietnam was highly desirable and sought after. It meant medals, excitement, extra money, and an invariable promotion. A unique volunteer system also existed at the time for the young enlisted men. Almost anyone who volunteered for Vietnam could be assured of three things: an instant change of location, an immediate furlough, and a bonus. These incentives were sufficient to ensure an adequate supply of voluntary "cannon fodder" until the further escalation of American troop involvement in the war after MyLai.

The case of a prototypical individual may serve to illustrate some aspects of the relationship between American society in 1968, its military, and the subgroup of the military fighting in Vietnam. Let us call this prototypical individual "Larry" and set the place of his origin as Iowa. The oldest of six children born to an alcoholic hired farmer and his tired wife, Larry was clearly a hell raiser from the time he hit puberty. Dropping out of high school as soon as he turned sixteen, in 1965, Larry vaguely supported himself with a series of odd jobs that proved inadequate to pay for his car insurance, gas, and a heavy-drinking life-style. In November 1966 he was apprehended attempting to rob a local gas station. The community was delighted to get rid of Larry but at the same time had no desire to increase the state prison population or their tax burden. After all, the money involved was recovered and no great harm had been done. So the county judge told Larry he had two choices: to join the Army or go to jail.

Things were simple from then on. The Army recruiter had his little office in the same county building as the judge. Needless to say, there were openings in the infantry. Larry enlisted for Germany because he'd heard that the girls were easy there, and within the week he was on his way to Fort Leonard Wood, Missouri, for basic training. Basic and then advanced infantry training (AIT) kept him so busy that he didn't even have time for trouble. But when he got to Germany it was different. The girls were as good as they were cracked up to be, and the beer was mighty fine. But prices were high. He borrowed money and had trouble paying it back. He sold a little hashish for a bigger dealer, which helped out, but then his supplier rotated. His debts mounted. Larry, almost nineteen now, could see the way things were going. Either his creditors would beat him up or they would squeal on him about the hashish. But there was a way out. He quietly volunteered for Vietnam, and within three days he was on a plane back to the United States, safely ahead of his troubles. He felt good. He had his bonus to blow on a ten-day leave back home in Iowa, seeing his old buddies and impressing the girls. As for the future after that, he didn't mind it at all. He'd heard the women in Nam were even better than in Germany, and, besides, it would be exciting to see some real action for a change. Shooting up some Gooks might be kind of fun.

Unfortunately, despite the obvious contribution it would have made to our understanding, a sociological analysis of the composition of Task Force Barker has never been performed. Consequently I can say nothing scientific. I do not mean to imply that the whole group was made up of petty criminals like "Larry." But I do mean to suggest that Charlie Company and Task Force Barker were not at all an average cross section of the American people. Its members all arrived at MyLai in March 1968, for reasons of personal history and self-selection, through a system of selection also established by the American military and by American society as a whole. It was not any random group of men. It was highly specialized, not only in its mission but also in its unique composition.

The specialized human composition of Task Force Barker (and countless other human groups) raises three significant issues. First is the question of the flexibility that can be expected of specialized human beings. Charlie Company was a specialized group of killers. The individuals in it had for one reason or another gravitated toward the killing role as well as being deliberately seduced into that role by the system. In addition, we trained them for the role and provided them with weapons to perform it. Is it surprising, then, given a host of other contributory circumstances, that they killed indiscriminately? Or that they apparently failed to experience great guilt over what we had led them to do? Is it realistic to encourage and manipulate human beings into specialized groups and simultaneously expect them, without any significant training, to maintain a breadth of vision much beyond their specialty?

A second issue is the subtle but definite scapegoating involved. The prototypical Larry was a petty cheat and thief, an unpleasant sort of chap for whom it is not easy to feel great sympathy. But he was also a scapegoat. When his community pushed him into the Army, they were not attempting to deal with the human, social problem he presented to them; they were simply getting rid of the problem. They purified their own community by dumping the dirt on the military, sacrificing Larry to the God of War. And they scapegoated the military as well. It is, of course, one of the unwritten functions of the military to serve as a dumping ground for some of the more misbegotten of America's youth—a sort of national reform school. But the fact that this system works rather smoothly, and not always for ill, should not blind us to the scapegoating nature of the process.

By then seducing him into Vietnam, the Army, of course, further scapegoated Larry. On the one hand, it makes a definite kind of social logic. Why shouldn't those individuals like Larry who are troublemakers and misfits be the most appropriate candidates for cannon fodder? If someone has to be killed, why not let it be one of apparent little social value? But the decision to kill was not Larry's. Nor Lieutenant Calley's. Nor his superior officer, Captain Medina's. Nor Lieutenant Colonel Barker's. It was America's decision. For whatever reason, America decided that there would be killing, and insofar as these men killed, they were all doing America's bidding. They may have seemed dirtier and less noble than the average American, but the fact is that we Americans as a society deliberately chose and employed them to do our killing—our dirty work—for us. In this sense they all were our scapegoats.

One way in which this scapegoating is highlighted is in the history of the antiwar movement. Criticism of America's role in Vietnam began to flourish in 1965 among "the intellectual left," but despite all the teach-ins and mass marches, the antiwar movement never gained any grass-roots support, and hence effectiveness, until 1970. Why this time lag? Certainly a number of factors were involved. But perhaps the most important factor—one that has gone largely unrecognized—was that it was not until 1969 that any significant numbers of drafted Americans *who had not volunteered to go there* began to be sent to Vietnam.

It was quite natural that the vast American public should not have been particularly aroused when everyone in Vietnam wanted to be there. Conversely, it is natural that the public began to be upset only when brothers and sons and fathers who did not want any part of it began to be sent to Vietnam. That was when the grass-roots support of the antiwar movement first started.

The point is that we had a sufficient number of specialized killers to fight a relatively large-scale war for six years without significantly, personally involving the American public as a whole. Since they were not personally involved, the public was mostly content to let the killers they had created "do their thing." The public did not begin to assume responsibility for the war until we ran out of specialists. And this is the third issue we must look at. It presents us with a dreadful reality we must not ignore. For the reality is that it is not only possible but easy and even natural for a large group to commit evil without emotional involvement simply by turning loose its specialists. It happened in Vietnam. It happened in Nazi Germany. I am afraid it will happen again.

What we need to learn is that whenever we create specialty groups, we are creating the dangerous possibility that our right hand will not know what our left is doing. I am not arguing that we should do without specialty groups entirely; that would be to throw out the baby with the bath water. But we must realize the potential danger, and structure our specialty groups in such a way as to minimize it. We are not yet doing so. For instance—because it does not hurt us as a whole—our society developed and currently maintains the policy of an all-volunteer military. Our response to the antiwar sentiment engendered by Vietnam has been to opt for an even more thoroughly specialized military, overlooking the danger involved. Abandoning the concept of the citizen soldier in favor of the mercenary, we have placed ourselves in grave jeopardy. Twenty years from now, when Vietnam has been largely forgotten, how easy it will be, with volunteers, to once again become involved in little foreign adventures. Such adventures will keep our military on its toes, provide it with real-life war games to test its prowess, and need not hurt or involve the average American citizen at all until it is too late.

A draft—involuntary service—is the only thing that can keep our military sane. Without it the military will inevitably become not only specialized in its function but increasingly specialized in its psychology. No fresh air will be let in. It will become inbred and reinforce its own values, and then, when it is once again let loose, it will run amok as it did in Vietnam. A draft is a painful thing. But so are insurance premiums; and involuntary service is the only way we have of ensuring the sanity of our military "left hand." The point is that if we must have a military at all, it *should* hurt. As a people we should not toy with the means of mass destruction without being willing to personally bear the responsibility of wielding them. If we must kill, let us not select and train hired killers to do the dirty job for us and then forget that there's any blood involved. If we must kill, then let us honestly suffer the agony involved ourselves. Otherwise we will insulate ourselves from our own deeds, and as a whole people we will become like the individuals described in previous sections: evil. For evil arises in the refusal to acknowledge our own sins.

I have spoken of the individual foot soldier and the regression experienced in response to the stress of combat. The tendency to regression of the individual in a group setting was also noted. Then we examined the forces of conformity and narcissism at work in small groups, particularly a military group such as Task Force Barker. From there we proceeded to explore the relationship between such a specialized small group and the larger group that spawns it, commenting on aspects of scapegoating in the relationship. Now let us turn to the large group itself—in this instance, the United States military.

The core of the military is the career soldier, the twenty- or thirty-year man, whether senior officer or NCO. These are the people who most determine the nature of the military organization. Certainly the organization must bend in certain ways to accommodate itself to draftees and to induce enlistments. And it must respond in certain ways to the direction of its civilian leadership, headed by the Secretary of Defense. But secretaries of defense come and go. Draftees and four-year enlistees come and go. The career men stay on, and it is they who not only give the military its continuity; they give it its soul.

Some aspects of the soul of the U.S. military are of great, even spiritual value. Civilians have more than they think to learn from military traditions, discipline, and styles of leadership. My purpose here, however, is not to present a fully balanced picture of the military but to examine one of the military's failures as an example of the phenomenon of group evil. Consequently it is necessary to focus on the less savory aspects of the "military mind" or soul.

We humans are so constituted that we need a sense of our own social significance. Nothing can give us more pleasure than the sense that we are wanted and useful. Conversely, nothing is more productive of despair than a sense that we are useless and unwanted. In a time of sustained peace the military man is disregarded—at best considered by his country as a necessary evil, and more often as a rather pathetic parasite on the body politic. In time of war, however, he suddenly becomes needed again, filling a role not only regarded as useful but absolutely essential by his society. The drudge becomes the hero.

The state of war is therefore not only psychologically satisfying to the career soldier but economically rewarding as well. In peacetime, promotions are frozen and dead wood is weeded out. Even demotions are the rule. Simply to economically and psychologically survive peacetime the career military man must possess a kind of emotional stamina greater than that of many. He must wait, unrecognized and forsaken, until wartime, when once again he comes into his own. Responsibilities suddenly and dramatically increase. Promotions are rapid. Salary increases, benefits, and bonuses pour in. Medals mount up. And once again he is the man of the hour, out of debt and despair, unquestionably important and significant.

It is inevitable, then, that the ordinary career military man, unconsciously if not consciously, desires—longs for—war. War is his fulfillment. A few military men of extraordinary stature and spiritual greatness succeed in overcoming the enormous natural inclinations of their career so as to work and argue on behalf of peace. But such rare martyrs and unsung heroes are hardly our right. To the contrary, we must fully expect, without rancor or recrimination, the military man to always vote and stand on the side of war. To do otherwise would be infantilely unrealistic.

One of the things this means is that the United States military was not in Vietnam in 1968 reluctantly. The prevailing attitude of career personnel was not one of doubt or caution or restraint. If anything, it was an exuberant "Whoopee, let's go at it, boys" sort of fervor, sanctified by the President and Commander in Chief, who himself went to Vietnam and instructed the troops to "bring the coonskin home."

Another factor to be considered is the technological nature of the American military in the 1960s. The military had not always been so oriented, but this was the time of the acme of our faith in technology in general and American technology in particular. In this regard the military reflected our whole society's infatuation with machines and devices and equipment that would make everything easy and efficient, including killing. Indeed, not only was Vietnam regarded at the time as a sort of ideally challenging testing ground for new military technology but the military itself was regarded as properly filling the role of the principal developer of innovative new technology for American society at large. One result of this was that we went technologically "hog-wild" in Vietnam, employing our bulldozers and weapons systems and precision bombing and chemical defoliants with a Strangelovian fervor. The other result was an emotional distancing from our victims, whom we usually did not even see. It was napalm, not we, that set fire to the bodies of Vietnamese. It was the planes and the tanks and the bombs and the mortars, not we, that killed. At MyLai the killing was face-to-face, but I believe our use of technology in the war had served to deaden our sensitivities. Several years of placing all our gadgetry between us and our victims had had the effect of insulating our consciences. I suspect that the similar use of technology will always have that effect.

Yet all our collective technology and military expertise and American know-how was not working. America was the mightiest nation on earth. In its entire history it had never lost a war. But now the unbelievable was happening. In 1967 and 1968 we were first beginning to perceive intimations of the reality of something so monstrous that we had never even conceived of it before: we were failing to win the war. With all our technology, in a tiny little country, against an unindustrialized and supposedly primitive people, we, the mightiest nation on earth, were losing.

Being on the spot, it was the military that first began to experience the unthinkable. And it was the military that had to bear the full brunt of the exquisite pain of America's humiliation. It was the unvanquished military that was failing in the performance of its very *raison d'être*. It was now unable to achieve the one thing for which it existed. What should have been its finest hour was now, suddenly and inexplicably, turning sour. Its cultivated esprit de corps, its proud tradition, was going down the drain.*

* A tiny personal vignette may serve to highlight what was happening to the psychology of the American military in those years. It should be prefaced by noting that the despair engendered by our defeat took a certain amount of time to spread beyond the confines of Vietnam and filter down into the psyches of those career soldiers who were not directly experiencing the insult. From 1968 until 1970 my family and I lived in a military housing area on Okinawa mainly occupied by career army officers. On Christmas Eve, 1968, a group of us and our friends went caroling throughout the neighborhood. It was a gay, almost magical occasion. As we sang, the families came to their windows, opened their doors, offered us refreshments, delightedly expressed their appreciation, and sometimes even joined us. The

At the time of MyLai, in early 1968, the military was like an enormous confident beast suddenly finding itself beginning to be hurt and wounded by a hundred little darts without even knowing where the blows were coming from. It was beginning to bellow in rage and confusion.

It is practically an axiom that cornered or wounded animals are particularly vicious or dangerous. America was neither seriously cornered nor threatened in Vietnam in early 1968, but its pride had definitely been struck to the quick, and the pride of the military in particular was badly wounded. Again and again we have noted the birth of evil from a condition of threatened narcissism. For the military the conditions were ripe for evil. Just as the highly narcissistic (evil) individual will strike out to destroy whoever challenges his or her self-image of perfection, so by late 1967 the American military organization—highly narcissistic, as all groups tend to be—began to strike out with uncharacteristic viciousness and deceit against the Vietnamese people, who were wreaking such havoc on its self-esteem. Suspected spies were tortured. Viet Cong bodies, dead or perhaps still alive, were dragged in the dirt behind armored personnel carriers. The era of the body count had begun. The lying and falsification, characteristic of our involvement in the Vietnam war from the beginning, escalated. Although the atrocity at MyLai was undoubtedly unique in magnitude, I have every reason to suspect that smaller atrocities were being committed by American troops throughout Vietnam at the time. I think we can safely say that MyLai occurred in the context of an atmosphere of atrociousness and evil that was pervasive not only in Task Force Barker but throughout the entirety of the American presence in Vietnam.

Although incisive, this conjecture of an atrocious atmosphere remains conjecture. As I have said, I was among several people

---

affair had been such a success, we attempted to repeat it on Christmas Eve, 1969. Our voices were largely the same and our spirits were full of anticipation. But something had radically changed. The houses were mostly dark. The windows were not thrown open. No one came to the door. No appreciation was expressed. No one joined us. As we disappointedly returned home, my wife and I commented to each other: "It's as if the whole damn community were depressed." At the time our vision was not complete, but in retrospect we know that the community was indeed depressed, and we know why.

who were asked to propose research that would contribute to the understanding of the psychological aspects of MyLai. Knowing full well that it would receive an unfavorable reception, our committee was nevertheless compelled by honesty to make the proposal—among others—that the incidence of atrocities committed by American troops elsewhere in Vietnam should be examined and compared, if possible, with the incidence of atrocities committed by American troops in other wars against other enemies. Between the Philippine Insurrection in 1899* and MyLai, there is nothing publicly written or documented about war crimes and atrocities committed by Americans. Are we to assume that American boys simply did not commit such brutalities in Korea or during World War II? Dozens of questions come to mind. Were atrocities committed with equal frequency in other wars, but were they unreported because the climate of the times was different? Were atrocities in Vietnam elsewhere than MyLai more or less frequent than we might suppose? Was the level of atrociousness in Vietnam unique? Are atrocities more likely to be committed by Americans against Orientals than against other Caucasians, such as the Germans?

We can never fully understand the group evil of MyLai without answers to such questions. Answers could be provided only through scientific historical research on the subject. Although there are technical difficulties (and immunity from prosecution would have to be granted those questioned), such research is quite theoretically feasible. Whether it is politically feasible is another matter. It was not  expedient in 1972, when we proposed it. My prediction is that these questions will go unanswered, not because the answers are unworthy of the trouble involved but because we as a people would simply rather not work toward discovering them. The potential for embarrassment is too great. We would rather not examine ourselves and our society so closely in this regard. Our poential for evil as a group is still sufficient for us to avoid looking squarely at it.

The purpose of our being asked in 1972 to make recommendations for research on the psychological aspects of MyLai was to make progress toward the goal of preventing such atrocities in the future. Since the proposed research was rejected *in toto*, I

---

* See Leon Wolff, *Little Brown Brother* (Doubleday, 1961).

have no fully scientific basis from which to discuss the issue of prevention. One major avenue toward prevention seems clear, however.

As long as we must have a military organization, I suggest that our society must seriously consider de-specializing it to the ultimate degree possible. What I would propose is a combination of several old ideas: universal service and a national service corps. In place of the military as it currently exists we could have a national service corps that would perform military functions but that would also be extensively utilized for peaceful functions as well: slum clearance, environmental protection, job training education, and other vital civilian needs. Instead of the corps being an all-volunteer force or being fed by some inequitable draft system, it could be based on a system of obligatory national service for all American youth, male and female. They would not be conscripted for cannon fodder but would be employed for a whole variety of necessary tasks. The requirement for all youth to serve would at one and the same time make military adventurism more difficult but would facilitate full-scale mobilization if necessary. Having major peacetime tasks to perform, a less specialized career cadre would be less eager for wartime. Sweeping though these proposals might be, there is nothing about them that is inherently unfeasible.

THE LARGEST GROUP: AMERICAN SOCIETY IN 1968

While the military may have been crashing around in Vietnam like a crazed bull, it did not get there of its own accord. The mindless beast was sent there and let loose by the United States government acting on behalf of the American people. Why? Why did we wage that war?

Basically, we fought the war because of a combination of three attitudes: (1) communism was a monolithic evil force hostile to human freedom in general and American freedom in particular; (2) it was America's duty as the world's most economically powerful nation to lead the opposition against communism; and (3) communism should be opposed wherever it arose by whatever means necessary.

This combination of attitudes comprising the American posture in international relations had its origins in the late 1940s and early 1950s. Immediately following the end of World War II, the

Communist USSR, with extraordinary speed and aggressiveness, imposed its political domination over almost the entirety of eastern Europe: Poland, Lithuania, Latvia, Estonia, East Germany, Czechoslovakia, Hungary, Bulgaria, Romania, Albania, and presumably Yugoslavia. Seemingly only by American money and American arms and leadership was the rest of Europe prevented from falling into the clutches of communism. Then just as we were bolstering the defense against communism's western flank, it exploded in the East, with the whole of China falling under Communist domination in 1950 almost overnight. And already the forces of communism were clearly threatening to expand through Vietnam and Malaya. The line had to be drawn. Given the explosive expansion of communism on all sides of the USSR, it is no wonder that we perceived it in 1954 as an evil monolithic force, so dangerously threatening to the entire world that we needed to become engaged against it in a life-and-death struggle that left little room for moral scruples.

The problem, however, is that by a scant dozen years later there was a wealth of evidence to indicate that communism was not (if, in fact, it had ever been) a force that was either monolithic or necessarily evil. Yugoslavia was clearly independent of the USSR, and Albania was becoming so. China and the USSR were no longer allies but potential enemies. As for Vietnam, any slightly discerning examination of its history revealed it to be a traditional enemy of China. The impelling force behind the Vietnamese Communists at that point in their history was not the expansion of communism but nationalism and resistance to colonial domination. Moreover, it had also become clear that despite the constraints on their civil liberties, the people in Communist societies were generally faring better than they had under their pre-Communist forms of government. It was also clear that the people in many non-Communist societies, with whose governments we had allied ourselves, were suffering violations of human rights that matched those of the USSR and China.

Our military involvement in Vietnam began in the period between 1954 and 1956, when the idea of a monolithic Communist menace seemed realistic. A dozen years later it was no longer realistic. Yet at precisely the time when it had ceased to be realistic, when we should have been readjusting our strategy and withdrawing from Vietnam, we began to seriously escalate our military involvement there in defense of obsolescent attitudes. Why? Why, beginning around 1964, did America's behavior in Vietnam become increasingly unrealistic and inappropriate? There are two reasons: laziness and—once again—narcissism.

Attitudes have a kind of inertia. Once set in motion, they will keep going, even in the face of the evidence. To change an attitude requires a considerable amount of work and suffering. The process must begin either in an effortfully maintained posture of constant self-doubt and criticism or else in a painful acknowledgment that what we thought was right all along may not be right after all. Then it proceeds into a state of confusion. This state is quite uncomfortable; we no longer seem to know what is right or wrong or which way to go. But it is a state of openness and therefore of learning and growing. It is only from the quicksand of confusion that we are able to leap to the new and better vision.

I think we may properly regard the men who governed America at the time of MyLai—the Johnson administration—as lazy and self-satisfied. They, like most more ordinary individuals, had little taste for intellectual confusion—nor for the effort involved in maintaining a "posture of constant self-doubt and criticism." They assumed that the attitudes they had developed toward the "monolithic Communist menace" during the preceding two decades were still the right attitudes. Although the evidence was obviously mounting to throw their attitudes into question, they ignored it. To do otherwise would have placed them in the painful and difficult position of having to rethink their attitudes. They did not take up the work required. It was easier to proceed blindly, as if nothing had changed.

Thus far we have been focusing on the laziness involved in "clinging to old maps" and attitudes that have become obsolete.* Let us also examine the narcissism. We are our attitudes. If someone criticizes an attitude of mine, I feel he or she is criticizing *me*. If one of my opinions is proved wrong, then *I* have been wrong. My self-image of perfection has been shattered. Individuals and nations cling to obsolete and outworn ideas not simply because it requires work to change them but also because, in their narcissism, they cannot imagine that their ideas and views could be wrong. They believe themselves to be right. Oh, we are quick

* See *The Road Less Traveled*, pp. 44–51.

to superficially disclaim our infallibility, but deep inside most of us, particularly when we have apparently been successful and powerful, we consider ourselves invariably in the right. It was this kind of narcissism, manifested in our behavior in Vietnam, that Senator William Fulbright referred to as "the arrogance of power."

Ordinarily, if our noses are rubbed in the evidence, we can tolerate the painful narcissistic injury involved, admit our need for change, and correct our outlook. But as is the case with certain individuals, the narcissism of whole nations may at times exceed the normal bounds. When this happens, the nation—instead of readjusting in light of the evidence—sets about attempting to destroy the evidence. This was what America was up to in the 1960s. The situation in Vietnam presented us with evidence of the fallibility of our world view and the limits of our potency. So, rather than rethinking it, we set about to destroy the situation in Vietnam, and all of Vietnam with it if necessary.

Which was evil. Evil has already been defined most simply as the use of political power to destroy others for the purpose of defending or preserving the integrity of one's sick self. Since it had become outmoded, our monolithic view of communism was part of our national sick self—no longer adaptive and realistic. In the failure of the Diem regime, which we sponsored, in the failure of all our "advisers" and Green Berets and massive economic and military aid to counteract the expansion of the Viet Cong, the sickness or wrongness of our policies was exposed to ourselves. Rather than alter these policies, however, we launched a full-scale war to preserve them intact. Rather than admit what would have been a minor failure in 1964, we set about rapidly escalating the war to prove ourselves right at the expense of the Vietnamese people and their self-aspirations. The issue ceased to be what was right for Vietnam and became an issue of our infallibility and preserving our national "honor."

Strangely enough, on a certain level, President Johnson and the men of his administration knew that what they were doing was evil. Otherwise, why all the lying?* It was so bizarre and seem-

---

* One of the tests for criminal responsibility is the question of whether the defendant knows the difference between right and wrong. If a criminal in any way, shape, or form attempts to conceal his crime, it is assumed he knew his action to be a crime—that is, to be wrong. By the very fact that

ingly out of character that it is difficult for us merely to recall the extraordinary national dishonesty of those days, a scant fifteen years ago. Even the excuse President Johnson gave in order to begin bombing North Vietnam and escalate the war in 1964— the "Gulf of Tonkin Incident"—was apparently a deliberate fraud. Through this fraud he obtained from Congress the authority to wage the war without Congress ever formally declaring it (which was its constitutional responsibility). Then he set about "borrowing" the money to pay for the war—diverting funds earmarked for other programs and extorting "savings bonds" from the salaries of federal employees—so that the American public would not have to immediately pay increased taxes or feel the burden of the escalation.

This book is entitled *People of the Lie* because lying is both a cause and a manifestation of evil. It is partly by their lying that we recognize the evil. President Johnson clearly did not want the American people to fully know and understand what he was doing in Vietnam in their name. He knew that what he was doing would be ultimately unacceptable to them. His defrauding the electorate was not only evil in itself but was also evidence of his awareness of the evil of his actions, since he felt compelled to cover them up.

But it would be a mistake and a potentially evil rationalization itself for us to blame the evil of those days entirely on the Johnson administration. We must ask why Johnson was successful in defrauding us. Why did we allow ourselves to be defrauded for so long? Not everyone was. A very small minority was quick to recognize that the wool was being pulled over our eyes, that "something rather dark and bloody" was being perpetrated by the nation. But why were most of us not aroused to ire or suspicion or even significant concern about the nature of the war?

Once again we are confronted with our all-too-human laziness and narcissism. Basically, it was just too much trouble. We all had our lives to lead—doing our day-to-day jobs, buying new cars, painting our houses, sending our kids to college. As the ma-

---

President Johnson took various actions and made up various lies to cover up his deeds, we may assume that he knew what he was doing was wrong or at least knew that it was unacceptable to the society that he was sworn to represent.

jority of members of any group are content to let the leadership be exercised by the few, so as a citizenry we were content to let the government "do its thing." It was Johnson's job to lead, ours to follow. The citizenry was simply too lethargic to become aroused. Besides, we shared with Johnson his enormous large-as-Texas narcissism. Surely our national attitudes and policies couldn't be wrong. Surely our government had to know what it was doing; after all, we'd elected them, hadn't we? And surely they had to be good and honest men, for they were products of our wonderful democratic system, which certainly couldn't go seriously awry. And surely whatever type of regime our rulers and experts and government specialists thought was right for Vietnam must be right, for weren't we the greatest of nations and the leader of the free world?

By allowing ourselves to be easily and blatantly defrauded, we as a whole people participated in the evil of the Johnson administration. The evil—the years of lying and manipulation—of the Johnson administration was directly conducive to the whole atmosphere of lying and manipulation and evil that pervaded our presence in Vietnam during those years. It was in this atmosphere that MyLai occurred in March 1968. Task Force Barker was hardly even aware that it had run amok that day, but, then, America was not significantly aware either in early 1968 that it too had almost unredeemably lost its bearings.

HUMAN KILLING

We must remind ourselves in this consideration that America is itself merely a group and not the whole. Specifically, it is one of the many political subgroups of the human race which we call nation states. And, of course, the human race itself is but one of the enormous number of different life forms of the planet. (That we need remind ourselves of this at all is another reflection of our human narcissistic propensity to think only in terms of our own species.)

We must also remind ourselves that evil has to do with killing—that evil is live spelled backward. We have been considering My-Lai as an example of group evil because of the particular kind of killing that occurred there. But that brand of killing was only a misstep in the ritualistic dance of death we call war. War is a form of large-scale killing that we humans consider an acceptable instrument of national policy. It is necessary for us now to examine the subject of killing in general and human killing specifically.

All animals kill, and not necessarily just for food or self-defense. Our two well-fed cats, for instance, routinely horrify us by bringing into the house the shattered corpses of chipmunks they have murdered for the joy of the hunt. But there is something unique about human killing. Human killing is not instinctual. One manifestation of the noninstinctual nature of human beings is the extraordinary variability of their behavior. Some are hawks and some are doves. In regard to a form of killing, some love to hunt and others abhor hunting, while still others are indifferent on the matter. Not so with cats. All cats will hunt chipmunks, given the opportunity.

The almost total lack of instincts—elaborate, predetermined, stereotypic behavior patterns—is the most significant aspect of human nature. It is our lack of instincts that is responsible for the extraordinary variability and mutability of our nature and our behavior. What replaces species-wide instincts in human beings is learned individual choice. Each of us is ultimately free to choose how we are going to behave. We are even free to reject what we have been taught and what is normal for our society. We may even reject the few instincts we have, as do those who rationally choose celibacy or submit themselves to death by martyrdom. Free will is the ultimate human reality.

Let us remember what so many theologians have said: Evil is the inevitable concomitant of free will, the price we pay for our unique human power of choice. Since ours is the power to choose, we are free to choose wisely or stupidly, to choose well or badly, to choose for evil or for good. Since we have this enormous—almost incredible—freedom, it is no wonder that we so often abuse it and that human behavior, in comparison to that of the "lower" animals, so often seems to get out of whack. Many animals may kill to protect their territory. But only a human could direct mass killing of his own species so as to protect his "interests" in a far distant land he has never set eyes upon.

So our human killing is a matter of choice. In order to survive, we cannot not kill. But we can choose how, when, where, and what we will kill. The moral complexities of such choices are enormous and often quite paradoxical. A person may become a vegetarian as an ethical choice in order to refrain from even the indirect responsibility for killing, yet to survive, he or she must still bear the responsibility for hacking living plants off at the roots and roasting the corpses thereof in ovens. Should the vegetarian, one wonders, eat eggs (the potentially unborn children of beautiful birds) or drink milk (taken from cows whose calves have been slaughtered for veal)? Then there are such matters as the issue of abortion. Does a woman have the right to bear to full viability an infant whom she neither wants nor has the capacity to care for? But does she have the right to kill that same potentially holy fetus? Is it not strange that many pacifists are advocates of abortion? Or that those who would seek to deprive others of their choice to abort on the grounds that life is sacred are so often those who champion capital punishment? And for that matter, what ethical sense does it make to kill a murderer as an example to convince others that killing is morally wrong?

Complex though the ethics of our choices to kill or not to kill may be, there is clearly one factor that contributes to unnecessary and obviously immoral killing: narcissism. Once again, narcissism. One manifestation of our narcissism is that we are far more likely to kill that which is different from us than that which resembles us. The vegetarian feels guilty killing other animal life forms but not plant life forms. There are specialized vegetarians who will eat fish but not meat; others who will eat chicken but not mammalian flesh. There are fishermen who abhor the idea of hunting and hunters who shoot birds but would shudder at killing a deer with its all-too-human eyes. The same principle applies when humans kill other humans. Those of us who are Caucasians seem to have fewer compunctions about killing blacks or Indians or Orientals than we do in killing our fellow white men. It's easier for a white man to lynch a "nigger" than a "redneck." I also suspect it's probably easier for an Oriental to kill a Caucasian than a fellow Oriental. But I do not know for sure. The matter of the racial aspects of intraspecies killing is yet another one deserving significant scientific investigation.*

* There are subtleties involved in the matter of interracial killing that not only deserve to be investigated but that are also extremely fascinating. One of the group of proposals (rejected *in toto*) made to the Chief of Staff of the Army in relation to the psychological aspects of MyLai was that research should be conducted on interracial and intercultural differences in nonverbal behavior.

War today is at least as much a matter of national pride as of racial pride. What we call nationalism is more frequently a malignant national narcissism than it is a healthy satisfaction in the accomplishments of one's culture. In fact, to a large extent it is nationalism that preserves the nation-state system. A century ago, when it required weeks for a message to get from the United States to France, and months to get to China, the nation-state system made sense. In our current age of instant global communication as well as instant holocaust, much of the international political system has become obsolete. It is our national narcissism, however, that clings to our outmoded notions of sovereignty and prevents the development of effective international peacekeeping machinery.

Wittingly or unwittingly, we actually teach our children national narcissism. The linear map of the world that stretches above our countless schoolroom blackboards shows that the United States is more or less at the center of that map. And on the maps of little Russian schoolchildren it is the USSR that is more or less at the center. The results of this kind of teaching can sometimes be ridiculous.

---

As we were driving along one of the back roads of Okinawa one day a small child ran out directly in front of the car. We screeched to a stop, barely missing him. We trembled with anxiety and horror at the terrible injury we had almost caused. The boy's mother, a young Okinawan woman, standing by the side of the road, looked at us and giggled. Smiling and giggling still, she went out on the road and collected her son. We experienced a wave of the most intense fury at her. Here we were, trembling at what we might have done to her child, and she was giggling as if she didn't even care. How could she be so callous? Goddamn Orientals, they don't care about human life, even that of their own children. We'd like to smash her with the car and see how she feels about it!

It was only after we had driven away a few miles down the road that we became calm enough to reflect on the fact that when they are embarrassed or frightened, Okinawans invariably smile and giggle. The woman had been just as frightened as we were, but we had misinterpreted her behavior. One wonders what the nonverbal behavior of the Vietnamese civilians was when they were herded at gunpoint at MyLai. Did they fall down on their knees, weeping and begging in the supplicant posture that we Caucasians would likely take in a similar situation and that might have stirred the troops' hearts to pity? Or did they, perhaps like the Okinawan woman, smile and giggle in terror, thereby possibly infuriating the Americans, who might have felt that they were being laughed at in derision? We do not know. But we need to know such things.

I am reminded of May 1, 1964, when my wife was awarded her citizenship along with two hundred other new citizens at a celebration attended by their families and assorted dignitaries and officials in downtown Honolulu. The festivities began with a parade. Three companies of spit-polished soldiers with rifles gleaming marched around the field and then took their formation behind seven howitzers. The cannon were then used to offer a roaring twenty-one-gun salute to the occasion. At this point the governor of Hawaii stepped to the podium, just in front of the still-smoking howitzers. "Today is referred to as May Day," he began, "but our nation has designated it as Law Day. Here in Hawaii," he quipped, "we might call it Lei Day. Anyway, the point is that here we are celebrating this day with flowers, while in the Communist countries they are having *military* demontrations."

No one laughed. It was as if the absurdity—the insanity—went unnoticed: this undoubtedly intelligent, certainly dignified man, with three companies of soldiers standing at attention behind him while the smoke of seven cannon encircled his head, chastising the Russians for the military nature of *their* festivities.

Organized, group, intraspecies mass killing—war—is a uniquely human form of behavior. Because this behavior has characterized essentially all cultures since the dawn of history, many have proposed that humans have an instinct for war—that war behavior is an immutable fact of human nature. It is, I suppose, why the hawks always refer to themselves as realists and to the doves as fuzzy-headed idealists. Idealists are people who believe in the potential of human nature for transformation. But I have already stated that the most essential attribute of human nature is its mutability and freedom from instinct—that it is always within our power to change our nature. So it is actually the idealists who are on the mark and the realists who are off base. Anyone who argues that waging war is something other than a choice ignores both the reality of evil and the evidence of human psychology. To wage war may not be always necessarily evil, but it *is* always a choice.

It is personally extremely tempting for me to think simplistically about war. I would like to take the Sixth Commandment literally, to believe that "Thou shalt not kill" means just that—at least, Thou shalt not kill other human beings. And it is similarly tempting for me to believe in the utter universality of that greatest of all ethical principles: the end does not justify the means. But thus far I cannot escape the conclusion that in rare previous moments of human history it has been necessary and morally right to kill in order to prevent even greater killing. I am profoundly uncomfortable with this position.

Not all, however, is ambiguity. I do remain sufficiently simplistic to believe that whenever war is waged, some human beings have lost their moorings and that some (more likely many) have succumbed to evil. Whenever there is war, someone is at fault. One side or both are to blame. A wrong choice has been made somewhere.

It is important to bear this in mind, because it is customary these days for both sides in a war to proclaim themselves victims. In days of old, when human beings were not so scrupulous, one tribe would not hesitate to kill another with the frankly avowed motive of conquest. But nowadays there is always the pretense of blamelessness. Even Hitler concocted pretenses for his invasions. It is likely that he and the majority of Germans even believed their own pretense. And so it has been since. Each side believes the other is the aggressor and itself the victim. In the face of this bilateral rhetoric and the complexities of international relations we tend to throw up our hands and think that maybe war really is no one's fault, that no one really is the aggressor, that no one made the wrong choice—that war somehow just happens, like spontaneous combustion.

I denounce this position of ethical hopelessness, this abrogation of our capacity for moral judgment. I can think of nothing that would fill Satan with greater glee or better signify the ultimate success of its conquest of the human race than an attitude on the part of humans that it is impossible to identify evil.

The war in Vietnam did not just happen. It was initiated by the British in 1945.* It was sustained by the French until their

* Britain, assigned by the terms of the Yalta agreement the task of "disarming and repatriating the Japanese and restoring order" in Southern Indochina at the end of World War II, chose to interpret its task as the reestablishment of the French colonial regime (despite the fact that this had been a Vichy regime, cooperating with the Japanese occupation). British troops found the Japanese already disarmed and a unified Vietnam under the control of the Vietminh. They proceeded to rearm the Japanese and use them to reinforce their own troops in forcefully wresting control of Saigon from Ho Chi Minh's forces. They then by force of arms maintained their

defeat in 1954. Then, with peace in sight, it was reinitiated and sustained by the Americans for the next eighteen years. Although there are many who still debate the issue, it is my judgment—and I am convinced it will be the judgment of history—that America was the aggressor in that war during those years. Ours were the choices that were most morally reprehensible. We were the villains.

But how could we—we Americans—be villains? The Germans and the Japanese in 1941, certainly. The Russians, yes. But the Americans? Surely we are not a villainous people. If we were villains, we must have been unwitting ones. This I concede; we were largely unwitting. But how does it come about that a person or a group or an entire nation is an unwitting villain? This is the crucial question. I have already addressed myself to this question at various levels. Let me return to it and discuss once again the issues of narcissism and laziness at this broadest level.

The term "unwitting villain" is particularly appropriate because our villainy lay in our unwittingness. We became villains precisely because we did not have our wits about us. The word "wit" in this regard refers to knowledge. We were villains out of ignorance. Just as what went on at MyLai was covered up for a year primarily because the troops of Task Force Barker did not know they had done something radically wrong, so America waged the war because it did not know that what it was doing was villainous.

I used to ask the troops on their way to battle in Vietnam what they knew about the war and its relationship to Vietnamese history. The enlisted men knew nothing. Ninety percent of the junior officers knew nothing. What little the senior officers and few junior officers did know was generally solely what they had been taught in the highly biased programs of their military schools. It was astounding. At least 95 percent of the men going off to risk their very lives did not even have the slightest knowledge of what the war was about. I also talked to Department of Defense civilians who directed the war and discovered a similar atrocious ignorance of Vietnamese history. The fact of the mat-

---

occupation of Saigon until masses of troops began arriving from France three months later. Handing Saigon over to the French, they then withdrew. The French Indochina War had begun.

ter is that as a nation we did not even know why we were waging the war.

How could this have been? How could a whole people have gone to war not knowing why? The answer is simple. As a people we were too lazy to learn and too arrogant to think we needed to learn. We felt that whatever way we happened to perceive things was the right way without any further study. And that whatever we did was the right thing to do without reflection. We were so wrong because we never seriously considered that we might not be right. With our laziness and narcissism feeding each other, we marched off to impose our will on the Vietnamese people by bloodshed with practically no idea of what was involved. Only when we—the mightiest nation on earth—consistently suffered defeat at the hands of the Vietnamese did we in significant numbers begin to take the trouble to learn what we had done.

So it is that our "Christian" nation became a nation of villains. So it has been with other nations in the past, and so it will be with other nations—including our own once again—in the future. As a nation and as a race, we shall not be immune to war until such a time as we have made much further progress toward eradicating from our human nature the twin progenitors of evil: laziness and narcissism.

## PREVENTION OF GROUP EVIL

As an example of group evil MyLai was not an inexplicable "accident" or unpredictable aberration. It occurred in the context of a war, which is itself an evil context. The atrocities were committed by the side that was the aggressor and that, in its aggression, had already fallen into evil. The evil of the small group—Task Force Barker—was clearly a reflection of the evil of the whole American military presence in Vietnam. And our military presence in Vietnam was directed by a deceitful, narcissistic government that had lost its bearings and that was mandated by a nation that had fallen into torpor and arrogance. The entire atmosphere was rotten. The massacre at MyLai was an event waiting to happen.

Let us remember that we have been examining MyLai as an

*example* of group evil. Group evil is not just something that happened one morning in 1968 on the other side of the world. It is
still happening all over the globe. It is happening here today.
Like individual evil, group evil is common. In fact, it is more
common—so common, indeed, it may be the norm.

We are living in the Age of the Institution. A century ago
the majority of Americans were self-employed. Today all but a
small minority devote their working lives to larger and larger
organizations.

I began this discussion by noting how responsibility becomes
diffused within groups—so much so that in larger groups it may
become nonexistent. Consider the large corporation. Even the
president or chairman of the board will say, "My actions may
not seem entirely ethical, but after all, they're not really a matter
of my prerogative. I must be responsive to the stockholders, you
know. On their account I cannot help but be directed by the
profit motive." Who is it, then, that determines the corporation's
behavior? The small investor who does not even begin to understand the operations involved? The mutual fund on the other side
of the nation? Which mutual fund? Which brokerage house?
Which banker?

So, as they become larger and larger, our institutions become
absolutely faceless. Soulless. What happens when there is no
soul? Is there just a vacuum? Or is there Satan where once, long
ago, a soul resided? I do not know. But I think the antiwar activ-
ists, the Berrigan brothers, are correct when they say that the task
before us is nothing less than to metaphorically exorcise our institutions. There is no word adequate to describe the urgency of
this task.

The military-industrial complex that played such a large role
in Vietnam, and continues to be a primary creator of the gro-
tesqueness of the arms race, is submitted to nothing but the profit
motive. This is no submission at all. It is pure self-interest. I am
not an enemy of capitalism per se. I believe it is possible for the
profit motive to be operative and at the same time submitted to
higher values of truth and love. Difficult, but possible. If we cannot somehow engineer this submission and "Christianize" our
capitalism, we are doomed as a capitalist society. The total failure
of submission is always evil—for a group, for an institution, for a
society as for an individual. Unless we can heal ourselves by

submission, the forces of death will win the day, and we will consume ourselves in our own evil.

Although the research has not been conducted that would establish a thoroughly scientific basis for the prevention of group evil, I think we already know from the examination of MyLai and similar phenomena where preventive efforts should be directed. Our study of MyLai revealed the operation of gross intellectual laziness and pathological narcissism at every level. The task of preventing group evil—including war itself—is clearly the task of eradicating or, at least, significantly diminishing laziness and narcissism.

But how is this to be accomplished? Although there are such phenomena as group identity, group narcissism, and group spirit, there is no way to influence such phenomena except through influencing individual members of the group. Customarily, when we wish to influence group behavior, we first attempt to do so by the most efficient means possible: influencing the individual group leaders. If our access to the group leaders is blocked, then we must turn to the lowliest of the members and start seeking grassroots support. Either way, it is to the individual that we turn. For the "group mind" is ultimately determined by the minds of the individuals who make up the group. As a single vote may be crucial in an election, so the whole course of human history may depend on a change of heart in one solitary and even humble individual. This is known to the genuinely religious. It is for this reason that no possible activity is considered to be more important than the salvation of a single human soul. This is why the individual is sacred. For it is in the solitary mind and soul of the individual that the battle between good and evil is waged and ultimately won or lost.

The effort to prevent group evil—including war—must therefore be directed toward the individual. It is, of course, a process of education. And that education can be conducted most easily within the traditional existing framework of our schools. This book is written in the hope that someday in our secular as well as religious schools all children will be carefully taught the nature of evil and the principles of its prevention.

At a dinner party recently one of the guests, speaking of a prominent film-maker, said, "He left his mark on history." Rather spontaneously, I remarked, "Each of us leaves his or her mark on history." The company assembled looked at me as if I had said something not only out of place but faintly obscene. Whether we affect history for good or for ill is, of course, each individual's choice. One fine means of teaching us our potential individual responsibility for group evil and history occurs in certain churches on Good Friday when, in reenacting the Passion according to Saint Mark, the congregation is required to play the role of the mob and to cry out, "Crucify him."

Children will, in my dream, be taught that laziness and narcissism are at the very root of all human evil, and why this is so. They will learn that each individual is of sacred importance. They will come to know that the natural tendency of the individual in a group is to forfeit his or her ethical judgment to the leader, and that this tendency should be resisted. And they will finally see it as each individual's responsibility to continually examine himself or herself for laziness and narcissism and then to purify themselves accordingly. They will do this in the knowledge that such personal purification is required not only for the salvation of their individual souls but also for the salvation of their world.

# THE DANGER
# AND THE HOPE

## ⊟ THE DANGERS OF A
## PSYCHOLOGY OF EVIL

There are a variety of reasons we have not yet developed a psychology of evil. Psychology is a very young science, as it is, and cannot be expected to have accomplished everything in its short lifetime. Being a science, however, it has shared in the traditions of science, which include a respect for value-free thinking and a distrust of religious concepts such as the concept of evil. Then again, it is only quite recently that the secular majority of society has seriously concerned itself with the social manifestations of evil. Slavery was abolished only a century ago. Child abuse was largely taken for granted until the present generation.

But perhaps the most important reason for our failure to scientifically examine the phenomenon of evil is fear of the consequences. We have good reason to be afraid. There are real dangers inherent in the development of a psychology of evil. This book has been written with the assumption that these dangers are outweighed by the dangers of *not* developing a psychology of evil. Nonetheless, anyone who seeks to participate in the endeavor of subjecting the phenomenon of evil to the scrutiny of science should begin by deeply considering that this endeavor in itself has potential for causing evil.

## THE DANGER OF MORAL JUDGMENT

As has been noted, it is characteristic of those who are evil to judge others as evil. Unable to acknowledge their own imperfection, they must explain away their flaws by blaming others. And, if necessary, they will even destroy others in the name of righteousness. How often we have seen it: the martyrdom of the saints, the Inquisition, the Holocaust, MyLai! Often enough to know that whenever we judge another evil we may ourselves be committing evil. Even atheists and agnostics believe in Christ's words: "Judge not, that ye be not judged."*

Evil is a moral judgment. I am proposing that it may also be a scientific judgment. But making the judgment scientifically will not remove it from the moral sphere. The word is pejorative. Whether we call a man evil on the basis of pure opinion or on the basis of a standardized psychological test, we are passing a moral judgment on him either way. Had we best not refrain from doing either? Science is dangerous enough. Moral judgment is dangerous enough. How dare we mix the two in the light of Jesus' admonition?

If we examine the matter more closely, however, we will see that it is both impossible and itself evil to totally refrain from making moral judgments. An attitude of "I'm OK; you're OK" may have a certain place in facilitating our social relationships, but only a place. Was Hitler OK? Lieutenant Calley? Jim Jones? Were the medical experiments conducted on the Jews in German concentration camps OK? The LSD experiments conducted by the CIA?

Let us also look at everyday life. If I am to hire an employee, should I take the first person who comes along or should I interview a number of applicants and judge between them? What kind of father would I be if I discovered my son cheating, lying, or stealing and failed to criticize him? What should I tell a friend who is planning suicide or a patient who is selling heroin? "You're OK"? There is such a thing as an excess of sympathy, an excess of tolerance, an excess of permissiveness.

The fact of the matter is that we cannot lead decent lives with-

* Matthew 7:1.

out making judgments in general and moral judgments in particular. When patients come to see me, what they pay me for is my presumably good judgment. When I seek legal advice, I am interested in the quality of my lawyer's judgment. Do we spend five thousand dollars on a family vacation or invest it in savings for the children's education? Do I or do I not cheat on my income tax? You and I go through our day making decisions that are judgments, most of which have moral overtones. We cannot escape from judging.

The sentence "Judge not, that ye be not judged" is usually quoted out of context. Christ did not enjoin us to refrain from ever judging. What he went on to say in the next four verses is that we should judge ourselves *before* we judge others—not that we shouldn't judge at all. "Thou hypocrite," he said, "first cast out the beam out of thine own eye; and *then* shalt thou see clearly to cast out the mote out of thy brother's eye."* Recognizing the potential for evil in moral judgments, he instructed us not to always avoid making them but to purify ourselves before doing so. Which is where the evil fail. It is the self-criticism they avoid.

We must also remember the purpose for which we judge. If it is to heal, fine. If it is to enhance our own self-esteem, our pride, then the purpose is wrong. "There but for the grace of God, go I" is a reflection that should accompany every judgment of another's evil.

The scientific exploration of human evil will, I believe, bear witness to the truth of that reflection. Consider some of the issues that this work itself has raised: the possibility of genetic causation or predisposition; the evidence for the role of unloving parenting and excessive childhood suffering; the mysterious nature of human goodness. The more deeply we examine the subject, the less cause for personal pride we discover.

Some interpret the truth of the reflection "There but for the grace of God, go I" to be a reason for fatalism. Since God rescues this person but not that one, since the degree to which we can save ourselves through our own efforts will probably remain unclear, why bother? But fatalism is just that: fatal. To throw up our hands is to die. While we may never ultimately discern the meaning of human existence—including just why this per-

* Matthew 7:5.

son is good and the other evil—it still remains our responsibility to live as best we can. Which also means to go on making the moral judgments necessary to support life. And we are permitted to choose whether to live in a state of greater or lesser ignorance.

The issue, then, is not whether to judge; we must. The question is how and when to judge wisely. Our great spiritual leaders have given us the basics. But since in the end we must make moral judgments, it makes sense to further refine our wisdom with the application of scientific method and knowledge of evil when appropriate—as long as we remember the basics.

## THE DANGER OF CLOAKING MORAL
## JUDGMENT IN SCIENTIFIC AUTHORITY

This is a major pitfall. It is a pitfall because we ascribe to science much more authority than it deserves. We do so for two reasons. One is that very few of us understand the limitations of science. The other is that we are too dependent upon authority in general.

When our children were infants we were blessed by the very best of pediatricians, a kind and dedicated gentle man of great erudition. When we visited him a month after the birth of our oldest child, he instructed us to start feeding her solid foods almost immediately, because such supplementation was needed for babies being breast-fed. A year later, when we visited him a month after the birth of our second daughter, he directed us to delay feeding this one solid food as long as possible so as not to deprive her of the extraordinary nutrition in breast milk. The state of the "science" had changed! When I was in medical school we were taught that the essential treatment for diverticulosis was a low-roughage diet. Now medical students are taught that the essential treatment is a high-roughage diet.

Such experiences have taught me that what is paraded as scientific fact is simply the current belief of some scientists. We are accustomed to regard science as Truth with a capital T. What scientific knowledge is, in fact, is the best available approximation of truth in the judgment of the majority of scientists who work in the particular specialty involved. Truth is not something that we possess; it is a goal toward which we, hopefully, strive.

What is worrisome about this is the possibility that scientists—specifically psychologists—will make public pronouncements on the evil of certain personages or events. We scientists, unfortunately, are little more immune than anyone else to jumping to unsound conclusions. Many psychiatrists who had never even met the man labeled Barry Goldwater in 1964 "psychologically unfit" to be President. In the USSR, psychiatrists systematically abuse their profession by labeling political dissidents "mentally ill," thereby serving the interests of the state rather than the interests of truth and healing.

The problem is aggravated by the fact that the public is actually eager to be guided by the pronouncements of scientists. As was earlier discussed in relation to the issue of group evil, the majority would rather follow than lead. We are content, even anxious, to let our authorities do our thinking for us. There is a profound tendency to make of our scientists "philosopher kings," whom we allow to guide us through intellectual labyrinths, when they are often just as lost as the rest of us.

In our intellectual laziness we forget that scientific thought is almost as faddish as taste. Since the current opinion of the scientific establishment is only the latest and never the last word, we must for our safety as a public bear the responsibility of being skeptical of our scientists and their pronouncements. In other words, we should never relinquish our individual leadership. Demanding though it may be, we should all attempt to be scientists at least to the degree that we make our own judgments on issues of good and evil. Although issues of good and evil are too important to exclude from scientific examination, they are also too important to leave entirely to the scientists.

Fortunately, in our culture, scientists love to argue with one another. I shudder to think of a time and place in which there is a "scientific" gospel on the nature of good and evil that is not subject to debate. I use "scientific" in quotes in this regard because debate is the cornerstone of genuine science, and a science without debate and exuberant skepticism is not a science at all. The best safeguard we have against the misuse of the concept of evil by scientists is to assure that science remains scientific and grounded in a democratic culture in which open debate is encouraged.

## THE DANGER OF THE MISUSE OF SCIENCE

The gravest misuse of science may be attributed not to those scientists themselves who proclaim personal opinions in the guise of scientific truth but to the public—industry, government, and poorly informed individuals—which employs scientific findings and concepts for dubious purposes. Although the atomic bomb was made possible through the work of scientists, it was the politicians who made the decision to build it and the military who dropped it. This is not to say that scientists bear no responsibility for the manner in which their findings are put to use. But it is to say that they don't have control over the situation. Once a scientific finding is published (and generally it must be, since science depends upon publishing and the free flow of information), it becomes part of the public domain. Anyone can use it, and scientists have little more to say about it than any other public-interest group.

The body of scientific knowledge of psychology is already misused in a variety of ways by the general public. Its employment—and the extent to which it is employed—by the judicial system is debatable in this country, let alone in the USSR. Although psychological tests are often of immense value to teachers, many children are falsely diagnosed and misclassified by them. Similar tests are used or misused to reject people for employment and higher education. At cocktail parties men and women bandy about such terms as "penis envy," "castration fear," and even "narcissism," with little idea of what they are talking about and little thought of the possible consequence of their prattle.

It is a bit frightening, therefore, to imagine scenarios of what might happen if and when the public gets hold of scientific information concerning evil. Suppose, for instance, that a psychological test might be developed that could identify evil persons. Many might want to use such a test for other than academic purposes: schools seeking to screen out undesirable applicants, courts seeking to determine guilt or innocence, lawyers fighting custody battles, and so on. Consider also how everyday people would look for the signs and symptoms of evil in a mother-in-law, an employer, or antagonist, and how quick they might be to use such stigmata to smear their opponents either publicly or informally.

But while it would be impossible to withhold scientific information about evil from the public, the picture is hardly as gloomy as it might at first glance seem. Psychiatric information about individuals can be kept confidential. The formal diagnosis of evil as made by psychologists and psychiatrists can be restricted solely to the purposes of strictly controlled scientific research. As for the reality that general psychological information is often misused by the general public, it does not mean that we are worse off in the balance for such information. Indeed, it is my firm belief that the increasing psychological awareness of the general public over the past few decades represents a dramatic moral and intellectual step forward.* While some may bandy their Freud about in a silly fashion, the fact that many have come to acknowledge the reality of their unconscious mind (and are even beginning to take responsibility for it) may be the seed of our salvation. Our burgeoning interest in the existence and source of our prejudices, hidden hostilities, irrational fears, perceptual blind spots, mental ruts, and resistance to growth is the start of an evolutionary leap.

Finally, an increasing public sophistication about the psychology of evil will itself serve to prevent the abuse of that psychology. Although we need research to know much more about evil, we already know a few things beyond doubt. One is the tendency of the evil to project their evil onto others. Unable or unwilling to face their own sinfulness, they must explain it away by accusing others of defects. As we develop a psychology of evil, this fact—already common knowledge among scholars—will surely be more widely publicized. We will become more rather than less discerning about those who cast stones. As scientific interest in the phenomenon of evil filters down to the public, our consideration of it should become increasingly thoughtful.

THE DANGER TO THE SCIENTIST AND THERAPIST

Thus far we have been talking of ways in which the public might be endangered by the work of scientists on the subject of evil. But what about scientists themselves? Might they not be endangered by their own research? I believe so.

The most basic scientific investigator of evil will always be a therapist. There is no method of looking into the core of a per-

---

* Some, notably Martin N. Gross, in *The Psychological Society* (Random House, 1978), bemoan the current emphasis on psychological-mindedness, but while they are eloquent about the abuses, they overlook the virtues. They fail to see the big picture or give a balanced view.

son's being that can approach psychoanalysis for its depth and discernment. There is no way to penetrate the disguise of the evil except in the role of a healer—one who, in the interests of healing, is willing, as a psychotherapist, to do battle with the malignant personality or, as an exorcist, to wrestle with the demonic behind the pretense. Our most basic data about the nature of evil will be won from hand-to-hand combat with evil itself.

Some literature on exorcism emphasizes the danger to the exorcist in this struggle. It is usually depicted in physical terms because these are concrete and easy to talk about. But greater, I suspect, than the risk of death and deformity is the risk the exorcist runs of having his own soul damaged or polluted. I believe that the psychotherapist who truly attempts to tangle therapeutically with an evil patient is facing somewhat similar risks. Because it is currently rare for an evil person to become engaged in psychotherapy, we do not know much about such risks. But if this book is successful in stimulating psychiatric interest in evil, more and more therapists will be experimenting with its treatment. I would advise them to be careful. They may be placing themselves in great jeopardy. I do not think such experiments should be attempted by a young therapist, who has enough to do learning how to battle with the more ordinary resistance and countertransference. Nor should they be attempted by one who has not yet thoroughly cast the beam out of his or her own eye, for a weak-souled therapist will be the most vulnerable.

The dangers exist not only for therapists, exorcists, and healers but for anyone who becomes preoccupied with the subject of evil. There is always the risk of contamination, one way or another. The more closely we rub shoulders with or against evil, the more likely it is that we may become evil ourselves. All scientists—even those whose work is restricted to the library or sterile laboratory—would be well advised to begin their research by reading Aldous Huxley's *The Devils of Loudon* (from which I quote below).* Until we learn more through the development of a psychology of evil, there is no better work on the subject of evil contamination than this historical analysis of evil events in a seventeenth-century French town. Let the investigator or therapist remember:

* Harper & Row, 1952, Perennial Library Edition.

The effects which follow too constant and intense a concentration upon evil are always disastrous. Those who crusade not *for* God in themselves, but *against* the devil in others, never succeed in making the world better, but leave it either as it was, or sometimes even perceptibly worse than it was, before the crusade began. By thinking primarily of evil we tend, however excellent our intentions, to create occasions for evil to manifest itself. (p. 192)

.  .  .  .  .  .  .  .  .  .  .  .  .  .  .  .  .  .  .  .  .  .

No man can concentrate his attention upon evil, or even upon the idea of evil, and remain unaffected. To be more *against* the devil than *for* God is exceedingly dangerous. Every crusader is apt to go mad. He is haunted by the wickedness which he attributes to his enemies; it becomes in some sort a part of him. (p. 260)

THE DANGERS IN PERSPECTIVE

The final concern one might have about the scientific investigation of human evil is that it could endanger the nature of science itself. The tradition of science as value-free would be seriously threatened. If we consider this tradition as basic to science, would not a "science" of evil—based as it is upon an a priori value judgment—undermine the very foundation of science as we know it?

But perhaps this particular foundation of science needs to be altered. With the rarest of exceptions, scientific research is no longer conducted in a simple laboratory by a solitary, independent seeker of truth for its own sake. It is instead mostly financed by government or industry in the form of group efforts according to executive agendas. The technology required for modern investigation itself has become so complicated that it can be dangerous. The fact is that modern science has become so inextricably interwoven with big business and big government that there is no longer such a thing as "pure" science. And the end result of a science detached from religious insights and verities would appear to be the Strangelovian lunacy of the arms race—just as the end result of a religion unsubmitted to scientific self-doubt and scrutiny is the Rasputinian lunacy of Jonestown.

There are profound reasons to suspect that traditional value-free science is no longer serving the needs of mankind—to suspect that science no longer can or should ignore issues of values. The most obvious of those values is the matter of evil. When we lived at the mercy of beasts in the forest, flood and drought, famine and infectious disease, our survival depended upon our race to control such vast external forces. We had neither time nor need for much introspection. But as we have tamed these external threats with our traditionally value-free science and its resultant technology, internal dangers have arisen with proportional rapidity. The major threats to our survival no longer stem from nature without but from our own human nature within. It is our carelessness, our hostilities, our selfishness and pride and willful ignorance that endanger the world. Unless we can now tame and transmute the potential for evil in the human soul, we shall be lost. And how can we do this unless we are willing to look at our own evil with the same thoroughness, detached discernment, and rigorous methodology to which we subjected the external world?

The dangers inherent in developing a scientific psychology of evil are very real. They should not be underestimated. The making of moral judgments, the confusion of opinion with scientific fact, the misuse of scientific information by the malicious and uninformed, and the risks of moving close enough to evil to examine it are not simply theoretical pitfalls. As we proceed in the development of a psychology of evil, some will fall into them. Although to a considerable extent it will be possible in ways suggested to avoid these pitfalls, I have no doubt that there will be casualties. But in the world of the conglomerate and the neutron bomb, of the Holocaust and MyLai, the way seems clear. The dangers of developing a psychology of evil do not approach in magnitude the danger of failing to subject human evil to strenuous and coordinated scientific scrutiny. Dangerous though a psychology of evil might be, it will be more dangerous not to have one.

## A METHODOLOGY OF LOVE

Evil is ugly.

Until now we have properly focused on its danger and destructiveness. But there is another aspect of its ugliness: its small, cheap, tawdry dreariness.

"Imaginary evil is romantic and varied," wrote Simone Weil

in her essay "Criteria of Wisdom"; "real evil is gloomy, monotonous, barren, boring." It is no accident that when C. S. Lewis depicted hell he described it as a gray British Midlands city.* Having recently visited Las Vegas, my own latest vision of hell is that it is an endless slot-machine emporium, far removed from the variety of night and day, monotonously noisy with the repetitive clamor of meaningless jackpots, jammed with dull-eyed people spasmodically yet regularly yanking machines for all eternity. Indeed, the tasteless glitter of Las Vegas is a pretense designed to hide all that terrible dreariness.

If one ever has the good fortune to meet a living saint, one will have then met someone absolutely unique. Though their visions may be remarkably similar, the personhood of saints is remarkably different. This is because they have become utterly themselves. God creates each soul differently, so that when all the mud is finally cleared away, His light will shine through it in a beautiful, colorful, totally new pattern. Keats described this world as "the vale of soul-making," and whether they know it or not, when they help their patients clean away the mud, psychotherapists are engaged in the activity of saint-making. Certainly psychotherapists know it is their task routinely to free their patients to be themselves.

At the other end of the human spectrum from the saints lie the least free, the evil. All one can see of them is the mud. And it all looks the same. In Chapter 3 I offered a clinical, nosological description of the evil personality. It is extraordinary how well the evil fit the mold. Once you've seen one evil person, you've essentially seen them all. Even psychotics, whom we are accustomed to thinking of as the most seriously deranged, are more interesting. (Indeed, there is some reason to suspect that in certain cases psychosis is chosen as a preferable alternative to evil.)

Then how is it that psychiatrists have until now failed to recognize such a distinct, rigid type? It is because they have bought the pretense of respectability. They have been deceived by what Harvey M. Cleckley called "the mask of sanity."† As my priest friend commented, evil is "the ultimate disease." Despite their pretense of sanity, the evil are the most insane of all.

* *The Great Divorce* (New York: Macmillan, 1946).
† *The Mask of Sanity*, 4th ed. (St. Louis: C. V. Mosby, 1964).

It is to the incredibly dreary insanity of the Adolf Eichmanns of this world that Hannah Ahrendt was referring when she spoke of "the banality of evil." Thomas Merton put it this way:

> One of the most disturbing facts that came out in the Eichmann trial was that a psychiatrist examined him and pronounced him *perfectly sane*. We equate sanity with a sense of justice, with humaneness, with prudence, with the capacity to love and understand other people. We rely on the sane people of the world to preserve it from barbarism, madness, destruction. And now it begins to dawn on us that it is precisely the sane ones who are the most dangerous. It is the sane ones, the well-adapted ones, who can without qualms and without nausea aim the missiles and press the buttons that will initiate the great festival of destruction that they, the sane ones, have prepared.*

What are we to do with the evil when their masquerade of sanity is so successful, their destructiveness so "normal"? First, we must stop buying the masquerade and being deceived by the pretense. It is hoped that this book will help us toward that end.

But what, then? It is an old maxim: Know your enemy. We must not only recognize but study these poor, dull, terrified people. And attempt to do what we can to either heal or contain them.

How is this to be done in view of the major dangers of a psychology of evil? In view of the possibility that we ourselves might become contaminated in the process? I think we can safely conduct scientific research on a subject to which we give an a priori negative value only with a methodology of positive value. Specifically, I think we can safely study and treat evil only through the methods of love.

A twenty-eight-year-old man had spent several years in therapy with me, coming to grips with the evil that had been done to him throughout childhood by his father. One night he had the following dream, which represented the beginning of a turning point in the healing process:

> It was wartime. I was wearing a combat uniform. I was standing in front of the Morristown house—you know, the one where

* *Raids on the Unspeakable* (New Directions Publishing Corp., 1964, paperback edition, pp. 45–46).

the worst years of my childhood took place. My father was in the house. I had a walkie-talkie and was in communication with a mortar platoon. I gave the platoon leader the coordinates of the house and was asking him to lay down a pattern on our position. I knew that I myself would likely get blown up along with my father and the house in the bombardment, but the fact didn't seem to bother me at all. The platoon leader, however, was giving me trouble. "We've had lots of requests to lay down patterns all over the place," he said. He doubted they'd be able to get to it. I was very upset. I pleaded with him. I even told him there'd be a case of Scotch in it for him if he came through. Finally he seemed to relent. He'd see what he could do, he said. I felt great. But then my father came running out of the house to talk to me. I can't remember exactly what he said, but it had something to do with guests or visitors or other people. He went back into the house. I looked down the drive and, sure enough, there was this group of people walking up to the house. I don't know who they were. They weren't family. Just visitors. And suddenly I realized they would get blown up in the barrage too. I frantically called back the platoon leader—only this time I was begging him not to hit us. I told him he could have the case of Scotch anyway. He said he'd cancel the order, and I woke up, feeling tremendously relieved. I knew I'd gotten back to him just in time.

Like the patient in the dream, we are all in combat against evil. In the heat of the fray it is tempting to take hold of some seemingly simple solution—such as "what we ought to do is just bomb the hell out of those people." And if our passion is great enough, we may even be willing to blow ourselves up in the process of "stomping out" evil. But we run up against the old problem that the end does not justify the means. Although evil is antilife, it is itself a form of life. If we kill those who are evil, we will become evil ourselves; we will be killers. If we attempt to deal with evil by destroying it, we will also end up destroying ourselves, spiritually if not physically. And we are likely to take some innocent people with us as well.

What to do, then? Like the patient, we must begin by giving up the simple notion that we can effectively conquer evil by destroying it. But this leaves us in a sort of nihilistic vacuum. Are we to throw up our hands—to regard the problem of evil as being inherently insoluble? Hardly. That would be meaningless. It is in the struggle between good and evil that life has its meaning—and in the hope that goodness can succeed. That hope is our answer: goodness can succeed. Evil can be defeated by goodness. When we translate this we realize what we dimly have always known: Evil can be conquered only by love.

So the methodology of our assault—scientific and otherwise—on evil must be love. This is so simple-sounding that one is compelled to wonder why it is not a more obvious truth. The fact is, simple-sounding though it may be, the methodology of love is so difficult in practice that we shy away from its usage. At first glance it even appears impossible. How is it possible to love people who are evil? Yet that is precisely what I am saying we must do. Specifically, if we are to safely conduct research on evil people, we must do so in love. We must start from an a priori position of love for them.

Let me return to the dilemma I faced in dealing with Charlene. She insisted that I love her unconditionally, as if she were an infant without stain. But she was not an infant. And I could not find it in my heart to affirm her in her evil as she so desperately wanted. Is it not evil itself to love evil?

The resolution of this dilemma is a paradox. The path of love is a dynamic balance of opposites, a painful creative tension of uncertainties, a difficult tightrope between extreme but easier courses of action. Consider the raising of a child. To reject all its misbehavior is unloving. To tolerate all its misbehavior is unloving. We must somehow be both tolerant and intolerant, accepting and demanding, strict and flexible. An almost godlike compassion is required.

One minister described such compassion of God for man by putting the following words into God's mouth:

> I know you. I created you. I have loved you from your mother's womb. You have fled—as you now know—from my love, but I love you nevertheless and not-the-less however far you flee. It is I who sustains your very power of fleeing, and I will never finally let you go. I accept you as you are. You are forgiven. I know all your sufferings. I have always known them. Far beyond your understanding, when you suffer, I suffer. I also know all the little tricks by which you try to hide the ugliness you have made of your life from yourself and others. But you are beautiful. You are beautiful more deeply within than you can

see. You are beautiful because you yourself, in the unique person that only you are, reflect already something of the beauty of my holiness in a way which shall never end. You are beautiful also because I, and I alone, see the beauty you shall become. Through the transforming power of my love which is made perfect in weakness you shall become perfectly beautiful. You shall become perfectly beautiful in a uniquely irreplaceable way, which neither you nor I will work out alone, for we shall work it out together.*

It is not an easy thing to embrace ugliness with the sole motive of hope that in some unknown way a transformation into beauty might occur thereby. But the myth of kissed frogs turning into princes remains. Yet how does kissing the frog turn it into a prince? How does the methodology of love work? How does it heal? I don't know exactly.

I don't know because love can work in many ways, and none of them are predictable. I know that the first task of love is self-purification. When one has purified oneself, by the grace of God, to the point at which one can truly love one's enemies, a beautiful thing happens. It is as if the boundaries of the soul become so clean as to be transparent, and a unique light then shines forth from the individual.

The effect of this light varies. Some on their way toward holiness will move more swiftly by its encouragement. Others, on their way toward evil, when encountering this light will be moved to change their direction. The bearer of the light (who is but a vehicle for it; it is the light of God) most often will be unaware of these effects. Finally, those who hate the light will attack it. Yet it is as if their evil actions are taken into the light and consumed. The malignant energy is thereby wasted, contained and neutralized. The process may be painful to the bearer of the light, occasionally even fatal. This does not, however, signify the success of evil. Rather, it backfires. As I said in *The Road Less Traveled*, "It was evil that raised Christ to the cross, thereby enabling us to see him from afar."†

I cannot be any more specific about the methodology of love

---

* From "Known" by the Reverend Dr. Charles K. Robinson, Nov. 4, 1973 (*Duke Divinity School Review*, Winter 1979, Vol. 44, p. 44).
† Simon & Schuster, 1978, p. 279.

than to quote these words of an old priest who spent many years in the battle: "There are dozens of ways to deal with evil and several ways to conquer it. All of them are facets of the truth that the only ultimate way to conquer evil is to let it be smothered within a willing, living human being. When it is absorbed there like blood in a sponge or a spear into one's heart, it loses its power and goes no further."*

The healing of evil—scientifically or otherwise—can be accomplished only by the love of individuals. A willing sacrifice is required. The individual healer must allow his or her own soul to become the battleground. He or she must sacrificially *absorb* the evil.

Then what prevents the destruction of that soul? If one takes the evil itself into one's heart, like a spear, how can one's goodness still survive? Even if the evil is vanquished thereby, will not the good be also? What will have been achieved beyond some meaningless trade-off?

I cannot answer this in language other than mystical. I can say only that there is a mysterious alchemy whereby the victim becomes the victor. As C. S. Lewis wrote: "When a willing victim who had committed no treachery was killed in a traitor's stead, the Table would crack and Death itself would start working backwards."†

I do not know how this occurs. But I know that it does. I know that good people can deliberately allow themselves to be pierced by the evil of others—to be broken thereby yet somehow not broken—to even be killed in some sense and yet still survive and not succumb. Whenever this happens there is a slight shift in the balance of power in the world.

* Gale D. Webbe, *The Night and Nothing* (New York: Seabury Press, 1964), p. 109.
† *The Lion, the Witch and the Wardrobe* (Collier/Macmillan, 1970), p. 160.